FULL RESPONSIBILITY

SUNY series in American Philosophy and Cultural Thought
———————
Randall E. Auxier and John R. Shook, editors

FULL RESPONSIBILITY
On Pragmatic, Political, and Other Modes of Action Sharing

Steven G. Smith

Cover image of Agora of Izmir in Turkey is from Shutterstock.

Published by State University of New York Press, Albany

© 2022 State University of New York

All rights reserved

Printed in the United States of America

No part of this book may be used or reproduced in any manner whatsoever without written permission. No part of this book may be stored in a retrieval system or transmitted in any form or by any means including electronic, electrostatic, magnetic tape, mechanical, photocopying, recording, or otherwise without the prior permission in writing of the publisher.

For information, contact State University of New York Press, Albany, NY www.sunypress.edu

Library of Congress Cataloging-in-Publication Data

Name: Smith, Steven G., author.
Title: Full responsibility : on pragmatic, political, and other modes of action sharing | Steven G. Smith.
Description: Albany : State University of New York Press, [2022] | Series: SUNY series in American Philosophy and Cultural Thought | Includes bibliographical references and index.
Identifiers: ISBN 9781438489810 (hardcover : alk. paper) | ISBN 9781438489834 (ebook) | ISBN 9781438489827 (pbk. : alk. paper)
Further information is available at the Library of Congress.

10 9 8 7 6 5 4 3 2 1

To Howard

Contents

Acknowledgments	xi
Introduction	1
Chapter One: Responsibility and Realization	15
The Appeal of Responsibility	15
The Subjective Basis of Responsibility in Practical Realizing	28
Shared Realizing and Shared Responsibility	33
Agency Responsibility	36
Theory of Responsible Realization versus Theory of Values	41
Chapter Two: Pragmatic Responsibility	43
The Ontological Structure of Pragmatic Responsibility: Actualizing	45
The World Scene of Pragmatic Responsibility: The Sifting of Existence	49
The Personal Coherence of Pragmatic Responsibility: Vocation	52
The Social Coherence of Pragmatic Responsibility: Ethos	56
Sympathy, Empathy, and "Affective Responsibility"	57
The Relation between Pragmatic Responsibility and Historical Responsibility: The Description Issue	59
The Relation between Pragmatic Responsibility and Ethical Responsibility: The Stringency Issue	61
Chapter Three: Political Responsibility	69
Political Responsibility and Power Wielding: The Motivation Issue	70

The Relation between Political Responsibility and Ethical Responsibility: The Obligation Issue	74
The Relation between Political Responsibility and Pragmatic Responsibility: The Organization Issue	88
The Relation between Political Responsibility and Historical Responsibility: The Collective Identity Issue	90
Touchstones of Political Responsibility: Heroes and Cautionary Examples	93
The Pursuit of Collective Political Realization	96
Chapter Four: Challenges in Four Spheres of Political Responsibility	**103**
Family Responsibility and Abortion	106
Organizational Responsibility and "Good Jobs"	114
Community Responsibility and Immigration	120
Global Responsibility and the Displacement of Persons	124
Chapter Five: Full Responsibility	**137**
Limiting and Maximizing Approaches to Full Responsibility	137
Models of Full Responsibility	140
Spirits of Responsibility	154
Your Vocation (in another sense)	158
Epilogue	**161**
Appendix 1: Notes on Ethical Responsibility	**163**
Ethical Apriorism and Its Limitations	163
Alternative Positionings of Ethics	169
Appendix 2: Notes on Historical Responsibility	**175**
The Historical Dimension of Responsibility	175
The Roots of Historical Responsibility	176
The Farmer's Historical Responsibility	182
The National Leader's Historical Responsibility	184
Historical Injustice and Historical Jeopardy	186
Appendix 3: Notes on Religious Responsibility	**191**
Exemplars of Religious Responsibility	191
The Threat of Religious Responsibility	200

Bibliography 205

Index 215

Acknowledgments

I'd like to thank Liz Egan, Shelli Poe, Tamar Shirinian, and Elise Smith for their helpful comments on the earliest version of this work, and two readers for SUNY Press for important suggestions for the book's enrichment. Thanks also to Randall Auxier for timely guidance on the project.

I am embracingly grateful to Howard Pickett for thinking with me about responsibility for a long time.

Earlier versions of portions of chapter 1 and appendix 3 appeared in my article "Responsibility in Religiosity," *Religious Studies* 57 (June 2021): 249–65.

Introduction

The phrase "full responsibility" has a common meaning tied to being the agent in charge of some practical concern, as in "Sam bears full responsibility for the work." This expression makes a kind of sense in amplifying two common assumptions about responsibility: that it is a provision for something being done that we care about, and that it involves an agent's commitment to doing the right thing. But the qualifier "full" here is problematic, apart from its possible legal or quasi-legal significance, since in reality no state of affairs is produced solely by what one agent did, nor could an agent ever demonstrate perfect devotedness in attending to a practical concern in the right way. We speak of full responsibility approximately and aspirationally. This is true also for a less commonly invoked but not less important sense of fullness in responsibility that envisions breadth—work responsibility *and* family responsibility *and* responsibility on a sports team *and* responsibility in still other frames of reference. A fully responsible person in this sense is responsible to all relevant parties for all relevant matters in all relevant ways. This is an ideal of maturity. But it could also be a nightmare of inordinate demand and a tool of disastrous manipulation.

What is a full recipe for full responsibility? What stance or set of stances does a fully responsible agent have? A great intellectual investment has been made in the category of the ethical partly to provide a one-stance answer to this question. We could call this approach responsibility monism. It stipulates that responsibility is an ethical function; we know what responsibility means at work, at home, in team sports, and so on because general ethical principles of duty, value, and virtue apply in all practical contexts, and our ideal "responsible agents" (in the sense of agents who "act responsibly") are those who follow these principles in whatever contexts they find themselves in.

While it is true that ethical standards apply in all contexts, it seems not to be true that all action is responsible just insofar as it is governed by ethics—at least, according to the common and well-motivated understanding of ethics as a concern with general standards of approvable conduct. On this understanding, ethical constraint is determined by principles formulated in advance of cases so that we have an ideally agreeable plan for handling all situations.[1] The great principles of fairness and maximized happiness are distinctively useful and authoritative because they stand up in unlimited discussion and reflection. In practice, we apply these effectively universal and unconditional principles of conduct as officers of a community that is ideally inclusive of members and occasions; in that way we fulfill our ethical responsibility to that community and to each other as its constituents. However, we may find ourselves in intrafamilial or intergroup conflict, where loyalty to our closest collaborators would sometimes require violating general rules or obeying general rules would cause personal betrayals. Or we may acknowledge responsibility to past or future generations, unable to calculate what is due them by the rules of justice or measurements of welfare we are ethically bound to apply to each other but concerned nonetheless to rectify or improve the larger shape of our shared existence in history.[2] Such considerations point to a difference in modes of responsibility.

One area of responsibility that is often claimed to elude ethical determination is political action. Contrary to the political moralists' assumption that political responsibility is a branch of ethical responsibility—that is, an application of general standards of human dignity and welfare to affairs of state—political realists claim that political responsibility is a direct response to the pragmatic demands of statecraft. Max Weber made a notable contribution to this debate in his late address "Politics as a Vocation," distinguishing a political "ethics of responsibility" (concerned with managing the consequences of actions involving a government's coercive power) from an "ethics of conviction" (defined by unconditional loyalty to ultimate ends).[3]

---

1. For fuller discussion of this conventional conception of the ethical with attention to its limits, see appendix 1 below.

2. On what divides historical from ethical responsibility, see my "Historical Rightness," *Soundings* 98 (Spring 2015): 127–45 and "What We Have Time For: Historical Responsibility on the Largest Scale," *Journal of the Philosophy of History* 13 (June 2019): 163–82, along with appendix 2 below.

3. Max Weber, "Politics as a Vocation," in H. H. Gerth and C. Wright Mills, eds., *From Max Weber: Essays in Sociology* (New York: Oxford University Press, 1948), 77–128.

Weber thought that these two "ethical" stances can coexist in the life of an agent but cannot be reconciled in principle, given that the ethics of conviction rejects the strategic manipulations and violence of the agent of responsibility while the ethics of responsibility rejects the pure, sometimes very costly idealism of the agent of conviction.

Our ethical guidance system is in serious trouble if we are forced to say that it is ethically right to do something ethically wrong. The British air marshal Sir Arthur "Bomber" Harris seems to have been caught in this paradox when he insisted on bombing German cities late in World War II.[4] While the attack on civilians was flagrantly unethical according to long-accepted *jus in bello* standards, Harris made a clear appeal to responsibility for the war and for (and to) his comrades: "Attacks on cities . . . are strategically justified in so far as they tend to shorten the war and preserve the lives of Allied soldiers. To my mind we have absolutely no right to give them up unless it is certain that they will not have this effect."[5] We are missing something if we conclude simply that Harris is irresponsible and his ethical critics are responsible, or vice versa. One might wish to say, following Weber's lead, that Harris exemplifies a pragmatic "ethics of responsibility," but then one would be giving "ethics" the broader meaning of "normative orientation" (what then distinguishes the more strictly ethical kind of normative orientation?) and "responsibility" the narrower meaning of pragmatic responsibility (but isn't the "ethics of conviction," ethics in the stricter sense, responsibly concerned with rectifying conduct in relationship with others?). And one would still have to explain how Harris can have a normative orientation that is somehow tenable even though it is ethically intolerable. I think we will be better set up for clear practical thinking if we keep the category of responsibility inclusive with a view to letting ethical responsibility be ethical and pragmatic responsibility be pragmatic. To do this, we will not only need adequate conceptions of ethical and pragmatic forms of responsibility, we will need an explanation of how ethical and pragmatic evaluations can overlap and interact. For it is obvious that the two categories cannot simply be kept separate. Even if Bomber Harris's position makes pragmatically responsible sense vis-à-vis his war colleagues, the ethical problem with it is a significant political problem as well.

---

4. See the ethically disapproving discussion of Harris in Michael Walzer's *Just and Unjust Wars* (New York: Basic Books, 1977), 254–61 and 323–25.

5. Letter to Sir Norman Bottomley (March 29, 1945), quoted in Dudley Saward, *Bomber Harris* (New York: Doubleday, 1985), 294.

I aim to show how the ideal of responsible life works well in encompassing and coordinating our responses to diverse directive appeals subject to manifold practical uncertainties. Lately, there have been two main conversations in philosophy about the nature of responsibility, one about the conditions for voluntary action and blameworthiness (the dominant concern of analytic philosophers) and one about the human subject's orientation to transcendence (with frequent reference to proposals by Levinas and Derrida).[6] My angle of approach is different, in two ways. First, I align with the common human interest in assigning and assuming responsibility for constructive purposes and view responsibility as a device of collaboration—a plan of action that is meant to be fulfilled and that appeals to us as a fulfillment. Responsibility in this aspect, even though pervasively relevant for practical reasoning, has gotten only a small amount of preliminary attention from philosophers.[7] But there is much here to observe and interrogate. Second, I divide the field of responsible action sharing into three domains corresponding to the primary temporal dimensions of the constitution of beings: the historically fraught reality of past actions, the ethically governed future possibility of actions on the drawing board, and the pragmatically charged present of actualizing, trying to do things, in which reality is bridged to possibility. The complexity of this view disturbs the slumber of responsibility monism and informs a more sensitive guide model for responsible life.

Another significant conversation has dealt not with the nature of responsibility as such but with how the criteria of political rightness and wrongness relate to the criteria of ethical rightness and wrongness—the issue of "political responsibility." It comes up in the long-running debate between political realists and moralists; it comes up among moralists as they

---

6. For an overview of the analytic terrain, see Matthew Talbert, "Moral Responsibility," *The Stanford Encyclopedia of Philosophy*, ed. Edward N. Zalta (Winter 2019), accessed October 20, 2021, https://plato.stanford.edu/archives/win2019/entries/moral-responsibility/; on ethical transcendence, François Raffoul, *The Origins of Responsibility* (Bloomington: Indiana University Press, 2010).

7. See Garrath Williams, "Responsibility as a Virtue," *Ethical Theory and Moral Practice*, 11 (2008): 455–70. A recent turn to the study of "forward-looking responsibility," though largely limited to issues of social injustice, is also germane; see Peter A. French and Howard K. Wettstein, eds., *Forward-Looking Collective Responsibility* (Boston: Wiley, 2014). This work has remarkably little connection with the blame-centered consequentialist work represented in Fraser MacBride, ed., "Forward-Looking Accounts of Responsibility," *The Monist* 104, no. 4 (October 2021)—except for Mark Alfano's "Towards a Genealogy of Forward-Looking Responsibility," in that same issue of *The Monist* (489–509), which pivots toward the desirability of assuming responsibility.

debate how to build an effective politics on ethical foundations;[8] it comes up among realists as they try to identify the distinctively political kind of constraint that should be binding on conscientious agents.[9] Because political responsibility is the form best recognized for combining concerns of basically different kinds—ethical and pragmatic, if not also historical and religious—and appeals to us, despite its slipperiness, as a fullest responsibility, it plays a featured role in the present inquiry.

Order of exposition reversing order of discovery, I can best illuminate the political form of responsibility by first examining its purer pragmatic component. The whole sequence of chapters is as follows:

1. Since deeply diverse guidances keyed to responsibility will have to be reckoned with, we must establish an adequately inclusive *concept of responsibility*, clarifying what is generally appealing in the role-related ways of comporting ourselves that we demand or aspire to as responsible and what being responsible generally requires in understanding and commitment, even as different personal and collective realizations motivate different framings of responsibility. We will begin to give the aspirational aspect of responsibility its due by pointing out some of the personal and social fulfillments that appeal to us under this rubric.

2. The premise of potentially divergent past-, present-, and future-related branches of responsibility must be substantiated by locating their centers of gravity and boundaries in our conscientious reckoning. We shall start with the most intellectually obscure but most necessary, the form of responsibility that relates directly to the present constituting of actions. *Pragmatic responsibility* is an appropriate designation of the target here, given that ordinary senses of "pragmatic" are closely tied to immediate or near-term problem-solving and a distinctive salient value of expediency. This kind of responsibility appears clearly in emergencies, such as in wartime, but also in everyday situations of compulsory pragmatism such as in helping friends or colleagues with their tasks. A major challenge in developing an adequate model of pragmatic responsibility is sorting out the claims of action sharing

---

8. A signal attempt to think through politics on the basis of radical commitment to the Other (as in Levinas and Derrida) is Simon Critchley's *Infinitely Demanding: Ethics of Commitment, Politics of Resistance* (London: Verso, 2007).

9. See Matt Sleat, ed., *Politics Recovered. Realist Thought in Theory and Practice* (New York: Columbia University Press, 2018). Many of the papers in this volume reference Bernard Williams's focus on a distinctively political principle of legitimacy in "Realism and Moralism in Political Theory," in *In the Beginning was the Deed*, ed. Geoffrey Hawthorn (Princeton: Princeton University Press, 2005), 1–17.

on various scales of shared action: should I finish moving this piano with my friends now (with rain threatening) if it means being late to work (again) or missing dinner with my family (again)?

3. We can take advantage of a clarified idea of pragmatic responsibility to do justice to the complexity of *political responsibility*, which incorporates all other forms of responsibility and assumes quite different profiles depending on which of our chief concerns about our scheme for action sharing—about the holding of power, justice, workable social organization, or collective identity—is uppermost. Since there can be no standard plan for fulfillment here, we will acknowledge that personal exemplars of success in handling these concerns in combination (political heroes like Martin Luther King Jr.) have great orientational relevance for the most ambitiously responsible agents.

4. We can then test the proposed conception of political responsibility by showing how it informs a distinctive relevant response to a representative range of *challenges of political responsibility*: (a) in the sphere of family relations, the abortion decision, which determines the composition of family networks of responsibility (and where we can observe the partial convergence of a feminist "ethic of care" with the pragmatic responsibility concept); (b) in the sphere of organizations, the aspiration to responsible work amid a scarcity of "good jobs"; (c) in the sphere of self-governing political community, immigration policy, where the collaborative facts on the ground may call for assigning civic rights and duties to relative newcomers to the neighborhood; and (d) in the sphere of global society, the international regime regarding displaced persons, where improvised protection of human rights on the disunified global stage provides some remedy for the failures of states.

5. Political responsibility can be a compelling approximation to the ambiguous ideal of *full responsibility*, but we can recognize a range of different ways of thinking about fullest responsibility that are helpfully guiding and motivating, depending on the circumstances. Here metaphysical and religious views of maximal responsibility raise special problems but cannot be dismissed.

6. In the appendixes I offer concentrated portraits of ethical, historical, and religious responsibility, partly in support of earlier arguments that were obliged to cross into those territories and partly to meet the general challenge of envisioning responsibility fully.

My main claims will be the following:

To bear responsibility is to be in charge of a delegated and evaluated share of action, a fulfillable role, in a community that discusses and judges how best to share action.

Being disposed to be responsible and capable of bearing responsibility is a requirement for prosocial (directively sensitive) human life.[10] Bearing basic social responsibilities is assumed in social life.

Being responsible is not to be equated with being sensitive to others or with being self-determined. It involves participating in a collaborative scheme.

Being *fully* responsible, in the sense of being fully sincere and competent in perception and action, is an aspirational ideal for the bearing of responsibility. Full responsibility in the extensive sense of being responsible in all possible ways is an inordinately demanding ideal and yet sure to be interesting to whoever values the prosocial condition. The fullness ideals are in tension with the equally essential responsibility goals of (a) specifying the agent's burden so as to limit it reasonably and enable the agent to handle it successfully, and (b) upholding the agent's freedom in deciding how to exercise responsibility.

To be responsible is not necessarily to be ethically responsible—unless the ethical (or moral) field is simply equated with the field of responsibility, confounding our broadest category of prosocial constraint with a narrower requirement to act on general principle.

The main branches of responsibility correspond to the main scenes of action sharing, which in turn correspond to the basic ontological permissions for action sharing: the historical past of things done, the pragmatic present of things being done, the ethically assessable future of things that might be done, and perhaps also the envisionable eternal whole of action. For purposes of constructive reflection on right conduct, this view is a highly suggestive alternative to both the dominant monism of ethical responsibility and a chaotic value pluralism.

Political responsibility is a comprehensively combinatory form of responsibility and so in a sense the fullest form, at least from a mundane

---

10. I intend "prosocial" as an uncontroversial qualification of the human mode of existence as oriented to the proper management of relations among agents. It can be read as a descriptive term (humans are prosocial just as wolves are prosocial) or with the directive force that it has for prosocial beings while engaging in their collaborative life. Occasionally I will say *spiritual* in these places, as I think it is the best term to represent our active engagement with issues of right relationship, for reasons I have laid out in *The Concept of the Spiritual* (Philadelphia: Temple University Press, 1988). I will also sometimes use *directive* as a broader concept than the ethically affiliated *normative*.

perspective, but it is also unavoidably unstable in its standards. Seeing it clearly in this character gets us past the standoff between the simplistic alternatives of political moralism and political realism.

A program for the fullest feasible responsibility can be headquartered in any of the ontological venues of shared action—past, present, future, perhaps even eternity—and so will always be subject to challenge from differently located programs.

The comprehensive ideal of *personal* full responsibility is eclectic; it is unified by a personal or cultural vision, not by a normative logic. Though rarely, if ever, a trump, it has considerable life-guiding persuasiveness.

§⋅

My arguments will be pragmatic. Since we are deeply embedded in the assigning and assuming of responsibility, one main task of a philosophy of responsibility is to elucidate its roles in the practical life we are living, measuring its demands and solving its puzzles to the extent possible. A philosophical account of responsibility will have value if it adds clarity and detail to our shared picture of what we are already trying to do.

In another way, responsibility is discretionary. I might or might not be a friend, a parent, an employee, a member of a profession, or the adherent of a religion. I might be generally leery of living in that burdened way. Our collective mood might be unenthusiastic about promoting responsibility beyond a bare minimum. But this lack of interest could be caused by ignorance. To speak to those who lack appreciation for responsibility as an ideal demand, if only to explain what is at stake, a philosophical account of responsibility may try to show that important assumptions about agentic life involve responsibility, so that the price of dismissing responsibility would be a serious disillusionment. Or it may try to show that what a normally enterprising agent would hope to be true of life involves responsibility.

I can start that argument on both fronts—for responsibility as assumed and as aspirational—with a responsibility-based description of that most constant of all human collaborations, the use of language.

When you encounter another person of presumed linguistic competence, and you endeavor to make conversation, or make an excuse, or request or give direction, you are assuming that the other person will work with you in specifically linguistic ways. You will start the exchange by speaking and the other will be a hearer and responder, those roles being already understood and accepted by all language users (even by the speakers of mutually unintelligible languages). Under normal circumstances, the speaker's responsibility is to speak relevantly, not deceptively or distractingly and not merely wasting the hearer's time; the hearer's responsibility is to form a reasonable understanding of what the speaker says, so far as possible, and to be reasonably helpful ("The time? 4:15"). If these responsibilities are not fulfilled, there is not a successful communication. If we could not assume that these responsibilities will normally be fulfilled, if linguistic conduct were not institutionalized and assured of success to this extent, language would not be the public utility that it is and we would not be the citizens of a large community of knowledge sharing.

That language use is responsibility-based we know both positively and negatively: positively, as in the sketch of linguistic role playing I just offered, but also negatively, in our experience of breakdowns in communication due to inappropriate conduct by speakers and hearers. To enter into linguistic interchange on a different understanding—thinking of interlocutors not as freely devoted collaborators in the formation of shared awareness but as puppets to be manipulated by aural tugs, for example, or purely as parts of a natural process—is not to speak or listen. That we can learn a lot about language by manipulating and objectifying it does not remove the pragmatic necessity of fulfilling the responsibilities of speaker and hearer in linguistic performance.

There is a similar point to be made from the unsatisfactory aspects of instituted language—the degrading terms prescribed for some entities and actions, the oppressive hierarchies of sex and class sometimes encoded in grammar, the marginalization of entire languages by conquest or commerce. We could not stage a helpful discussion of such impediments to speaking and listening without the support of basic presumptions of responsibility in communication.

A certain aspiration for responsible conduct is just as unavoidable for language users as assuming the most basically responsible conduct. It is embedded in the terms with which I described language's functioning: usually in serious communications one cannot but hope for a *sincerely* and *intelligently* helpful interlocutor, one who will speak and answer *very* relevantly, as would be likely to happen only if the interlocutor is committed to mastering the roles of linguistic guide and follower. One wants to be able to *trust* one's interlocutor for communications of the highest possible value. Hoping to benefit from reciprocity, hoping not to be abused, one wishes to be a trustworthy communicator oneself.

Obviously, much of our linguistic activity is effective to some degree without being exemplary. We are often disappointed by our fellow speakers and by ourselves. If you are immune to this kind of disappointment, if your attitude toward all language use is purely that of a strategic manipulator or detached observer, then you will not be motivated to play the most fully responsible roles in it. But then if you were to speak to us in perfect indifference to the exercises of linguistic responsibility that we normally care about, we would probably detect your lack of hope, trust, and trustworthiness. You would be like a scary pitcher who might or might not choose to throw the ball where the catcher can catch it, and who therefore would be dropped from the team.

The sports team model serves as a reminder that norms of responsibility are constitutive of what we often understand ourselves to be engaged in doing. An active collaborator cannot ignore appeals to act responsibly and to strive to be more responsible. The issue is inescapable because normal human life is a tissue of collaborations. Anyone who wholly demurred from everyday helpfulness would be in a profoundly anomalous and unpromising position.

Whether an appeal to act responsibly does elicit greater dedication to collaborative role playing depends on a free response, for this is a personal matter, but it also depends on how revealingly the appeal exhibits the meaning of the choice, which is a rational matter. The philosopher's task is to devise revelations: to show what will and will not work in playing a game, and how to understand the game's key terms. Terms of interest here include collaboration, responsibility, obligation, the ethical, the pragmatic, and the political.

Each of the terms just mentioned has a broader meaning that gets confusingly mixed with a narrower meaning. In some cases I will want to link my claims to a broader meaning than what is more commonly assumed (collaboration, political) while in others the key meaning for my purposes is narrower (obligation, ethical, pragmatic).

Now is a good time to explain what I want to mean by "collaboration," which I am using as broadly as many other writers would use "cooperation" but still with a distinction in mind. It makes sense to think of *cooperation* as the mode of existence that generates considerations of practical rightness and wrongness because cooperation is liable to succeed or fail; it can be in good order, so that it continues, or be undermined, so that it breaks down. For example, I cooperate with strangers on the sidewalk so that the foot traffic keeps flowing smoothly. For the most part, I do this merely by making physical adjustments as I move forward; I cooperate similarly with dogs and even with insects. But there is a more commanding mode of cooperation in cases where agents are intentionally trying to accomplish something together, and the term *collaboration* expresses this. Collaboration fits the situations in which responsibility can be assumed or imputed. I could not say to an insect, "That's not helpful," but I could speak to a human who was blocking me on the sidewalk about our shared project of getting expeditiously to where we're going and the responsibilities this implies for all of us. Often when "cooperation" is invoked in social and political philosophy what is meant is "collaboration"—or it is the possibility of undertaking cooperation as collaboration that prompts a serious and open normative discussion. A Rawlsian liberal who refuses to posit that we are all working to realize the same agreed good, and who has a reason therefore to demand only a cooperative, not a collaborative, society, still needs everyone to subscribe to liberal justice as a shared project, not a mere *modus vivendi*; otherwise there would be no reasonable appeal for the scheme.[11] At the level of normative concurrence, then, cooperation must be a collaboration.

I grant that there is another way of looking at cooperation and collaboration. Suppose the model for our shared life is a ship voyage. It is as though we are on a ship (this represents all our logistical requirements), and we all have a stake in sailing safely and in the right direction. We also share an interest in a smooth flow of activities on board, so we tend to stay in our lanes. To the extent that our purposes and activities intersect, we make sure that they mesh. But in any given phase of the voyage some of us are crew, sharing the work of operating the ship, while the rest of us are passengers, free for our individual projects. The crew *collaborates* on sailing the ship while the passengers merely *cooperate* with them and each other. (Collaboration is a more focused and constrained mode of cooperation.) Even if the ultimate point of the voyage is to enable passengers to fulfill their individual goals, we would not say that the passengers are collaborators in sailing the ship. So too, the less intentionally demanding relationship of cooperation—not collaboration—is the appropriate inclusive standard for action sharing on the level of a whole society.

This view does capture how we would specify different parties' responsibilities in many sets of circumstances. But I would note that (1) the passengers (at least, those who are aboard willingly) all share in *sponsorship*

---

11. On justice versus a *modus vivendi*, see John Rawls, *Political Liberalism*, expanded ed. (New York: Columbia University Press, 2005), 146–48; and see Rawls's specifications for "social cooperation" on p. 16.

of the voyage in such a way that they all share in executing a governing plan for it—their cooperation is not as passive as it may seem at a given moment during the voyage; and (2) the division of roles between crew and passengers is a luxury that everyone understands might have to be suspended in an emergency. (An emergency would, in effect, re-create older conditions of human existence in which everyone is crew.) In these ways collaboration underlies cooperation.

A general assumption motivating and supporting the following discussions is that we can determine what is satisfactory, best, or necessary for our practice by relating a choice or action positively to the project of rectifying relationships between beings. This general life-project involves conducting one's own parts in relationships in such a way as to support the greatest mutual benefit of beings in them. The sharing of being is the supreme good and norm. No argument will be offered against selfishness and indifference. (We must not, however, overlook the pervasive influence of competition and the constant possibility of disaffection in the field of socially sensitive conduct.)

I will be examining shared action just in the respect that it generates directively charged issues of assumable responsibility in several major modes—pragmatic, ethical, historical, political, and religious—subject to an aspiration to full responsibility. While my account intersects with other theories of responsibility rooted in action sharing, notably Margaret Gilbert's plural subjects theory in chapter 3, I will not offer a distinct theory of the intentional mechanics of joint planning and action.

I will not defend the freedom premise of responsibility from determinist attack.[12] In my view, the relevant kind of agent freedom is not precluded by natural or social causation properly understood, but in any case I foresee that freedom-assuming responsibility games will continue to be played in our reason-sensitive dealings with each other. My discussion is within this game, where for serious players the more important considerations about involuntariness have to do with who we find ourselves responsible to and what we find or can make ourselves responsible for rather than with dimi-

---

12. See Bruce Waller's determinist argument against moral responsibility in *Against Moral Responsibility* (Cambridge, MA: MIT Press, 2011).

nution or removal of responsibility by general conditions of our existence. That practical intention takes the lead in our "participant attitude."[13]

Nor will I (thinking now of politically militant friends on my left) ground my claims in a critical analysis of existing society or gear them to a transformation of that society. I would be in deep trouble if it could be shown that my account of responsibility supports an unjust status quo against better alternatives. But I posit that the best justification for the best politics will incorporate a philosophically broadened and refined view of human aspirations for relationship—a corrective for all inspirational and polemical oversimplifications, though with due respect for the need for such oversimplifications in the cut and thrust of political action.

Finally, in this discussion I will not look beyond issues in human relationship, but I do affirm that responsibility extends to nonhumans as well. That humans use a linguistic, concept-negotiating mode of communication almost exclusively among themselves admittedly makes an immense practical difference and guarantees that issues of interhuman relation will take the highest spiritual priority. It is a mistake, however, to think that we can only have responsibility *for* and never responsibility *to* nonhuman beings simply because we are not talking with them in human fashion—for we can take cues directly from nonhuman beings that constrain how we relate to them, supposing a commitment on our part to mutually beneficial relations.[14]

---

13. The notion of a "participant attitude" is from Strawson, but my prime consideration is not emotions, as in Strawson, but actions. P. F. Strawson, "Freedom and Resentment," *Proceedings of the British Academy* 48 (1962): 1–25.

14. The work of Bruno Latour and his allies on assemblages of concern shows how we can make sense of an unlimited range of meaningful relations with nonhuman beings, relations that are codetermined by all beings in their various ways of acting. Bruno Latour, *Reassembling the Social* (Oxford: Oxford University Press, 2005); *Making Things Public: Atmospheres of Democracy*, ed. Bruno Latour and Peter Weibel (Cambridge, MA: MIT Press, 2005); and see my "The Structure of Unlimited Action Sharing," *Philosophical Frontiers* 4 (July–December 2009): 57–71.

Chapter One

Responsibility and Realization

The Appeal of Responsibility

Responsibility is a word we cannot do without that we have only been using for a couple of centuries; it appears almost nowhere in pre-Enlightenment texts.[1] As Roland Pennock pointed out, it is an essentially modern, liberal concept that we apply when we want to allow for an agent's exercise of discretion in relation to a social demand.[2] Unlike more rigidly predefined

---

1. An ancestor of our idea is the political concept of an executive's "accountability" to a council. This is found in classical Greek authors' statements that a tyrant is "completely unaccountable," *anupeuthunos*. See Kinch Hoekstra, "Athenian Democracy and Popular Tyranny," in Richard Bourke and Quentin Skinner, eds., *Popular Sovereignty in Historical Perspective* (Cambridge, UK: Cambridge University Press, 2016), 15–51, 19–22.
2. J. Roland Pennock, "The Problem of Responsibility," in Carl J. Friedrich, ed., *Responsibility* (New York: Liberal Arts, 1960), 3–27, 4–5, 9. Dewey and Tufts articulated the key premises of this view in 1908: "The more comprehensive and diversified the social order, the greater the responsibility and the freedom of the individual. His freedom is the greater, because the more numerous are the effective stimuli to action, and the more varied and the more certain the ways in which he may fulfill his powers. His responsibility is greater because there are more demands for considering the consequences of his acts; and more agencies for bringing home to him the recognition of consequences which affect not merely more persons individually, but which also influence the more remote and hidden social ties . . . the opportunities for an effective circulation of sympathetic ideas and of reasonable emotions have only newly come into existence. Education as a public interest and care, applicable to all individuals, is hardly more than a century old; while a conception of the richness and complexity of the ways in which it should touch any one individual is hardly half a century old." John Dewey and J. H. Tufts, *Ethics*

"duties" and "obligations," responsibilities allow room for spontaneity and personal authenticity. If you fail to fulfill a duty or to meet an obligation, you are simply at fault, but if you fail to fulfill a responsibility, the rest of us wonder if a conversation needs to be reopened about how your responsibility should be understood and assigned, and what your attitude really is.[3] (Thus, in *philosophizing* with his son about "duties" in *De Officiis*, Cicero was getting at "responsibilities" *avant la lettre*.) Apparently *responsibility* has become our term of choice for the most desirable general orientation because we prefer to trust each other in social collaboration via the communicative dynamic of "answering for" our freely chosen actions rather than merely by monitoring the presence of standard virtues or the fulfillment of standard duties.[4] We are contemplating the field of shared and sharable action not simply with a view to assuring group coherence, as on the military model

---

(Okitoks, [1908] 2017), 150, 154. Tracking the same point, H. L. A. Hart distinguishes a soldier's "sphere of responsibility" from mere "duty" as involving "duties of a relatively complex or extensive kind . . . requiring care and attention over a protracted period of time"—*Punishment and Responsibility* (New York: Oxford University Press, 1968), 213.

3. In Robert Brandom's reconstructed Hegelian account of normatively directed life, the term "responsibility" expresses the general status of being subject to a normative demand (identified with "dependence" in Hegel's argument) in distinction from "authority," the status of making a normative demand (identified with "independence")—*A Spirit of Trust* (Cambridge, MA: Harvard University Press, 2019), chap. 9, consistent with Brandom, *Making It Explicit* (Cambridge, MA: Harvard University Press, 1994), 172–75. Slaves would then be "responsible" to the masters who determine their duties and their liability for reward and punishment, but for us that is an incongruous expression, even if master and slave agree that obeying the master is *right*. The dialectic of normativity will, to be sure, arrive at modern "responsibility," correcting the spiritual deficiency of traditional hierarchical duty—see *Spirit of Trust*, chap. 10, and compare Brandom's own explicitly collaborative responsibility system of "deontic scorekeeping" in *Making It Explicit*.

4. In his critical synthesis of modern and classical perspectives, Alasdair MacIntyre argues that virtues are always connected to forms of social collaboration: "[1] when any virtue has been specified with sufficient adequacy to provide guidance for moral practice and moral education, it will turn out to be functional in respect of some forms of political and social life and dysfunctional in respect of others. . . . [2] debate and conflict as to the character of *sophrosune* [one of the strongest classical counterparts to "responsibility"], debate as to which rival account of it is the best, must therefore be inescapably linked to political debate and conflict as to which forms of social and political life merit our allegiance." "*Sophrosune*: How a Virtue Can Become Socially Disruptive," *Midwest Studies in Philosophy*, Vol. 13: *Ethical Theory: Character and Virtue*, ed. Peter A. French, Theodore E. Uhling Jr., and Howard K. Wettstein (Notre Dame: University of Notre Dame Press, 1988), 1–11.

of ordering everyone to do their duty according to their station—nor in the individualist counterposition of assuming sovereign self-control over one's participation in society—but in recognition that the terms and meaning of our intentional action sharing are subject to discussion.[5] We no longer believe that a permanently established social design dictates the functional roles "for which we were made." And apparently we are optimistic that a common rationality will support our discussions and that agents will follow through on their conclusions.[6]

Another way of thinking about the rise of responsibility is that in an increasingly atomized, higher-mobility type of society we cannot rely as much (although we do still rely heavily) on the felt importance of continuing personal *attachments*—partialities that can be counted on for prosocial conduct, such as helping one's family or standing by one's patron—and must instead plan for appropriate responses to interruptive *appeals* as they are made by new circumstances that we notice and new communicators' initiatives that we hear. This is a structural reason why groups seeking to control individuals' behavior tend more to operate on the premise of their responsibility ("responsibilization" as a power formation),[7] but at the same time it is a reason why a school of hyperethical philosophers resist all calculation of responsibility by tying it to the advent of the Other as a singular Event ("responsibilization" as an original upsurge of spiritual sensitivity).[8]

---

5. In an ideal modern army, responsibility would enfold duty, not abolish it; the responsible soldier, able to respond optimally in all eventualities, would most often recognize and fulfill the duty of a station.

6. Richard McKeon, "The Development and the Significance of the Concept of Responsibility," *Revue Internationale de Philosophie* 11 (1957): 3–32, 25f. Philip Pettit's account of discursively controlled freedom reinforces these premises—*A Theory of Freedom* (Cambridge, UK: Polity, 2001), 70–72.

7. See Pat O'Malley, "Responsibilization," *The Sage Dictionary of Policing*, ed. Alison Wakefield and Jenny Fleming (London: Sage, 2009), 276–78, and Frieder Vogelmann, *The Spell of Responsibility: Labor, Criminality, Philosophy*, trans. Daniel Steuer (London: Rowman & Littlefield, 2017). To the extent that the discourse on responsibilization is guided by Nietzsche's genealogy of "responsibility" (*On the Genealogy of Morals* II/II) it is skewed by Nietzsche's identification of all normative constraint (duty, guilt, punishability) with the liberal ideal of responsibility.

8. See Matthias Fritsch, "Sources of Morality in Habermas's Recent Work on Religion and Freedom," in Craig Calhoun et al., eds., *Habermas and Religion* (Cambridge, UK: Polity, 2013), 277–300, sketching a synthesis of constructive senses of responsibilization in Levinas (for whom asymmetrical encounter with the personal Other is primary) and Habermas (for whom symmetrical communicative action is primary).

Responsibility is reckoned in many ways, and any student of the concept must consider this range:[9]

1. *A determinative explanatory factor.* "He was (the fellow agent) causally responsible for the accident." If everyone had done just what drivers normally do, the accident would not have occurred, but because he swerved suddenly out of his lane, he is the culprit.[10]

2. *Attributability.* This is a condition on praising or blaming an agent for an action: "He is responsible for causing just such an accident."[11] It was his swerve, and his swerve expressed a reckless impatience that was truly his. A higher degree of attributability involves *sponsorship* of an action or goal: "He actually planned that stunt; he's fully responsible for it."

3. *Accountability.* "He is responsible to the rest of us for driving safely." "He is responsible to his friend for how he drives the car he borrowed." Now that bad driving has occurred, interpersonal accountings are in order—but perhaps not dictated by causal or purposive attribution, because someone else could step up to answer for the situation ("I take responsibility for what my son did"). Accountability is more practically pointed than the general answerability involved in persons taking a personal interest in each other.[12]

---

9. For a similar taxonomy more fully discussed, see Nicole A. Vincent, "A Structured Taxonomy of Responsibility Concepts," in *Moral Responsibility: Beyond Free Will and Determinism*, ed. Nicole A. Vincent, Ibo van de Poel, and Jeroen van den Hoven (Dordrecht: Springer, 2011), 15–35. For social-psychological perspectives see Ann Elisabeth Auhagen and Hans-Werner Bierhoff, eds., *Responsibility: The Many Faces of a Social Phenomenon* (London: Routledge, 2001).

10. There may of course be multiple culprits with different shares of causal responsibility—the other driver who waved distractingly, the designer of the oversensitive steering system, and so on. This idea is logically related to the idea that (in this example) the accident that happened to *the driver* is the indisseverable consequence of *his* actions, so that he must recognize that he made the accident happen. Lucien Lévy-Bruhl cites this as a primary datum of responsibility in *L'idée de responsabilité* (Paris: Hachette, 1884), 30. But the perception of one's own causation does not figure as evidence of responsibility if it is not placed in a social arena. It is only the responsibility-for component without responsibility-to.

11. My senses (2) and (3) roughly follow the attributability/accountability distinction drawn by Gary Watson in "Two Faces of Responsibility," *Philosophical Topics* 24 (1996): 227–48.

12. Christine Korsgaard runs the two ideas together in *Self-Constitution: Agency, Identity, and Integrity* (Oxford: Oxford University Press, 2009), 129–31. What makes sense of this is thinking of being the person one is as fulfilling the *role* of being that person in a *scheme* of "We're going to be persons, each in his or her own way." But I think that this most-basic *allotment* of initiative and interest among persons in a scheme of social

4. *Liability.* "He is responsible for the accident" in the sense that he must pay the costs. This obligation might be the driver's, but it might belong instead to the driver's parent or guardian or employer, depending on how legal liability is assigned.

5. *A general purposive role assignment.* "She is responsible for investigating the accident." An equivalent expression is "charged with," suggesting the granted authority of "being in charge" of a matter. Work duties have been assigned so that this investigation is hers. Others expect her to do this and depend on her doing this (it would contradict the premise of responsibility, but not of duty or obligation, for others to make their plans on the assumption that she may well not do this). Unless there are overriding considerations, she is in the wrong if she fails to perform the investigation; if she does perform it, then (so far as that goes) she proves herself worthy of her job. By extension, any other instrumentality by which a role is to be fulfilled can be called responsible in the same sense: "The police department is responsible for investigating the accident." By implication, when we fault someone searchingly for a wrongful action, it may seem appropriate to treat them as though they had been given a responsibility in which they failed, such as "driving responsibly."

6. *A purposive role in a specific relationship or at a specific juncture.* "He is responsible for that cat now." Because he started feeding the stray cat, he is the one who should take it to the vet to be neutered. Contextually specific responsibility can be attributed to an agent due to an opportunity: if the cat is coming onto his porch, then he is the one who should try to catch it and get it to the vet. (Sen's "responsibility of effective power" is in this category.)[13]

7. *A capacity and a virtue.* "He is a responsible person," responsive to relevant facts and sound values, bearing a known competence and sanity in his public comportment and a sufficiency in his resources,[14] and therefore *should not* and *would not* have negligently or passionately swerved out of his lane; or *would not* have failed to do her job investigating the accident; or *would* be a fully engaged cat keeper, or is a good bet to catch the cat;

---

existence that *could not* be different, the scheme of answerability, is always already in place when we *assign* and *assume* responsibilities in schemes that *could* be different.

13. Amartya Sen, *The Idea of Justice* (Cambridge, MA: Harvard University Press, 2009), 205–7, 270–71.

14. Hart discerns a "capacity-responsibility" relative to legal culpability: one is or is not "responsible" in the sense of being able to intend or act in the way that punishment presupposes (227–30).

or *is* generally self-controlled and considerate of the legitimate needs, concerns, and questions of others—not simply due to natural equanimity and amiability, but as an intent sponsor of that kind of conduct.[15] By extension, an action or policy or habit that would be worthy (or unworthy) of a responsible person can be called responsible (or irresponsible).

A significant thread running through all this usage is what we might call the *setup* of life as responsible: in these various ways we are actually or hypothetically placing someone in an evaluated relationship, the holding-and-held-responsible relationship, which assumes both the autonomy of the agent and the solidarity of the community.[16] We maintain the autonomy and solidarity requirements knowing that they do not always pull in the same direction. When Henry David Thoreau refused to pay his taxes in protest of slavery and Sam Staples put him in jail, both Thoreau and Staples embodied responsibility. We see the responsible agent as self-directive and discerning, not merely compliant, and the responsible action as sincere and well-informed, not merely lawful, which opens the possibility of rebelliousness and illegality (Thoreau must protest). At the same time we are putting the claims of a community first, insisting on compliance and correctness (Thoreau must be jailed; Staples must do his job). Agents are allowed to be self-directive just so long as they are committed to fulfilling the legitimate expectations of their colleagues, including that they answer for their actions; and the claims of the community take precedence only so long as the community is composed of independently thinking and speaking self-directive agents.

A third principle has to do with the practical format of autonomy-in-solidarity: the agent whom we regard as responsible *plays* (or is ready or able to play) an *assigned role*, that is, operates (or is ready or able to operate) voluntarily in an agreed (or demanded or imagined) collaborative scheme. If such a scheme obtains, there is some shared understanding of what needs to be done and how it can be accomplished. In the sketches made so far,

---

15. Garrath Williams would add that a responsible person is characteristically responsible in plural frames of reckoning—otherwise personal judgment and initiative would not be required of the responsible as distinct from dutiful person. "Responsibility as a Virtue," *Ethical Theory and Moral Practice* 11 (2008): 455–70, 459.

16. On the Strawson-inspired discussion of the relationship between being responsible and holding responsible, see Michael McKenna, *Conversation and Responsibility* (Oxford: Oxford University Press, 2012). For present purposes it suffices to note their connection without considering arguments for the explanatory or metaphysical priority of one or the other. I think McKenna is right that the two are mutually dependent.

this aspect was explicit only in the (4) legal liability and (5) job description senses of being responsible, but it was implicit in the others. For

(1) even purely causal responsibility assumes a collaborative scheme—in the accident example, the scheme for driving—as a basis for remonstrating with the agent and entering credit or blame in the agency ledger;[17]

(2–3) even unforeseen attributions and answerings figure the responsible agent as having taken a definite share of the sponsorship of action within a larger social economy of sponsoring action;

(6) even an emergent, particular assumption of responsibility, as for a stray cat, can be characterized as "responsible," as distinct from "competent" or "kind," only by reference to the playing of a role in a recognized scheme for attending to some matter of concern; and

(7) even the general virtue of being responsible, as distinct from being competent or kind, refers prospectively, if not also actually or historically, to the playing of roles in schemes.

A vast modern investment in the responsibility ideal encourages the thought that personal responsibility is a basic good or authentic disposition more original than role assignment and broader in its reach. This is connected with the thought that the original spring of responsibility is perception of need.[18] Another spring is the desire to be attached to other agents in some degree of friendly interdependence, perhaps in direct desire for that sociable good or perhaps in fear of the alternative of anarchy.[19]

---

17. Moreover, the presence of a quasi-collaborative mechanical scheme of prescribed actions of things, as in the design of a car, would make it more natural to say "the car's steering system was the culprit" than to say "the sudden rainstorm was the culprit." That we frequently identify nonpersonal beings as culprits shows, I think, our intuitively social framing of situations, or, if you like, a background animism; but Dieter Birnbacher considers this a "marginal" usage of the concept of responsibility ("Philosophical Foundations of Responsibility," in Auhagen and Bierhoff, 9–22, 11).

18. As in Robert E. Goodin, *Protecting the Vulnerable* (Chicago: University of Chicago Press, 1985); see also Hans Jonas's use of encounter with the compellingly needy newborn child as a paradigm for the motivation of responsibility in *The Imperative of Responsibility* (Chicago: University of Chicago Press, 1984), 130–35.

19. Pettit argues that there is an a priori connection between our ordinary concepts of freedom and responsibility in that "fit to be held responsible" and "free" require each other (18–31). He comes at this connection in a Strawsonian way, citing the psychology of reactive attitudes like gratitude and resentment, whereas I come at it in a Hobbesian way: we realize that we need a scheme of holding each other responsible because otherwise our mutually unpredictable and uncontrollable conduct is too dangerous. I further suppose that the Hobbesian scene undergoes a Rousseauvian shift: in holding each other

(We can say for collaborative life what is sometimes said for employment schemes: the purpose is partly to get some things done and partly to keep agents safely occupied.) I contend that when we conceive a basic good or authentic disposition as responsibility we are relating it to role expectations and to the functional needs of the collaborations for which such roles are specified, once collaborative efforts have been evoked by perceived needs. (Compare Gabriel Marcel's more open concept of "availability" to others.)[20] This claim requires more discussion, as it goes against the grain of some major theoretical appeals to responsibility.

When thinking agents find themselves acting together, for their guidance they either rely on a preexisting idea of the purpose and normal style of the activity or frame a new idea. Thereby they give an appreciable form to the basic social conception of partners' shares in a shared endeavor. Thus even mutual strangers who fall into frolicking together in a park and who are consciously enjoying freedom from role expectations will nevertheless form some notion of a *game* they are engaged in, generating role responsibilities, after all, and the possibility of letting each other down. Or if one person is pitching in to help another there will be some notion of a *task* and of *jobs* to be done. There is a hazard of discord and disappointment here so long as such notions are formed tacitly and separately in the space not determined by custom. But the means of reaching agreement and a kind of ostinato of active collaboration are always at hand in speaking and listening. Quite often we will discuss and formalize our collaborative relationship, bringing responsibilities into focus; an early-phase exercise of responsibility is to offer one's partners an articulation of the form ("If you take notes, I'll lead the discussion"). By this means we migrate from the hazardous situation of each of us wanting an optimal collaboration by our own lights (the force field in which reactive emotions like resentment and indignation are generated) to the safely regulated situation of agreed-on roles.

The simplest overt scheme of responsibility is the contract or covenant under which you and I each undertake to meet expectations we have determined for each other. For more complex collaborations, work organizations offer a clear model. The responsible agent is committed to a shared enterprise and to fellow agents according to their positions in the enterprise. Thus I

---

responsible, our normative psychology changes, which accounts for the constraints on responsibility that Pettit and I both recognize. A prosocial meaning of freedom is layered over its threateningness.

20. Gabriel Marcel, "On the Ontological Mystery," in *The Philosophy of Existentialism*, trans. Manya Harari (New York: Citadel, 1956), 39–43.

will be responsible *to* my practical community C (say, a storage company) *for* X (patrolling the warehouse), an object of shared concern in pursuit of collaborative goal G (security for the sake of profitability), *under* the agreed terms of an arrangement A (my work and pay schedule) for pursuing G and a collaborative scheme S for implementing A (the definition of my job, including my rights, and other jobs with which mine is interdependent). I may be responsible for X in the backward-looking sense that I may properly be identified as the cause of X obtaining or not; or in the present-oriented sense that I can be expected to report on how X is going and make relevant recommendations; or in the forward-looking sense that I can be expected to deal with X-related developments, within my recognized limitations. On this understanding, responsibility can never simply be unconditional: I *bear* responsibility only if I am included in the collaborative scheme, and I can *take* responsibility, claiming to be in charge of certain states of affairs, only if I am *given* an allowance to do so by a collaborative scheme. (I cannot take responsibility for being collaborative in the first place.) Whenever we have occasion to reexamine these allocations of responsibility ("We're asking too much of our security officers!"), the constitution of our community and the envisioning of our goal are in the background of our deliberations and can themselves come up for reexamination.

On this conception of responsibility, it must be said that one *has* responsibilities as one has rights, by assignment. Our expressions for *being* responsible would be uninterpretable apart from *having* responsibilities that have been assumed or given[21] and that are adequately understood.[22] To say that one *is* responsible for X, not merely by assignment but as an actual personal qualification, means that one identifies with that responsibility (as in "I feel obligated to take care of X") or that one is identified with it by others ("Don't worry, she'll take care of X"). To say simply that an agent *is* responsible, as a general characterization, implies that she or he has fulfilled and can be expected to fulfill responsibility assignments.[23] Viewing responsibility as a social competence, the relevant expectations and performance

---

21. Hart, 213.

22. For recent work on epistemic issues see Philip Robichaud and Jan Willem Wieland, eds., *Responsibility: The Epistemic Condition* (Oxford: Oxford University Press, 2017).

23. On the self-control and responsiveness to reasons requirements for acting responsibly, see John Martin Fischer and Mark Ravizza, *Responsibility and Control* (Cambridge, UK: Cambridge University Press, 1998) and Jeanette Kennett, *Agency and Responsibility* (Oxford: Oxford University Press, 2001).

vary by social context.[24] An agent comes to *be* responsible in submitting to the particular claims of collaborations (caring for a cat, holding down a job) while learning to bear a responsible identity and to appreciate the general ideal of intelligent fidelity in roles.

While responsibility is geared to assignments, not all assignments are codified. Some agents might *be* responsible in the sense that they are regarded as reliable role fulfillers in an ideal community of helpfulness in which what constitutes the relevant helpful action is often freshly determined ad hoc. In another sense, agents might *be* responsible as a matter of temperament if they spontaneously seek to fulfill responsibilities, whatever those are, in contrast with others who avoid responsibilities or fulfill them only in a conformist or selfishly convenient way.

Finally, responsible agents are not necessarily fully *successful* agents. Even the most robustly responsible human agents can fail to accomplish what they intend. The most we can realistically say is that if their responsibilities are well conceived and assigned they should have a good chance of not falling short in the most important respects. A responsible approach to a problem is definitely a "practically minded" teleological strategy and not merely the adoption of a righteous style. It is formed by reckoning with the problem. But it is not of its very nature the solution of that problem.

If the social ideal of responsibility is not completely fantastical or hypocritical, some agents, on some occasions at least, are sincerely responsible. We need to understand why an agent would spontaneously seek to fulfill responsibilities. An account of what responsibility is should not leave out what is appealing about it.

But let us give due notice to the burdens. When I become responsible for something, I no longer have an acceptable option of not being concerned about it or not tending to it; I am denied liberty to do various pleasing things I might like to do, even if I am being held responsible only by myself. I am prevented from doing some creative things for the good of a cause if they are too risky. I am not allowed not to have answers for persons to whom I am responsible. Often this means that I am not allowed not to have a definite plan that is acceptable to certain others for this part

---

24. See Andrew Sneddon's contextualism about being responsible in "Moral Responsibility: The Difference of Strawson, and the Difference It Should Make," *Ethical Theory and Moral Practice* 8 (2005): 239–65.

of my life. I am not allowed to avoid the blame, along with appropriate punishment, for any incorrect action or lack of action for which I am responsible—and this imputation sticks to me for the rest of my life, as part of my biography. What is worst, holding any responsibility exposes me to the treacheries of an uncontrollable world that can always prevent me from acting satisfactorily.[25] (The child learns this early; he is given some money to get milk at the corner store . . . and look what happens!) The parameters of my responsibility change surprisingly according to the changing demands of my collaborators and changing conditions of practice, sometimes forcing a difficult recalibration of my commitment (as when contracted workers are required to adapt to new technical requirements).[26] Of its very nature, responsibility seems to violate the principle that responsibility should never be assigned without a commensurate empowerment.

There is moreover a serious shame in being relieved of a responsibility because one is considered to have failed in it. A parent who loses custody of a child, for example, may lose intimately necessary forms of respect from his or her peers for being thought to have failed the child. But this is the discipline of the responsibility system: you stand or fall according to the satisfaction you give.

As long as we are thinking of responsibility as a preoccupying constraint, a liability for stigma and punishment, and a practical dilemma, it is obvious why anyone would wish to limit or avoid it. To minimize responsibility is human.

But it is also human to seek responsibility and rejoice in it—more specifically, to rejoice in the possession of responsible awareness and in the exercise of responsible power precisely under responsibility's constraining

---

25. Hegel declares that the will has the right to accept responsibility only for what it purposed, not for uncontrolled consequences. G. W. F. Hegel, *Elements of the Philosophy of Right*, trans. H. B. Nisbet, ed. Allen W. Wood (Cambridge, UK: Cambridge University Press, 1991), 145 (§118). (Dewey, with his eye on a purely self-realizational conception of responsibility, concurs: "There is no responsibility for any result that is not intended or foreseen. Such a consequence is only physical, not moral"—"Outlines of a Critical Theory of Ethics," in John Dewey, *The Early Works, 1882–1898*, Vol. 3 [Carbondale: Southern Illinois University Press., 2008], 341.) But the more responsible agents do not compartmentalize their causation so neatly, and indeed Hegel goes on to add: "An old proverb rightly says, 'The stone belongs to the devil when it leaves the hand that threw it.' By acting, I expose myself to misfortune, which accordingly has a right over me" (148 [§119]). On the Hegelian unity of intentional and consequential characterizations of actions see Brandom, chap. 11.

26. I owe this example to Marc Anderson.

aspect. Consider family responsibility: even more than it is avoided it is voluntarily undertaken. No doubt responsibility-incurring choices like the choices to marry and to have children are socially conditioned at the level of one's acquired vision of meaningful life, but nevertheless the responsible way of life really is ideally attractive to us and not merely a set of constraints we cope with. Nor can the appetite for responsibility be resolved simply into a desire to raise one's social profile, since accepting responsibility is sometimes not conducive to eminence and may even work against it. (That has been many women's experience in bearing responsibility for family care.)

Like any mode of intent action, responsibility is a way of being more alert—more perceptive and intellectually engaged—and more mobilized, more competitive against disfavored possibilities, and more a positive maker of the world that comes. Like any mode of effectiveness, responsibility carves out a share of the action, maintaining the agent's standing among agents. Like any allocation, responsibility gives the agent something of his or her own. Like any stance with a justification, responsibility has the partly adventurous, partly reassuring appeal of binding the agent to a worthy cause even in adversity or chaos. As a role assignment, responsibility gives the agent something to be in charge of, like a vehicle to drive; at the same time, defined responsibility brings some limitation and manageableness to the otherwise scary proposition of affecting other people's lives. More specifically, responsibility draws positive value from the advantageousness of collaboration and from an intrinsic good that we can see in several desirable qualifications of the collaborator's agency:

1. A conscious agent is unavoidably fascinated with the links between agent-caused effects and quality of life; this fascination engages a larger, more complex array of effects and qualities when agent efforts are combined in a collaborative enterprise. As long as the effects and qualities seem to be good on balance, the individual agent is bound to be impressed by the collaborative advantage in efficacy and by the relatively definite prospect of being able to explain and justify his or her exercises of power. More immediately, the problem-solving capacities of the agent are satisfyingly engaged by the challenge of complex coordination. The role assignments of responsibility are often essential to the sense of this engagement.

All of these advantages are found in some measure just in directing one's own life seriously, collaborating as it were with oneself. But if self-direction were not tributary to social collaboration it would seem, at best, an incomplete staging of responsibility and a lesser enrichment of agency.

2. To play a role responsibly in a collaborative scheme one must understand how the scheme is supposed to work and to what end. A good team member in an organization must have some of the head's or planner's perspective, and a good head or planner must have some of the perspective of each kind of member. These perspectives determine not only what the agent understands technically but what the agent cares about. They are satisfying enlargements of practical understanding beyond the horizons of solo endeavors.

3. Acting responsibly requires acting as effectively as possible in awareness that the success and well-being of others depends on what one does, possibly to an even greater extent than anyone expected.[27] As the sites of impact are multiplied beyond oneself the importance of acquiring and exercising relevant skills is enlarged and the exercise of those skills is more ideally satisfying. The American World War I hero Alvin York is more important as a good army sniper in France saving hundreds of lives than as a good turkey shooter in Tennessee.

Note that all of these enhancements of agency are appreciable regardless of whether responsible actions earn social rewards. One can imagine a praise of responsibility citing only social enhancements of the agent's standing, but I hope I have already shown that there is much to be said for the good of responsibility from a responsible agent's own point of view without appealing to a desire for social approval or a transactional bargain.

If public approval of responsible agency might be lacking in the form of paying honor to the agent, a kind of validation is nevertheless always present in the felt worthiness of collaborative intent and of the collaborative enterprise on its own merit. As an inflection of social relationship, the essential character of responsible action is *the help* given someone by someone. As a technical asset, responsibility serves *the cause* to which the agent subscribes. An agent acting responsibly acquires worth in understanding something of others' needs and something of the technical requirements of joint efforts. (In any line of endeavor that can be conceived as a *profession*, the twin ideals will be mastery—being equal to the normal challenges of collaborative occasions of some kind—and continual improvement of one's understanding.) Helping and technically collaborating are never separate:

---

27. Collingwood points out that if you agree to go on a walk with someone you may end up having to defend your partner's life. R. G. Collingwood, *The New Leviathan* (Oxford: Oxford University Press, 1992), 145.

even if I nurse you back to health from a helpless state, we are team members in that cause; even if we are equally empowered colleagues, like a pitcher and a catcher in baseball, we need each other's help to fulfill our roles.

An episode of help or joint exertion in a cause might be very short-term—as when two Home Depot shoppers lunge together to stop a large sheet of plywood from falling over—but in principle it is always possible to ask in the middle of the enterprise, "How are we doing?" with reference both to the need-state of collaborators and the progress of the effort. The responsible agent has the worthy capacity of relevantly asking and addressing that question, wherever he or she is practically placed.

From the foregoing I think it is evident that a much different discourse on responsibility will proceed from the interests of the ambitiously prosocial agent than from the social interest in holding deviant agents responsible in a punishment system. Bruce Waller argues in *Against Moral Responsibility* that blaming and punishing are unjustifiable given that we cannot regard agents as free authors of their actions.[28] For Waller's purpose, the crucial point at issue is the causal *independence* of the agent which, as a determinist, he denies. But pro-responsibility agents have their eye primarily on outcomes that depend on their modulations of the *interdependence* of agents. Responsibility, for them, is power. When the power is considerable, when we know that the well-being of others is deeply affected by someone's holding of responsibility, then we want to prevent oppression and abuse not by canceling responsibility (except in certain unfortunate situations) but by making the right forward-looking specifications for it.

As far as I can tell, nothing said so far implies that responsibility is confined to the sphere of ethically regulated action. Ethics serves one sort of scheme for collaborative action—a scheme for forming and judging action according to general standards of approvable conduct.[29] There may be others.

The Subjective Basis of Responsibility in Practical Realizing

I addressed the question of motivation by pointing out how responsibility involves a desirable (though hazardous) enlargement of agency. Does this suffice? Consider how much we ask for under the rubric of responsibility,

---

28. Bruce N. Waller, *Against Moral Responsibility* (Cambridge, MA: MIT Press, 2011).
29. For fuller discussion of the conception of the ethical that I am working with, see chapter 2 of this book, 61–67 and appendix 1.

in hopes of sustaining our vitally important collaborations despite technical and psychological uncertainty: that the agent act harmoniously with colleagues of various human sorts; that the agent study and understand the bigger picture and never fail to react appropriately to a particular development that matters for that role, even a very challenging and unforeseen element; and that the agent pull his or her weight relative to what other responsible agents are contributing. We expect a fully responsible agent to accept whatever is entailed in fulfilling the assignment, first embracing the necessity of performing the proper actions and the risk of failing to do so, then embracing every practical necessity of execution. But we also want the responsible agent to be a freely pledged trusty colleague, willing to prosecute our shared venture from an unshakable autonomous base. This seems far too big an assignment to expect most ordinary agents to accept on the basis that it can be personally rewarding. But what other basis is there?

Behavioral training can do a great deal to keep shared action on track, and no doubt plays a large part in the life of human communities, but it does not provide responsible motivation. An account of becoming-responsible as undergoing a socialization to role-playing might fill the bill for schemes meant to reduce bad behavior, but it would be of limited use in elucidating the meaningfulness of the ideal for responsible persons since it leaves out the appeal to the agent's freedom. What is wanted here, from the perspective of promoters of responsibility, is a way of enrolling agents in responsible living that is subjectively compelling in proportion to the importance of the need for it.

Habermas has asserted the need for an "intersubjective recognition of moral norms or customary practices that lay down for a community *in a convincing manner* what actors are obliged to do and what they can expect from each other," without which morality "would have no advantage over other, more costly forms of action coordination."[30] We see that he is on the trail of transsubjective validity, the sort of cognitive solidity that is possessed by basic principles of justice like the Golden Rule or Kant's categorical imperative; but what about the "convincing" part? Without assuming automatic reasonableness or sure-fire temperamental niceness, and without resorting to intimidation, we must hope that our fellow subjects will become serious about collaboration on the basis of practical insight.

---

30. Jürgen Habermas, "A Genealogical Analysis of the Cognitive Content of Morality," in *The Inclusion of the Other*, ed. Ciaran Cronin and Pablo De Greiff (Cambridge, MA: MIT Press, 1998), 3–46, 3–4.

A term we might use for the subjective condition in which understanding combines with commitment is *practical realizing*. We can define the practical realizer as one who has become aware of what needs to be done—sees it in its aspect of needing to be done, overcoming uncertainties and distractions—and sees also something of what is required to accomplish it, crucially including the agent's own contribution. For the realizer these elements are welded together. *That* is the situation.

Moreover, there are degrees of realizing: the fullest realizers grasp not only the pragmatic complex at hand (including the essential involvement of other agents, when that is true of the situation) but also the generality of *other beings like these* and *other situations like this* so that now they know, like it or not, that their actions are moves in a bigger game and they could not lucidly choose to play a lesser game. (They may realize this with or without being intellectually convinced by a model of the larger situation like utilitarianism or Marxism, and with or without reliance on a powerful model of realizing itself like Platonic recollection or prophetic inspiration.) Realizers may also have comparative realizations: it may become impossible to deny that *more* is at stake, for oneself or for one's world, in the content of one realization than in another, for instance in a duty to one's child compared with a duty to an employer. This is the firmest subjective practical basis for saying that one claim on the responsible agent is "stronger" than another.

To say "Now I have realized X" is to assert an unchangeableness of the practical situation as far as I and X are concerned, for better or worse. This can be a very serious move in relation to others; for example, one spouse telling another "I've realized that we can't live together" announces the beginning of separation. Above all, it is a serious move in relation to one's own agency, because it commits one to a particular centering of one's intentions and efforts. One can hold off an inconvenient commitment only by being in denial, a faulty condition both epistemically and practically.

Irresponsibility might reflect a nonattainment of realization due to thoughtlessness, impulsiveness, or selfish bias (someone hasn't "grown up"); or it might reflect the loss of a realization, as when a relationship or work situation goes sour. There is also a more fraught and erratic kind of irresponsibility caused by an insoluble conflict between realizations—as, for instance, when Jonah flees the undoubted command of his God, convinced that he can't handle the command—which underlines painfully the general point that realization is a work in progress.

Any realization can be invalidated or require updating, if there are changes in its data or framing assumptions. Nevertheless a realization controls the agent's practical horizon throughout the time that it obtains: things *are* sticking together and staying in focus with *this* significance. Starting from the onset of a realization, the agent faces the world on that premise.

Some realizations are lightly hypothetical, engaging no rooted commitment. For example, if I want to go further on this path, I see that there is no way around a wide puddle and I will have to jump it. (Here "I see" is a realization because it occurs on another level than merely noticing the puddle: I am seeing the impossibility of advancing without jumping.) But some realizations are more seriously binding. Perhaps the situation is that I have to get over this puddle right now or I will be late to work again and surely lose my job.

When the realization is serious, no further argument is needed to connect the realizer with the practical challenge. Having seen the situation, the realizer is past asking "What's this got to do with me?" The dots have been connected, the train has left the station: the agent's life is now bound to the admitted practical requirement—bound just as tightly as the person is capable of being serious. The agent cannot willingly be the person who evades the requirement or live in the world that would result from evading the requirement.

Hobbes offers a "cannot want that world" model of practical realizing for our civic life. Anarchy is a fearful and frustrating condition no one could sanely choose over a more peaceful, orderly, generally accepted alternative, nor could a sensible person risk unleashing anarchy in pursuit of some particular good. We see further that without a fully empowered enforcer, an agreement cannot keep us in line. Thus we see that we have to have a government and we have to obey it consistently; rebellion cannot make real practical sense, except in a limit case of self-preservation. However our governors obtained their position, their power now is authoritative not because it is intimidating (though it does need to be intimidating) but because we see the necessity of the scheme. This solidly registered seeing is the cognitive core of a Hobbesian's politically responsible attitude.

Kant's ethics relies in contrast on a "cannot be that person" model.[31] The Kantian agent sees that rationally inconsistent willing is *self-contradicting*, because the self that rules a person's life authoritatively *is* reason, that is, the centering of the will by universal principle. One could

---

31. The "cannot want that world" constraint appears in the Law of Nature formulation of the categorical imperative (*Groundwork of the Metaphysic of Morals*, AA 4:421), but its Kantian significance is that it is a way of exhibiting the requirement of rational consistency.

try to avoid identifying with this reason by viewing oneself purely as a creature of naturally given impulses and inclinations—not an unpopular tack to take—but that evasion cannot finally make sense, since one's reason is active in any self-understanding. Like it or not, the "I" of "I will chase my pleasures" is still the universalizing judge of all conduct. Seeing this, the agent is bound to go ahead and think through what constitutes a universalizable policy for all agents for every sort of choice, and to uphold these fair policies in practice. That seeing is the core of a Kantian's ethically responsible view of life.

A Hobbesian realizer could still break the law or revolt, and a Kantian realizer could still lie or cheat, but these acts would be seriously distressing for themselves in proportion to the seriousness of their enrollment in responsibility. Their inconsistency would cause them to fall off the train that had already left the station, putting in doubt their arrival anywhere. No less importantly, they would have let down their colleagues. For the essence of each of those realizations was an imperative of fair collaboration, so that collaboration on certain terms could be counted on by all. When the setup for collaboration is at stake, the defection of the inconsistent realizer causes a crisis in the community. This is the grave danger we are indicating when we say that an agent or action is "irresponsible," and why, when we consider whether an agent who normally would be held responsible might have a diminished responsibility or none in a given instance, we stage that evaluation very seriously.

Realizing goes beyond mere knowing, in the epistemic dimension, and mere deciding, in the dimension of volition, in just the way that serious enrollment in responsibility requires. It binds the subject to an understanding of how the world works by revealing connections of significance among elements within the world, and it includes in its synthesis an understanding of how the subject's own life works by revealing connections among the subject's desires and judgments. The agents who would assent to the proposition "We have realized that policy P is necessary for an acceptable practical future" would be the same agents who would most intently uphold P and thus would be considered, and would hope to be trusted as, responsible in that area. Conversely, the people who in fact reliably uphold P would have sufficient motivation and insight to act in this responsible fashion in realizing that P is necessary.[32]

---

32. This equivalence assumes ideal sets. In actuality, among realizers there are weak-willed people who cannot be trusted to act responsibly although they genuinely feel and could

Realizing and being responsible fit together so well that one might wonder whether the supposed event or state of realizing is nothing more than an ideal stipulation for the subjectivity of responsibility. But realizing is a much broader platform than responsible action, as the puddle example shows. It is a condition of our intelligent life. Thus the cognitive priority belongs to realizing. The earliest contractual agreements would have had little hope of success if the contractors had not seen with the conviction of realizers that breaking their contract could not end well.

Shared Realizing and Shared Responsibility

Both the Hobbesian political realization and the Kantian ethical realization have to do with the sharing of action among agents, which gives them a more precarious status than an individual's simplest realizations about what he has seen or what she can do. Others may not have the understanding and commitment needed to sustain the necessary scheme, so that the shared action that levies an overriding claim on the realizer may not come off at all, leaving the realizer in the lurch. To minimize this danger, Hobbes and Kant carefully explain principles that should be engagingly comprehensible and strongly motivating for all partners in their schemes. They want to secure the politically or ethically necessary shared action on a base of shared realization. They want everyone who is in this situation to recognize that they are in this situation. And they are off to a good start: just in using language and reason they are taking advantage of our common realization that life is shared with one's fellow subjects and thus has a general social meaning that is continually being specified in the working out of interintentional relations.

A shared realization that is pointedly mobilized, as in Hobbesian politics and Kantian ethics, may be called a collective realization, placing it among collective acts.

A skeptic might challenge the premise of shared realization and with it the possibility of sincerely concerted conduct. The skeptic can argue that even if we grant a shared sense of communal belonging and accept an individual's explicit claim that he or she has realized something about the

---

effectively explain their realization, and among the responsible there are people lacking insight who could not explain or offer a justification for their practice but nevertheless can be trusted to fulfill their roles.

terms of collaboration, we can never ascertain that two subjects share a specific subjective commitment. For example, if two people have agreed that a collaborative job needs to be done, we can tell that they do *not* fully share a commitment to the job if one of them fails (avoidably) to pitch in with the other, but if they do complete the job, we cannot fully know their reasons and how they might have acted under different circumstances. In cases of successful collaboration it is reasonable to think that individual agents are strategically sharing their *efforts*, aiming at *results* in which they are convergently interested; but it is not a tenable assumption that agents are sharing their *commitment*. (We often talk as though they share a realization, as though we knew full well how things look from their own points of view—"Sam and Ted looked at each other and realized they would have to move that log"—but the question is whether the postulation of a shared intentional state can be verified.) Thus the skeptic can deny that Hobbesians and Kantians have a realistic expectation of shared commitment on which to base their schemes. Perhaps the collaboration their schemes require will come about only through behavioral conditioning or transactional calculation.

One might counter the skeptic with cases in which shared realization seems very hard to doubt, such as the realization shared by a basketball team, down 90–89 with 0:05 to play, that they need to score on this last possession, or the realization shared by ardent lovers that they cannot live apart. Perhaps most to the point, consider the case of getting married, where two lovers enter a covenant to maintain an irrevocable commitment. Now that they have publicly stated what they are both committed to, it would be obtuse to insist that we cannot know their exact states of mind. As the marriage progresses, they may of course reveal that they do not share an identical commitment—perhaps one is more devoted or the other is more conflicted. But if they are normal enrollees in marriage they understand and accept the suasive appeal of the norm of sharing the publicly defined marital commitment; the norm herds them together. On this basis one can remonstrate with a spouse whose attitude seems iffy. While we cannot assume a perfect identity of subjective states of realizing, we can expect individuals to *track* sharable realizations with their own recognitions and choices and hopefully with their own convergent realizations.

It seems that this tracking idea can support a moderately optimistic Hobbesianism or Kantianism. We cannot expect people's hearts to be in exactly the same place, but we can standardly expect people to be politically or ethically responsible in the prescriptive sense that we can ask them to understand and be responsive to ideally shared realizations of the requirements for an approvable shared life, and also in the predictive sense that we can foresee that agents who use reason extensively and are trained in prosocial behavior will for the most part keep faith with their essential role assignments in the political and ethical covenants.

Another application of the tracking idea would allow differences between harmonious realizers to count positively. Suppose we grant that multiple agents embrace Hobbes's and Kant's principles seriously, and that their realizations are sufficiently convergent to keep those political and ethical schemes afloat. It still seems likely that agents will differ precisely *in* their well-motivated conduct in how they understand and adhere to the scheme. They will have their own views on the best way to proceed, with conscientious rivalries and sometimes even fights. For the sake of not abdicating from collaboration, then, they are obliged not only to track the ideals of the scheme as loyally as they can but to track each other's intentions and patterns of action. A comprehensive shared realization must admit an unending stream of new practical experiences; the shared realization is a work in progress and so is held studiously and flexibly by conscientious agents.

We do see this conscious-work-in-progress quality in the committed relationships of spouses and other teammates. People can accept that their lives are bound together by defined goals and role assignments while seeing also that they must be students of each other and of their interactions so that their relationship can evolve properly. In committing to life in the state, the Hobbesian realizer commits to the study of government and the myriad pressures affecting the maintenance of a legal and political system. In committing to a perfect universalization of maxims of conduct, the Kantian realizer is ready to examine every alternative universalization that is offered under every set of circumstances, in effect becoming a student of the lives of all persons of goodwill. A memoir written by any of these realizers might have a strongly unifying theme of friendship, citizenship, or morality while also revealing a dramatic history of realization-refining.

The revisability of realization is as much a part of our conception of being responsible as is firmness in basic realizations. An agent lacking in prosocial realizations would be untrustworthy, but a know-it-all agent whose prosocial realizations were fixed ideas would be hard to work with in many situations.

Collective realizing is more obviously a responsibility ideal in some contexts than in others. For Hobbesian political agents and Kantian ethical agents collaboration is consciously sociable and agreement on principles is a primary concern, but in the very different case of an individual who realizes one evening that the thing that must be done is to feed a stray cat, the agent cannot expect to share any sort of realization with the cat and may never have to answer for the cat to anyone. Still we can point out in the background of any assuming of responsibility a scheme shared by a multiplicity of committed agents who determine what counts as responsible conduct by assigning roles and tasks according to commonly acknowledged needs and constraints. The cat feeder who resists taking the cat to the vet needs to be helped toward a more systematic understanding of cat and community welfare. The individual's realization of what must be done with the cat at hand needs to track the collective realization of what must be done with such cats generally.

Many controversial *historical* realizations have been proposed with difficult responsibility implications, often concerning one group's bad treatment at the hands of another. Some of the responsibility that would be shared going forward may be implied by a shared accountability for what happened in the past. Many individuals must decide for themselves whether to join in the backward-looking realization of accountability and how to relate that stance to a forward-looking realization concerning what needs to be done.[33] Ideally they will be historically well-informed and active in reasonable discussion of the issues.

Agency Responsibility

Seeing that something needs to be done, practical realizers are sometimes able to do what is necessary straightway. But often they need to consider and discuss and make a plan for the doing, and an adequate plan may involve delegation of responsibility, as in the usual social contract delega-

---

33. On the issue of individuals' acceptance of shared responsibility see Larry May, *Sharing Responsibility* (Chicago: University of Chicago Press, 1992). May's focus is on responsibility as accountability. On backward-looking assessment of causal responsibility for unacceptable conditions as a motivator for forward-looking collective responsibility and guide for defining and distributing roles in it fairly, see on the first point Marion Smiley, "Future-Looking Collective Responsibility: A Preliminary Analysis," in *Forward-Looking Collective Responsibility*, ed. Peter A. French and Howard K. Wettstein, *Midwestern Studies in Philosophy* 38 (Boston: Wiley, 2014), 1–11, and on the second Christian Neuhäuser, "Structural Injustice and the Distribution of Forward-Looking Responsibility," in French and Wettstein, 232–51, 242–49.

tion of enforcement responsibility to the government. Thus our model of realization-based responsibility must include not only personal and collectively shared responsibility but what I will call *agency responsibility*.

An agency of collective responsibility, whether it is the whole group, a smaller group, or an individual, must be able to process information, make decisions, and stage action in its own way—otherwise there would be no transition from shared felt responsibility to collectively sponsored action. It can be considered responsible insofar as it can be in charge of some matter of concern—otherwise it would not have been constituted as an agency. And it can be called to account—otherwise it would be too dangerous to allow.[34] If the agency were not a distinct site of responsibility, the members of an agency would not share in the distinct charge given that agency; for example, police officers would not participate in a police department's responsibility for keeping a community safe under a professional and legal discipline, and thus would not have the challenge of reconciling their individual feelings about what police should do with the departmental perspective.[35]

It is possible to interpret the ethical community—its competent adult members, at least—as an agency of collective responsibility, and even as the supremely authorized agency. If we are Kantians, we are all honesty officers; if utilitarians, welfare officers. But to see the ethical community this way is to see it as a political arrangement like a government or legal order. In practice, the determinations that set up collectively responsible agencies and the ground rules for holding them responsible must reckon not only with ethical standards but with particular historical and pragmatic challenges. Different forms of responsibility will be in the mix together. (We will be attending to those forms for their own sake in later chapters, but while we are on the subject of responsibility sharing I want to sketch in this important piece of the practicality of responsibility.)

The creation of distinct agencies adds new wrinkles to the scene of holding-responsible compared to the basic scene of distributed individual roles in a collaborative ensemble. Once collective responsibility has been

---

34. Christian List and Philip Pettit, *Group Agency: The Possibility, Design, and Status of Corporate Agents* (Oxford: Oxford University Press, 2011), chap. 7. I am adding to their specifications for group responsibility the possibility of being put in charge of a matter of concern.

35. A determined normative individualist could interpret all alleged responsibility in such situations as either individually borne or invalid, following the principle that it is never fair to blame an agent for what was not in the agent's control. But responsibility is not always a matter of blame, and control is sometimes shared diffusely.

implemented it is possible to deal with the sponsoring group as having assumed responsibility for what its agency is addressing, and it is possible to deal with the agency and its members as responsible for their roles in that implementation. Thus I encounter the city in the police officer, who answers for the city in matters of public safety, and I encounter that individual as responsible to the city and the police department as well as to me in working to fulfill the responsibility taken by the city for public safety. I also have an accumulating encounter with the city in the institution of the police department, which might, as its personnel come and go and different civic challenges arise, be policing the community helpfully or unhelpfully. If I am dissatisfied with the police department, there are ways of making the city answer for this that are not as direct as holding individuals responsible in their roles but are potentially more definitive since policies can be implemented to govern matters of concern. I can address the city about this by speaking to one of the supreme city agencies, the mayor or city council or city assembly.

Most of the existing discussion of shared responsibility is backward-looking, concerned with culpability and duties to change behavior or make amends.[36] Even when we know who did what, these issues can be hard to resolve because of the role of agencies in the structuring of responsibility. Agents may not be consciously or visibly organized in such a way that anyone has the assignment of answering to the charge of class-, sex-, or race-based discrimination, for example. Even when agencies have been set up and their causal preeminence is clear, they can disappear before it becomes possible to hold them responsible (as after 1865 there was no more Confederate government over the Southern states in the US) or they can come under new management (as a Republican administration is not responsible for much of what the previous Democratic administration did, and vice versa). In sharing out blame and liability among the constituents of a collective agent we often have to pretend to know just how intent or agreeable or unwilling they were.

Things seem much clearer on the forward-looking side, where responsibly charging an agency with a goal is typically motivated by realizers' dedication to making a needed difference to the world in the future. Here the intentional sponsorship of what is to be done is expressly avowed by

---

36. A notable exception is Iris Marion Young's "social connection" model of assumable collective responsibility in *Responsibility for Justice* (New York: Oxford University Press, 2011).

the sponsors and knowingly accepted by whoever joins the enterprise. Nevertheless the forward-looking reckoning of responsibility cannot be *wholly* clear, for even if we have a well-defined plan for collectively responsible action we must expect to be faced not only with surprising occurrences but with ambiguous relations between agents of collective responsibility at different levels. There are always at least the two levels of individuals and society to consider as sharers of the responsibility, with any number of agencies in between (government, administration, department, unit, program, task force, support group, etc.), and the recognition of shares among these parties depends somewhat unforeseeably on what can be ascertained about their various intentional states and actions as the test of their responsibility unfolds, with changes in circumstances and personnel over time.

Consider this simple model of such a plan: a small, poor forest community has learned to avoid some delicious-looking but deadly mushrooms that grow all around their village. (We suppose also that they currently have no safe way to move to a different location.) Any adult who sees a young child approaching those mushrooms realizes the urgent necessity of warning the child away from them and shares that realization in principle with all other adults. The whole pattern of activity in the village is such that a child's death by mushroom is most reasonably regarded as a community rather than family failure. Because of a shared realization of practical need, the community appoints a group of teenagers to keep special watch over the children. Now a hierarchy of responsibilities obtains: the assigned guardians are responsible to the community for the children's welfare, but the ground of the guardians' responsibility is the community's responsibility. A failure by the guardians is a failure by the community, just as fulfillment by the guardians is fulfillment by the community; for the guardians are *entrusted*. Unfortunately, the time arrives when the guardians fail to prevent a death, and then there are recriminations against those individuals and everyone who went along with the guardian plan.

Several important observations can be made about this scenario.

First, an advantage of assigning responsibility to an instituted agency like the guardians is that the agency can be held responsible for adequate performance in a way that the whole complexly occupied community cannot. The whole community can only wring its hands when a child dies, but guardians can be disciplined or replaced. However, the community cannot evade its own responsibility for its strategic decision to appoint guardians and for appointing *those* guardians. The responsibility that the guardians bear is a focused extension of the community's responsibility. The guardians are punishable and rewardable as the community is not, and yet grieving parents might reproach the community for appointing just a few guardians, or *those* guardians—indeed, would blame the community more than the guardians if the latter are innocently overmatched by their job. Most members of the community would be alive to the danger of putting too much blame on individuals, let alone on teenagers.

Second, the community must always already be functioning for some purposes like a committee of the whole, that is, as a collective agent. The members may never have had a chance to charter that agency, and there may not have been any formalized consultation or recognized offices before the appointment of guardians, but there were proper-seeming ways of making such a provision and a shared sense that the community was in charge of moral coordination as only the community could be. Even if the "appointment" was really just someone making a suggestion and a few others saying "Okay," the community did act, and it acted with a relatively more definite shared intention, and correspondingly more responsibly, in the measure that its action was grounded in realization. In this case the community knew with conviction that something must be done about the deaths of children, that it needed to address this, and (perhaps with a bit less conviction) that the appointment of guardians was the thing to do.

Third, however definite the realization and the plan were, it would be impossible to control the variable degree to which the capacities, intentions, and performance of the guardians match the capacities, intentions, and complementary performance of the community. The sharing out of collective responsibility between the authorizing community, the instigators of the plan, and the instruments of the plan creates a circuit in which the buck never definitively stops. As a matter of political responsibility, laws and procedures may be instituted to stop the buck somewhere in cases where it is too awkward not to do so, and good laws and procedures will have some intuitive and customary support, but at its heart collective responsibility is a spiritual adventure. Even while we are still at the drawing board we can see that dilemmas will arise between wrongly granting individuals immunity and wrongly scapegoating them as ways of registering collective responsibility.

It might be objected that my small, high-solidarity *Gemeinschaft* exercising responsibility as a committee of the whole differs greatly from a large *Gesellschaft* in which the political problems and solutions emerge complexly in relations among diverse social vectors, and so the possibility of collective responsibility in a large *Gesellschaft* has still not been elucidated.[37] I reply

---

37. For a more realistically complex model of issues in the social distribution of respon-

that the principles that support collective responsibility in the village case are necessary in any group inasmuch as they reflect the structurally basic possibilities for sharing action *and* realization *and* responsibility. Therefore a *Gesellschaft* needs procedures that emulate the intentional unity of a *Gemeinschaft* if it is to sustain a reality of being collectively responsible in the minds of its constituents. This is why there is so much interest in figuring out how to make democracy work properly and how we can appropriately hold bureaucratized agencies responsible. Later I will consider how a Rawlsian liberal society can meet this requirement.[38]

Theory of Responsible Realization versus Theory of Values

By shifting the discourse on responsibility from culpability to collaborative ambition, we allow the concept to do much more work in our models of a worthy life. We catch up with the everyday prevalence of positive references to responsible choices and actions.

By appealing to realization as the subjective basis of responsible commitment we come in line with the commonly drawn, strongly felt, and motivationally crucial distinction between merely knowing the facts of a situation and realizing the practical significance of a situation. We also avoid the detour of value theory, which incurs theoretical difficulties in trying to explain what sort of thing values are, how they have normative force (by virtue of a strange property of "oughtness"), and why agents differ in sensitivity to them. Whereas the directive force of value as such is enigmatic, the directive forces of responsibility are plainly inherent in our hastening to be in harmony with our sufficiently trusted fellows on the basis of realized practical necessities.

I admit that a responsibility theory *could* start by identifying relevant values (the high-ranking preferablenesses of equity, dignity, fidelity, etc.) and positioning responsible subjects as competent observers of those values, which would then regulate their conduct toward their fellow beings in each value domain. Proceeding in this way could indeed generate recognizable profiles of the genres of responsibility. And it might help us identify confusions and conflicts among targets of desire. But putting values ahead of individual existents and their relationships tends to disguise the high

---

sibility, with some suggested general normative guidelines, see Hans Lenk and Matthias Maring, "Responsibility and Technology," in Auhagen and Bierhoff, 93–107.

38. See chapter 3, 96–99.

importance of the collegiality (the to-whom) and the material seriousness (the for-what-specifically) in responsible action. This is because values are merely ideal directions to appreciate or respect kinds of thing, directions that always wait to be applied. A values perspective is best fitted to the ethical form of responsibility, facilitating the ethical demand for consistency across all situations; it loses its grip when situational particularities and live communication are decisive, as in personal relationships most obviously but also in the actions of historically and politically concerned communities. The structure of responsibility seems therefore the more fundamental consideration.

The values premise is a convenient way of designating different realms or domains of concern, since values can be defined and grouped however seems appropriate, but the idea of responsible shared action based on shared practical realizing seems to me a more insightful way of setting the scene for the major branches of responsibility. For it can be made evident that the "we" involved in sharing and the sharable "what must be done" are determined differently when we are reckoning the right course of action *in this juncture* of trying to do something with someone (pragmatically), *in this era* of building on certain cumulative accomplishments (historically), *in principle* in all occasions (ethically), and perhaps also *in this whole of being* (eternally) or *in relation to ultimate being* (religiously).

We will now look into these differences, starting where action sharing starts in our experience of it, in direct active collaboration.

Chapter Two

Pragmatic Responsibility

We are thinking of responsibility as ethical when we think of it as fulfilled in generally approved typical actions. The ethically responsible agent does what anyone should do under such-and-such circumstances, mindful of what everyone should always be mindful of (such as human dignity or vulnerability). But the ethical conception of responsibility may be of uncertain relevance when we find ourselves in a particular practical partnership that seems likely to enter a better or worse condition depending on how we act right at this moment. The strain is felt in the obliging prompt being different—a concrete constraint and opportunity versus a general standard, an action in hand versus an action merely contemplated—and it may even be felt in a divergence between seemingly right things to do.

Suppose that I've been recruited by a friend to help him move a piano from a truck into his new house. I'm quite busy at work, but I use my lunch hour to go to the site, having been assured that the task will take less than an hour. Four of us assemble to move a heavy upright grand, one at each corner. We manage to get the piano down the truck's ramp and onto a path leading to the house, but the unpaved path is long and hazardous due to recent rains, and we are only halfway to the house when my hour strikes. From one point of view, it is clearly permissible for me to leave—I only promised my help for an hour—and it is clear to me also that I owe my contracted presence to my work organization during work hours. But I realize that I am now coresponsible for getting the piano to the house, so that it is immediately wrong to leave my fellow piano movers in the bad position of lacking a fourth. Distinct from the relation I assumed with my friend in making a promise of an hour's help is the relation I assumed with my fellow movers and the particular task once we got involved in moving this beast of a piano.

Note that the practical priority I am pointing to is not based on my special fondness for my friend or my personal dependence on close relationships.[1] The point here is not that the needs of friends and relatives automatically qualify for special consideration and may take precedence over purely impartial considerations. It is that actively shared action takes precedence. In practice, friend and family relationships are usually hotspots of active collaboration; for *that* reason, sometimes more than for other reasons, they have a tendency to take priority. It is true that I would not have driven across town to help a stranger move a piano. But if I *had* gotten involved in helping a stranger, I would probably not drop out to go help my best friend with something else.

Responsibility comes into such cases with direct regard to others but also in a self-regarding way that has an important implication for worthy collaboration generally. To the extent that I keep accounts with myself, monitoring my own agent competence and the progress of my practical career, I feel responsible for finishing what I started whenever I undertake anything. This sense of being responsible is based in a realization that if I fail to complete an action my practical life will to that extent have failed to amount to anything—an hour or a day wasted—and if I make a habit of this I will waste a considerable part of my life. When I am collaborating with other agents, the responsibility to finish what has been started takes on additional importance to the extent that they depend on me to finish what *they* started. Thus there is a prima facie imperative to support them via the action we are sharing. *Don't let go.* Many sorts of consideration could override this imperative—the action might be perceptibly futile, it might be leading to imminent harm, it might be immoral, we might suddenly realize that we would all rather do something else. But those possibilities are appreciable only in some detachment from the actual doing of the action. *In* the doing, it is understood that we are in a mutually supportive relationship that depends on an appropriate performance.

We can call this mode of responsibility *pragmatic* because present practical performance and concretely estimable success (usually near-term success) are its essential concerns. It deserves its own designation because it

---

1. There is a strong tendency in the literature on special obligations to put them on this basis; there seems to be a widely shared assumption that this is the only basis they could have. On the priority issue see Susan Mendus, "The Magic in the Pronoun 'My,'" *Critical Review of International Social and Political Philosophy* 5 (2002): 33–52.

occupies a distinctive major zone in practical life. It is naturally associated with the value of *expediency* in the positive sense of getting problems solved (which is not to say that ethical or historical scruples are irrelevant to it). The problems that are to be solved are the ones that are *right in front* of *us*, a particular collaborative ensemble. Thus pragmatic responsibility may be associated with competitive, conflictual actions by groups as opposed to ethically approved actions from which conflict has been scrubbed out.[2]

The concept of pragmatic responsibility is by no means unintuitive, but explaining it in its full originality is a major challenge in an intellectual environment dominated by the category of the ethical. Ethical subcategories like "applied ethics" and "special obligations" along with proposed general reorientations like "ethics of care" and "embodied ethics" have variously reached into pragmatic experience, coloring it with ethical idealization.[3] The very idea of responsibility is often treated as an ethical principle, forestalling any discussion of different basic ways of being responsible. To correct this monism of responsibility we need to see the grounds for a basic discrimination.

The Ontological Structure of Pragmatic Responsibility: Actualizing

Three general forms of being are worth distinguishing in practical philosophy because of the broad differences they make for our orientation. We address the *reality* of constituted being mainly as seekers of knowledge; we address the *possibility* of constitutable being as prescribers of goals and standards; and we address the *actuality* of constituting being as wranglers of ever-changing relations between given realities and available possibilities. Actuality, the active present, is the primary ontological setting for pragmatic responsibility.

Actuality. In the actualizing present, an agent composes action in conscious continuity with given facts (like the weight of a piano or its position on a path), purposefully reaching toward the most immediately relevant possibilities (as in advancing the piano toward its new home or preventing

---

2. Samuel Scheffler has pointed out that members of "special responsibility" relationships are committed to preferential treatment of each other in a way that could entail unethical treatment of others. He calls this the "distributive objection." "Relationships and Responsibilities," in *Boundaries and Allegiances* (Oxford: Oxford University Press, 2001), 97–110, 99.

3. On the ethics of care in this connection see appendix 1, 172–174.

it from tipping over), and bearing the immediate weight and chance of the action together with whoever else has their hands on it. The agent tries to impose a design on what is happening in this episode of achieved realities turning into certain continuation-realities and not others. Often the design must be adjusted. Within the present of action, a well-oriented agent needs to be aware of established facts and accessible possibilities and yet can never take assessments either of reality ("It's so heavy . . .") or of possibility ("We could get a dolly . . .") as wholly determining—not while the joining of realities and possibilities is being thrashed out. Here the responsible agent's mission of rectifying relationships is carried out in the midst of the thrashing, the agent envisioning, affecting, and reacting to others according to present action's necessarily shallow focus on the *pragmata* (the elements of the developing situation that can be intentionally engaged) and its uncertainty as well as its intended payoff.

When someone calls me from work, I may say, "Actually, I'm helping these guys move a piano right now . . ." Or I may feel the overriding pull of what is waiting to be done at work and say to the piano crew, "Actually, I have to go now." This "actually" holds a plea or apology: I am admitting that the resolution of the current episode may differ from what had been projected, but I am also insisting that I am in a developing situation that imposes exigency, including the requirement to bear with it and watch over its maturation while trying for the best result. To say that my action should be dictated just by a relevant fact, or just by a relevant possibility, is to deny my full actuality, my engagement in the task at hand.

Action sharing. The general phenomenon of action sharing is screened off by the individualizing focus that often rules our determinations of responsibility. Monitoring each other, we put credits for agents in our ledger to keep track of their participation and impact: *Sam did (did not do) X, accomplishing (not accomplishing) Y; Janet ought (ought not) to have done X.* For myself, I often need to concentrate on the particular moves that are within my own power to perform in the next moment, gauging their likely impact on the developing situation. The individualizing perspective is not simply false: it is indeed true for each of us at each moment that the world becomes different from what it would have been had we acted differently. On occasion, much depends on one agent—as when my colleagues leave me balancing the piano by myself while they go for sodas. But no agent or action is an island. Every action is a symphony of cooperations, its causal power codetermined by a host of supporting and constraining conditions and its meaning codetermined by a host of actually or potentially involved parties, in various modes of interdependence.

The sharing of all action in past reality must be borne in mind when we are working out more historically adequate, necessarily more complicated ideas of *what happened* and *how it happened*; and the possibilities of action sharing are important for ethical reckoning for the future, given that we are required to implement ideals of justice and virtue. Distinctively in the present of actualizing, agents have a detailed awareness of the opportunities, constraints, and moment-by-moment changes of balance in the action they are sharing. The piano movers in my example must be vividly aware of each other's lifting and shifting as well as their own. Such awareness is salient in a distinctively pragmatic sense of responsibility: I *know* how awkward it would be for the others if I dropped my corner now or staggered to the left, I *know* how hard the piano would be to move for just three people if I departed; when someone else provides less lift, I know I must immediately provide more; when my grip starts loosening involuntarily, I know I can't keep lifting beyond the next couple of seconds; when the piano does move in the right direction, I perceive and appreciate that all four movers are doing what it takes to enable success for all. I judge good and bad, right and wrong by these points of reference at each moment of the effort. This sympathetic sensitivity to others in present action is an ideal for the present aspect of responsibility generally.

Scales of action. Any action we can identify is composed of smaller actions and embedded in larger actions. The piano moving is composed of the efforts of the movers and nerve and muscle actions in the movers' bodies (among other things) and embedded in the larger action of moving a family into a new house (among other things). Pragmatic responsibility focuses on actions and outcomes that are directly manipulable, yet its scale varies according to the pressures and stakes of acting. I may drop my corner of the piano because of a sensation of something going wrong in my back, shifting my pragmatic focus to what had previously been an unobserved component of action; or I may keep lifting, despite my back pain, despite slacking by other movers, looking beyond the piano to the larger goal of getting your family moved in.

Pragmatic responsibility can also attend a collaboration in which contributions are widely distributed in time and space, as long as they are understood to belong to an action in hand.[4] Such understanding may not

---

4. Colin Dansby provides a lovely example of the construction of college teaching as a presently shared action.

> Suppose a student asks for special treatment in my class on account of illness. I am not sure what to do. I wander down the hall to ask a colleague who

be fully shared in the absence of immediate, vivid, piano-moving-grade contact with other agents' efforts. There may be debate about whose hands are actually on the actively shared action, or should be. There will be rival imaginings of the active ensemble. A woman who had thought that her pregnancy was her own affair may be told that the national government and the gods are involved in it.[5] (She can disprove this claim by moving to another country, changing her religious view, and then having her baby. The piano mover, in contrast, cannot leave the other movers and still move that piano.)

Ethical ideals may be invoked to ground pragmatic responsibility—but they need not be. When I "take my turn" cooking or cleaning in a household, or "do my share" keeping my part of a neighborhood litter-free, we need not suppose that in performing these responsible acts I must be motivated by gratitude for benefits received from membership in the collective, or by a general rule of fair turn-taking, or by a calculation of future benefits—or by investment in a historical identity—but only that I accept that I *am* one of the enactors of *this* shared action. I uphold the action that I understand myself to be in, responsible to *those* collaborators and for the foreseeable results of the collaboration. (If I detach myself from actively

---

listens to my story, asks a few questions about the student and class, then perhaps tells me a story of his own. Another colleague walks by, I retell my story, and further chat follows. Neither of them tells me what to do, though they may mention alternative ways of handling the situation that had not occurred to me. But by the end of fifteen minutes the situation is much clearer in my mind. Several things have happened. First, I had to organize and structure my thoughts in order to articulate my dilemma to a peer, which I would not have done had I just brooded on my own. Second, I was asked questions and gently prodded to see the situation in new ways. Third, through these conversations I both drew on the existing teaching culture of my program and reproduced it; for all of the participants, the conversation will update our sense of how we, collectively, approach our students and their needs. And fourth, by seeking advice, I acknowledged that my decision in this case affects my colleagues should the student come to expect similar accommodation from other teachers. So I acknowledged my responsibility to them (it might also be said that I implicated them).

"Lupita's Dress: Care in Time," *Hypatia* 19 (Fall 2004): 23–48, 27.

5. William R. LaFleur, *Liquid Life. Abortion and Buddhism in Japan* (Princeton: Princeton University Press, 1992), 107–111 (on neo-Shinto arguments against abortion in the Edo period).

shared action in order to consider how I *might* collaborate with others, then a principle of gratitude or fair taking of turns or maximizing of benefits might well govern my deliberation.)

Part of pragmatic responsibility is setting the scale of shared action in the most satisfactory way, being responsible *to* others and *for* shapes of action and outcomes with regard for what seems to matter most. If I have a greater responsibility to your family to get you all moved in than I have to fulfill my original promise to help you move the piano, then in fidelity to the greater goal I could even urge abandoning the piano.

There is not just one spatiotemporal scale for the actively shared action or developing situation that pragmatic responsibility is directly responsive to. Moving the piano has been my developing situation; the piling up of trash is a developing situation in Rome; Christianity was a developing situation for Luther and the popes; the whole of cosmic history might be a developing situation for a divine creator. In a great variety of ways, with a great variety in mental demands, pragmatically responsible agents find themselves in the midst of significant change and moving the levers of change.

The World Scene of Pragmatic Responsibility: The Sifting of Existence

Agents who consider generally how change happens will be aware that action in the present always selects among possible continuations of what has previously obtained. Awareness of the inevitability of selection is essential to intelligent practice; without it, an agent could not understand what is at stake in a situation. But there are different ways of conceptualizing selection that have importantly different implications.

Since Malthus and Darwin it has been common to characterize the whole scene of selection as a "struggle for existence." The struggle model has undoubted heuristic value for drawing attention to the competitive aspects of events and processes and the displacements of losers by winners. But it can falsely suggest that struggling is universal and constant and that the facts of existence are always best explained as the results of struggles. A common "realist" or "Social Darwinist" mistake is to compound the error of granting a universal explanatory priority to struggle by placing a practical priority on struggling as well, so that the actions deemed most intelligent and justifiable would always be actions in aid of conquest. Such a view arbitrarily undermines responsible action sharing by putting mortal competition ahead of mutuality.

Yet it is not necessary to defend responsibility by asserting the opposite thesis that cooperation is the most important factor in human affairs. The concerns of pragmatic responsibility prompt a view of the selection scene that is more fully dimensioned than either the "struggle for existence" view or its mutualist antithesis. This larger view is worth stating to serve as a standing corrective to the oversimplifications.

At the point of acting, the pragmatically sensitive actor who is poised to respond to new data at any moment, including the claims of other actors, is thereby poised to accept or reject the continuation of any presently occurring action or plan for action. Such an actor addresses the present moment as a gatekeeper who is also a representative—responsible *to* the actors, intentions, and projects that are passed through the gate or blocked, responsible to self and others *for* selected contents of future situations, and responsible also *for* the better or worse style in which selection is carried out. The gatekeeper has the basic concepts of "right" and "wrong" as "what goes through" and "what doesn't go through." From this point of view the whole scene of selection is aptly characterized as a sifting of existence—a formulation that allows for struggle but also for responsible discrimination and various forms of coordination.

For a consciously self-positioning agent attending to the sifting of existence, the models of competition and cooperation will both prove indispensable and ought not to interfere with each other. For it can always be observed that continuations determined in the present to be incompatible were competing for future existence—the success of X did preclude the success of Y—while continuations determined to be compatible were cooperating in the forging of the next continuation of reality, seeing that they did in fact work together toward that result (whether or not in sympathy).

Competition tends to be disvalued or repressed in discourses of justice and virtue because we want to restrain the selfishness in self-assertion and coordinate action so that no one is conquered or otherwise victimized. But competition is not necessarily adverse to any living existents; the X that beats out Y might be one *state* of an existent beating out another, and it might be the more desirable state from most points of view (as when the *best* contestant *wins*). Nor are competition and cooperation simply disjunctive, with responsible worth and practical advantage all on the side of cooperation; we see them supervene on each other in ecological systems and we deliberately arrange for their mutual enhancement in many of our practical schemes, very conspicuously in politics and sports.

Cooperation itself can be more competitive or less so, just as competition can be more cooperative or less. At many junctures an action sharer can intensify either or both of these elements to a desired degree. In a philosophical conversation, for example, as I make my argument ever more reasonably, discussing your possible objections, I can be ever more insistent and brilliant; or I can reduce the monological insistence and give you more space to contribute to our sharing of thought. The competitive element in the conversation could easily become a problem—but you would probably not want to eliminate it altogether.

Agents whom we admiringly characterize as "pragmatic" take stock of facts and possibilities of competition and cooperation in their attention to gatekeeping prospects; "impractical" agents are the ones who are relatively unconscious about this. The outstandingly pragmatic agents have an impressive grasp of gate issues in various dimensions and on various scales of occurrence, recognizing certain sets of gates as significant trials of practice. Their pragmatic "realism" is something quite different from an exclusive interest in facts. It is a strategic understanding of possibilities and realities in relation, subject to foreseeable impositions of gatekeeping. That is what Weber meant by "the realities of life" to which the most admirably responsible agents face up.[6]

"The sifting of existence" is an apt description of the pragmatic situation for at least five reasons:

1. It indicates that actions are always already affecting what will obtain next, supporting some outcomes and precluding others. If you fail to pay attention to this you will lack understanding and influence.

2. It speaks to the core of agent motivation by highlighting the dangers, costs, and opportunities of action. While it challenges any blithe optimism about survival or inclusive harmony it nevertheless admits cooperation no less than competition as possibly decisive. It allows the agent to be the intentional sponsor of fateful action that might in one way or another be a benchmark specimen of competitive and cooperative strategy and tactics.

3. It directs our attention to the larger field of difference making that surrounds pursuit of the focal objective in an episode of sharing action. We may get your piano through the gate of placement in your house but not get our relationship through the gate of continued mutual respect if certain unfortunate things are said.

---

6. "What is decisive [for the ethics of responsibility] is the trained relentlessness in viewing the realities of life, and the ability to face such realities and to measure up to them inwardly." Max Weber, "Politics as a Vocation," in H. H. Gerth and C. Wright Mills, eds., *From Max Weber: Essays in Sociology* (New York: Oxford University Press, 1948), 77–128, 126–27.

4. It implies the flexibility in the best pragmatism: consciously sifting agents can always let alternative means or alternative conceptions of ends come to the fore in their quest for successful completion of shared actions. Pragmatically satisfactory solutions must very often emerge, different from what was prefigured (though not disloyal to essential ends).[7]

5. It implicitly relates the intentional direction of present action to the larger stream of occurrence in which the natural and cultural formations of life are changing according to the differential viability of their potentials and actual variations. The sifters are sifted. Although pragmatically responsible agents should not follow Social Darwinists in modeling the intentional sculpting of human affairs directly on the natural sculpting of species and ecosystems, neither should agents be incurious about larger processes they participate in—and the good or bad cumulative effects of human gatekeeping they might share responsibility for. At the present juncture, it may be pragmatically responsible to support some of our fellow citizens' traditional jobs in the energy sector; it cannot be pragmatically responsible to ignore pollution and climate change.

Appreciating the charge of pragmatic responsibility in these terms, when we enter into other frames of responsibility we can better appreciate the freedom they obtain by detaching (to the extent that they can detach) from the sifting of existence.

The Personal Coherence of Pragmatic Responsibility: Vocation

In his *Philosophy of Right* Hegel repeatedly invokes a "right of particularity"—the right of an individual to strive for his or her own economic success, for example, or for Germans to insist on German national interests

---

[7]. American pragmatism has been chided for fostering such disloyalty. Randolph Bourne warned bitterly against the complicity of Dewey's pragmatism with the catastrophe of World War I: "The American, in living out this philosophy, has habitually confused results with product, and been content with getting somewhere without asking too closely whether it was the desirable place to get. It is now bumming plain that unless you start with the vividest kind of poetic vision, your instrumentalism is likely to land you just where it has landed this younger [pragmatist] intelligentsia which is so happily and busily engaged in the national enterprise of war." "Twilight of Idols," *Seven Arts* 11 (October 1917): 688–702, accessed October 20, 2021, http://www.expo98.msu.edu/people/bourne.htm.

even to the point of war if necessary.⁸ The background metaphysical thought is that the full unfolding of the sovereign Idea must incorporate existence as well as essence, concrete multiplicity as well as unifying form, variation and conflict as well as anchoring structure. Germans need Reason but Reason needs Germans (along with the English).

One need not believe in Hegel's metaphysical plenitude to recognize a "right of particularity" inherent in the placement of the agent as the keeper of particular gates. The presently acting agent is the decider of just *those* continuations—whether to feed *that* cat on *that* occasion, whether to buy *that* expensive phone charger or look elsewhere, and so forth. Each decision takes place in a larger context of decisions made by this agent. If some of these decisions conform to socially intelligible patterns, they can be assigned to roles and role responsibility. If they can be incorporated in a biographically coherent form, the agent has the opportunity to intentionally affirm that larger formation of pragmatically responsible conduct and thereby undertake a *vocation* that will be better or worse fulfilled. The "calling" idea of vocation signifies that this higher-level decision and performance is itself responsible; the vocation bearer acknowledges that he or she has become concerned in a specific complex of action, not only immediately, hands-on, but as a planner of life, and now faces all fellow agents in this approvable posture, with a pragmatically justified project.

Attributing vocation to an agent implies a deserved respect, a "right of particularity," at the level of pragmatic strategy. The agent is one of the ones who is figuring out what is most properly to be done based on his or her own placement in the complex of what is actually being done. When the "Where are you?" call comes from work and a piano mover replies, "Actually, I'm helping these guys move a piano right now," the mover may lack an adequate justification for not being at work, or for not immediately heading back to work—in fact, if his regular job performance has been spotty he may be egregiously in the wrong, everything considered—but nevertheless it would be wrong of his work colleagues to insist that he drop what he is doing without considering at all what he *is* doing at the moment or what he *thinks* he is doing in the larger complex of ongoing action. That might be disrespecting a vocation.

---

8. G. W. F. Hegel, *Elements of the Philosophy of Right*, trans. H. B. Nisbet, ed. Allen W. Wood (Cambridge, UK: Cambridge University Press, 1991), 221 (§184), 238 (§207), 361 (§324).

It is possible to appreciate the vocational claim of pragmatic engagement mainly in terms of the outcomes that the agent assumes responsibility *for*. Also relevant may be the more formal consideration of good agent style, a fidelity to standards of best practice: "I *promised* him I'd help move the piano, and it turns out that *keeping my word* involves working at this longer than we expected." But the overridingly important aspect of the situation may be the agent's responsibility *to* the others with whom he or she is now pragmatically entangled. Vocation on this side involves maintaining a game plan for action that supports concretely given relationships. The commitment to helpfulness in relationship is a theme not only of friendship but of all vocational models for providing service—to "my clients," "my patients," "my students," even "my customers" on a serious view of commerce—in contrast to the transactional model of dealing with "the public" with whom one is required merely not to do anything objectionable.

The ideal of vocation implies some channeling of responsibility to and for others so that the claims of present situations do not become unmanageably numerous and diverse. The agent who helps move the piano, and then stops on the highway to help someone change a tire, and then takes an injured beaver to the animal hospital, and then listens supportively to a busker's concert, and so on, never ceasing to accept shared action opportunities, will probably have a hard time holding down a job or a home front; more concentration in the higher-priority areas might be needed. A vocation-deficit term describing such a life is "scattered." But should we nevertheless respect the consistently responsible present-mindedness of such an agent and allow that such a life can be well-lived, even though at a noticeable cost of practicality?

The life of spontaneously varying responsibility is an object of respect but also of regret. It seems that for the sake of responsiveness the agent is cramping responsibility in larger-scale relationships and formations of action in a larger gatekeeping. The agent might have found inspiration in the thought that one's practical life cannot amount to something approvable as a whole if one does not take care that each piece of it is lived responsibly. This is related to the competency concern to finish whatever one starts. But in the scattered life it seems that absorption in small-scale episodes has interfered with adequate engagement in larger-scale episodes and with vocational coherence.

When we evaluate pragmatic responsibility on the larger scale of a career or a lifestyle, we bring certain expectations to bear. Without them it would be impossible to secure a discernment of responsibility. They define the pragmatic versions of virtue. One of these expectations is that the agent *choose* intelligently the juncture of present action in which his or her responsible agency is to be activated. Within one's pragmatic embeddedness one usually has choices. If on the way home one of our piano movers, overdue for dinner with his family, stops to listen supportively to a busker, it seems clear that he has made a bad choice of relevant shared action. I would not generalize that agents should be ultracautious about honoring their greater responsibilities so that they never fall into an awkward involvement by responding to emergent claims; the piano mover's day began by quite reasonably agreeing to take an hour off to respond to his friend's previously unscheduled need. I can say "reasonably" here because there is a culturally maintained common sense about the feasibility of such an endeavor, although if one had known more about the particular task, or the people involved, one might have held back.

The choice issue may not be easy to focus. Some choices are forced to such an extent that the agent is simply submitting, not responsibly choosing (for instance, taking the only available job for the sake of making ends meet); at the other extreme, some choices verge on being too whimsical, having too little to do with generally recognized exigency, to count as responsible at all (like the choice to stop to listen to a busker). That the aptness of a choice is arguable does not mean that it cannot be responsible, however. Any choice that aims to support action sharing has something in its favor.

Another expectation is that the agent *respond*, even if inconveniently for others, to compellingly overriding demands. No one could fault an agent for being late to work if the reason was preventing someone else's imminent death. The exigency there would be the pragmatic analogue to an ethical perfect duty; stopping to save a life is the only conceivably acceptable way for the gatekeeper of that moment to have operated the gate to the future. But an overall consistency will be expected in the agent's vocational concerns, as in attending to work or family. That will be a test of the agent's responsiveness to the demands of larger structures of the present.

The pragmatically responsible life characteristically poses problems of choosing or mediating between the claims of differently sized, differently composed presents and is never safe from the possible tragedy of failing in one important responsibility for the sake of fulfilling another. At least a common sense about what agents should be expected to do protects us from this tragedy to a considerable extent.

The Social Coherence of Pragmatic Responsibility: Ethos

As a young man attracted to the craft, fellowship, and prestige of riverboat pilots, Mark Twain booked passage on a boat and watched the crew closely. One morning the mate called for a capstan bar. When Twain offered to go get one, the mate looked at him as if he were a completely irrelevant interloper. The mate knew a lot about how things are done on a riverboat that the young Twain did not; the collaboration that was wanted at that moment was prefigured by long experience.[9]

Even for our most spontaneous collaborations we have already a physical format for how our bodies are able to relate in space and time, together with a gestural and linguistic format for possible communication. On the level of teachable behavior there are universal dos and don'ts, some of which have the status of moral standards but many of which are simply default procedures. A coherent totality of appropriate ways of collaborating in a community might be called *ethos*. Ethos is for the life of a society what vocation is for the life of an individual.

Ethics has been in tension with *ethos* (Greek for "custom") since its birth, as ethics provides a platform on which one can criticize any existing community custom—even custom in the normatively charged guise of morality.[10] *Ethos* as the social parallel to personal vocation is not a haphazard assemblage of practices and preferences, however. It is an *ideal* coherence that solves a shared responsibility problem. Other types of large-scale responsible solution—ethical, political, religious—can be at odds with ethos. Throughout my own life spiritual battles have raged over patriarchal and racialist elements of my society's ethos. In those respects the ethos has been figured as a problem. It is difficult to see something as a problem for right living and at the same time recognize it as a responsible solution for right living. However, to the extent that a society really is guided by an ethos rather than simply being in the grip of inertia, it is important not to underestimate the pragmatic relevance and durability of the ethos and not to disrespect the agents who share in its responsibility.

---

9. Mark Twain, *Life on the Mississippi* (New York: Collier, 1917), 40 (chap. 5).
10. For more discussion of the categories of the moral and ethical see appendix 1.

Sympathy, Empathy, and Affective Responsibility

It is a fixture of our practical wisdom that feelings are involuntary and one cannot be held responsible for them; one can be responsible only for intended actions.[11] On the other hand, we would not even be disposed to be responsible and we could not sustain structures of responsibility if we did not reliably have strong prosocial feelings.[12] Sympathetic and empathetic feelings are such important psychological supports of *pragmatically* responsible choosing and acting that it seems at least almost true to say that a person totally lacking in sympathy or empathy in a juncture of shared action—totally unresponsive to fellow beings in those ways—would be, by that fact, pragmatically irresponsible and incapable of vocation. Responsive feeling seems closer to being a necessary condition for pragmatic responsibility, which lives in present contact, than it would be for more abstractly judged modes of responsibility.[13]

We can use the piano moving example again to suggest working definitions of sympathy and empathy and illustrate their practical importance. In ordinary usage the terms are nearly interchangeable and their philosophical uses have varied, but for present purposes we can assign them a definite distinction.

I shall understand sympathy, "feeling with," as resonance. In piano moving, sympathy occurs in my sensing that your load has grown when the weight of the piano shifts too much to your side. Because I am sympathetic I am aware of what others are feeling. A good musician or midfielder is *essentially* sympathetic because of the coordinative requirements of those

---

11. The point of this principle is not solely to excuse people for their feelings; it is because our feelings are not chosen that they can subject us to claims and gifts of others. "The idea of being able to command affective responses by our will, to innervate them as we innervate a movement of our limbs, would by implication deprive them of their meaningful relation to the importance of the other . . . No one who realizes the nature and meaning of joy, love, or veneration could even desire that his affective responses should be accessible to the command of the will. For we can see that this would be incompatible with the dignity of these responses." Dietrich von Hildebrand, *Ethics* (Chicago: Franciscan Herald, 1953), 319.

12. See Charles Darwin's convincing treatment of this point in the chapter on "Moral Sense" in *The Descent of Man*.

13. For a discussion of the limitations and hazards of sympathizing (here called empathizing) in the context of ethics see Jesse J. Prinz, "Is Empathy Necessary for Morality?" in Amy Coplan and Peter Goldie, eds., *Empathy: Philosophical and Psychological Perspectives* (Oxford: Oxford University Press, 2011), 211–29.

roles. As a sympathetic violin player, for example, I can play well in a string quartet because I am not only engaged with the music, I am highly sensitive to my partners' engagements with it. Good piano moving is like this too in its rougher way.

What got me into the piano moving adventure in the first place, however—what made me dedicate my lunch hour to such a risky errand—was that I understood and entered into my friend's need to get his household moved. Sympathetic awareness of his experience did not, by itself, draw me to his project. It *may* be that my sympathetic awareness of another's pain or pleasure is so compelling that I cannot but want to help or to join in. But it is empathy, "feeling in" to another's situation and the endeavors that answer to that situation successfully, that makes the situation not merely affecting but interesting and in that way involving. A musician playing Beethoven's music will probably empathize with whoever else is trying to play the piece successfully but may not have empathy for Beethoven himself, whereas a writer dramatizing Beethoven's life must have it. A politician lacking sympathy ("the common touch" in relation to constituents, professional tact in relation to coworkers), can, despite this handicap, still have the motivation of a responsible leader, while a politician lacking empathy could be only, at best, a competent minder of the store, or somehow luckily a cause of beneficial change or preservation, but not a political leader of the best sort.

Trust is usually requisite for collaboration, and it is hard to trust collaborators who seem to lack sympathy and empathy. They may fulfill their roles perfectly through a long series of challenges, building up a strong inductive case for their reliable helpfulness, but if we cannot tell that there is something in their personal nature that *makes* them sensitive to and collegially caring about their fellow beings—emotional proof that they have indeed been recruited into the sharing mode of life—then we lack confidence that we are placed with them in the normal linkage of pragmatic responsibility, sharing actions not merely as causal episodes but as matters of importance. Without sympathy and empathy they may be with us physically, interacting with us under shared circumstances, perhaps even under the flag of an explicitly undertaken commitment, but they are not yet *here* with us in a fully human intentional sharing.

Feelings are often determinative of the meaning we ascribe to our actions, and "moral sentiment" is a perennially attractive base for moral principles. Yet responsibility is firmly affiliated with voluntary choice and action rather than involuntary feeling. Moreover, the spirit of limitation in a system of responsibilities would protect responsibility holders in many instances from being desolated by bad outcomes or needing too desperately to find comprehensive validation in their successes in this capacity. It seems nevertheless that there is a layer of social feeling in which the adequately *responsive* person rises to the goodness of feeling the humanely illuminating and motivating sympathy and empathy that normally attend responsible choice and conduct. In so rising, the agent can be said to be affectively responsible. Although the concept of due diligence is not really at home in this context, it is as though the agent has been duly diligent in opening him- or herself up to appropriate feeling. The pragmatic correlate and proof of affective responsibility would be in the agent's reaching out to engage the actions of others, actually implementing a fundamental decision to work sincerely with others as opposed to working only his or her own angle.

Appeal might be made to affective responsibility as a necessary component of historical or ethical or religious dedication. The subject would be expected to respond positively to other beings figured as worthy forebears or vulnerable neighbors or eternal souls. The subject's *activated* responsibility would be historical or ethical or religious, according to the dimension of action sharing in which its dominant practical concerns are located; its focus plane would accordingly be in the past, or the future, or perhaps in eternity. But in the *actual* accepting of any kind of responsibility there must be an appropriate feeling for those with whom one intends to share situations. This is proven by the negative case: a fanatic or dreamer can be insensitively attached to a program of right conduct, and that is a deficit in responsibility even if the program is determined by unimpeachable historical or ethical or religious values.

The Relation between Pragmatic Responsibility and Historical Responsibility: The Description Issue

The acting agent is always putting the finishing touches on the historical base of shared action in his or her own practical location. What has just been done joins everything else that has been done and warrants a new narrative of what has come to pass. To perform and share action appropriately in light of the fact that a new total accumulation of action is being created is the general mandate of historical responsibility.[14] Part of that responsibility is to

---

14. For a fuller discussion of historical responsibility, see appendix 2.

be as well informed as possible about the facts of past action and equipped with a historically sound interpretation of those facts.

Historical responsibility could be a problem for the obliging piano mover. What if his boss at work can justifiably complain, "Today you're involved in piano moving—yesterday you were helping someone whose car wouldn't start, the day before it was something else . . . It's always *something* that keeps you from coming to work"? His actions seem not to be adding up well. Or: "You keep taking on too much. You never learn, do you?" He seems not to be as aware of his capacities and the causal ways of the world as he would be if he had been paying attention. On the other hand, a historical series of misfortunes incurred by the piano family might be important to know for judging the urgency or the appropriate means of helping them.

Some appeals to history will be controversial and may need to be challenged. Suppose one of the piano movers is the first person in his family to cross a supposed racial line in helping his friends move in, and his relatives rebuke him for it. There may be a strong historical pattern of principled racially discriminatory action that we would now agree should not be perpetuated. On the other hand, we would not give the agent credit in this dimension if he never gave historical precedent a thought, or simply shrugged it off without reflecting on what the facts of human experience are or what the totality of shared action ought to look like.

Our historical comprehension of what we have done and who we have become preforms our practical intentions and determines the evaluative descriptions of the actions we might undertake. Many of our actions are typed as loyal or disloyal in relation to collective identities and their understood agendas. In wartime, a great proportion of our actions are typed this way in relation to our national identities. But war experience is full of flashes of responsibility that clash with one's partisan historical responsibility; you may encounter someone from the other side who is seeking to avoid evil not only *like* you (the ethical consideration) but *with* you (the pragmatic) by not shooting when not necessary.

Illegal immigration can provoke a kind of low-intensity warfare in which members of national collective A are supposed to prevent nonmembers from entering A's territory (possibly for valid national-political reasons). In the absence of overt hostilities there can be many passages of cooperation between members of these historically divided collectives, although citizens of A who help migrants can get into trouble with authorities and fellow citizens for doing so. The historically pertinent description of the migrant as "non-A" clashes with the pragmatically pertinent description "neighbor." Reconciling the prompts of these different kinds of responsibility is one of the great political challenges—which I propose to consider again after we have thought through the definition of political responsibility.[15]

The Relation between Pragmatic Responsibility and Ethical Responsibility: The Stringency Issue

The relation between pragmatic responsibility and ethical responsibility does not correspond simply to the relation between attention to means and attention to ends, since pragmatic concern no less than ethical concern is about ends (though primarily near-term) and ethical concern no less than pragmatic concern is about means (though construed more abstractly as typical elements of approvable actions). Nor does it correspond to the relation between attention to particulars and attention to general rules, since ethically responsible action can hardly be dismissive of particulars and pragmatically responsible action can hardly be dismissive of rules. Should pragmatic responsibility be viewed as "applied ethics," a branch of ethical responsibility concerned with specifying ethical courses of action in distinctively challenging actual situations? That view would maintain the priority of ethics over pragmatics. Or does pragmatic responsibility have its own priority, so that we might think of ethics as generalized pragmatics? Reasons can be given for both views.

In favor of the priority of ethical responsibility it may be noted that moral and ethical norms saturate our responsible reckoning.[16] Our recognitions of present needs, our intentions of meeting them appropriately, and the terms we use in evaluating our actions are always preformed by general notions of right and wrong held by cultural consensus and personal commitment. In the piano moving case I would probably lend myself to a piano moving effort because I expect myself to *care* about my friend as I am committed to caring about all friends, or neighbors; I would show up for the move because I know that showing up is entailed in keeping a *promise*; and I would have known that I could not rightly *lie* about my availability. Acts of caring, fulfilling obligations, and truth telling are all

---

15. See chapter 4, 120–124.
16. On the relation between the moral and the ethical see appendix 1, 163–169.

implementations of general principles that are constantly demanded and approved by my conscience.

It may also be affirmed that action in the present is *directly* ethically responsible inasmuch as the agent unavoidably chooses from among types of action that are known to bear ethical value and is responsible to fellow beings who are known to have ethical dignity. These forms of ethical validity apply to the present situation because they apply to all situations. Pragmatic responsibility does not project universally in this way; it is always already framed by ethical responsibility, which does.

On the other hand, it is also true that future actions are always subject to the authority of pragmatic responsibility inasmuch as we should always take into account the likely conditions and actual workings of action—including likely advances or failures in supporting specific relationships—when we decide whether actions are eligible or required in principle. In the event, any purportedly ethical action might fail a pragmatic test by betraying a relationship. (This is what I rightly worried about when my hour for piano moving was up.) To the extent that keeping faith in relationships is an acid test for ethical validity, we can say not only that pragmatically responsible actions are applications of ethical standards but also that our ethical standards are generalizations from pragmatically responsible conduct, confirming a priority of the pragmatic. Further, it is plausible that some important practical rules that we think of as ethical, such as "Treat others as you would wish to be treated" or "Maximize desirable consequences for everyone," were originated and are continually renewed as distillations of pragmatic wisdom. The idea of a standing "obligation" or "right" may well have been generalized from extensions of collaborative partnership that seemed obviously appropriate to pragmatically responsible parties—as the obligation to care for one's children or parents extends naturally from the immediate demands of family life, or the right to access to water emerges naturally from experiences of neighborly problem solving.[17] When our ethical calculations run the other way, from settled universal rules toward improvisations, it is plausible to think that we are influenced by prompts of pragmatic responsibility.

The dual priority of the two modes of responsibility can be illustrated on both sides of the pro-life/pro-choice divide in thinking about abortion. On the pro-life side, many people with a general moral objection to abortion want to make exceptions in cases of rape or incest. It is presumed that the

---

17. The principle of obligation is pragmatically derived in chapter 3, 78–84.

eventual mother-child relation would be terribly distorted by the traumatic or inappropriate conception, so that carrying the pregnancy to term could not be expected to lead to a tolerable result. On the pro-choice side, many who would prioritize a woman's free choice about her pregnancy would draw the line at late-term abortions, which have too much of the character of disloyal interaction with *someone* considerable, whether or not a full-fledged person—the fetus having come so far, there seems to be a palpable pragmatic irresponsibility in breaking off cooperation with it.

A richly suggestive text on this issue is Judith Jarvis Thomson's famous ethical defense of abortion.[18] Thomson seeks to strengthen intuitive support for the idea of a woman's normative freedom to dispose of her own body. She imagines that a woman wakes up one morning to find that a distinguished violinist has been plugged into her for life support. (Her dependent is a distinguished violinist so that nothing in the pro-choice argument depends on denying the personhood or human value of the unborn.)[19] The woman is informed that the violinist would die for lack of the kidney function she alone can provide—although the violinist will be well again in nine months. Thomson claims that we would think the woman very *nice* for putting up with this inconvenience in order to help the violinist but nevertheless is well within her rights to unplug herself, and this despite the violinist's "right to life" that we often treat as overriding.

Four intuitions aroused by Thomson's thought experiment illuminate the relationship between ethical responsibility and pragmatic responsibility, showing how each can be dominant in responsible reckoning.

First, despite the outrageous imposition, the actual dependence of the violinist on the healthy woman *does* generate a pragmatic responsibility from which it would be spiritually painful to abdicate. Regardless of how we order the relevant rights in ethical perspective, there is a wrongness about stopping *this person's* life support *now* that is not adequately indicated by stating that it would be nice of the woman to help the violinist. The particular horror of causing an actual person's death (even by an indirect means, and with no previous involvement between the two parties)—the

---

18. Judith Jarvis Thomson, "A Defense of Abortion," *Philosophy and Public Affairs* 1 (1971): 47–66.

19. The pro-life view Thomson grants does not coincide with the pro-life view held by pro-lifers who believe in an essential teleological ordering of human lives, as Frances J. Beckwith points out in "Does Judith Jarvis Thomson Really Grant the Pro-Life View of Fetal Personhood in her Defense of Abortion? A Rawlsian Assessment," *International Philosophical Quarterly* 54 (2014): 443–51.

realization that one would have preempted that person's continuation of life—will no doubt encourage a general disapproval of unnecessarily occasioning death, which in turn will prompt affirmation of a "right to life" in a range of cases; but the pragmatic realization is not the same thing as the ethically reflected "right to life."[20]

Second, an apparent disanalogy between ordinary pregnancy, which most females experience, and the violinist case, which strikes the life-supporting woman out of the blue, is best stated for some purposes locating the relevant action in the present of enactment. One sees that Thomson means to turn the tables on a common view of abortion by making pregnancy rather than abortion the disturbing interruption of an action in hand. And she has succeeded: we feel that the life-supporting woman in Thomson's example quite possibly *ought* to go on with what she was doing before her activities were interrupted. On this basis we feel that she definitely *ought to be able*, that is, has a "right" to act as she would otherwise see fit. Life supporting was not what she was doing, nor is there reason to think that the life supporting of a sick violinist is a kind of thing she would have been doing. In gestating, in contrast, one is always positioned in the midst of a nine-month action of which abortion would be an interruption. (It makes a great difference of course whether a particular pregnancy is regarded as belonging to the class of "normal" and desirable gestations or rather as an undesirable process calling for interruption, more like a disease.)[21]

---

20. David B. Hershenov argues that *projective grouping* (a term of Peter Unger's) makes an intuitive difference: many would give themselves permission to unplug from Thomson's violinist, with whom they previously had no practical relation, but would not feel free to occasion someone else's death by detaching themselves from the other, even for the sake of avoiding serious damage to themselves, if the need for decision arose while the two were doing something together. "Abortions and Distortions: An Analysis of Morally Irrelevant Factors in Thomson's Violinist Thought Experiment," *Social Theory and Practice* 27 (January 2001): 129–48. Hershenov claims that this difference is morally irrelevant (139); it is surely not pragmatically irrelevant, however, even if "grouping" intuitions do not exactly correspond to degrees of actual pragmatic entanglement.

21. Thomson introduces other analogies on the premise that the normal and desirable action is sexual activity and pregnancy is a mishap. "If the room is stuffy, and I therefore open a window to air it, and a burglar climbs in, it would be absurd to say, 'Ah, now he can stay, she's given him a right to the use of her house—for she is partially responsible for his presence there, having voluntarily done what enabled him to get in, in full knowledge that there are such things as burglars, and that burglars burgle.' It would be still more absurd to say this if I had had bars installed outside my windows, precisely to prevent burglars from getting in, and a burglar got in only because of a defect in the bars" (58–59).

A third line of intuitive response to Thomson's case is to protest that if *everyone* needed nine months of kidney help to survive some preterminal stage of their careers, then a shared realization informing our ethics would be that the right to life is inseparable from a right to kidney support, implying that whoever is providing someone the necessary support in the usual way has a duty not to break it off (assuming a fair-enough distribution of this burden). Our basic relevant realization would be that if people could be terminated at the discretion of their kidney sponsors, then human life would be intolerably insecure and often regrettably shorter. But the strange violinist scenario is not governed by such a realization. (Here the difference between established humans like the violinist and unborn human life can be turned in Thomson's favor: zygotes, embryos, and fetuses evidently *can* be terminated at the discretion of their sponsors without overly disrupting our social-practical relations, given that the unborn beings are not yet practically functional.)[22]

A fourth intuition worth discussing is brought up by Thomson, who notes that although nine months of life support seems an unallowable imposition, a mere hour of life support seems a very different case. As Thomson puts it, even if the violinist had no *right* to the woman's life-support, surely it would be *indecent* of her to refuse it if doing so would subject her to no serious inconvenience.[23] (Thomson also thinks it would be indecent of a woman to obtain an abortion in her seventh month merely to avoid having to reschedule a vacation.) The move from what is decided on the basis of rights to what is decided on the basis of decency can be read at least in some cases as the move from ethical to pragmatic responsibility. The telltale vagueness in the norm of decency indicates its base in our overlapping personal experiences of finding what we can and cannot do when we are responsibly engaged with fellow beings in action. (But one should be wary of questionable cultural prompts in this pool of experience, as for instance women have been prompted to think that avoiding the vocation of motherhood is indecent.)

These considerations show that ethical responsibility and pragmatic responsibility are mutually entangled and influence each other, but that

---

22. But some abortion critics argue that a larger effect of allowing individual abortions is a cumulative classist or racist genocide, with one or more socially disadvantaged groups being disproportionally reduced in numbers by the practice. For discussion and feminist critique of such arguments see Jennifer M. Denbow, "Abortion as Genocide: Race, Agency, and Nation in Prenatal Nondiscrimination Bans," *Signs* 41 (Spring 2016): 603–26.

23. Thomson, 59–64.

we can distinguish their bases. Present action gets its responsible meaning crucially from particular pressures of action sharing; ethical standards get their responsible meaning crucially from their reflective depth and universal applicability. Each form of responsibility has its own original character and priority.

Recognition of priority depends on what we want to understand or prescribe. If we want to explain the ontogeny of moral action and character, for example, it seems that we must be able to point to an original pragmatic responsibility in advance of moral and ethical conceptions. For moral words when we first learned them must have resonated somehow with our experience; and even if one thinks moral meanings can be learned from scratch in new experiences tied to new words, we know from interactions with nonlinguistic infants and nonhuman animals that considerateness in relationship exists apart from language comprehension.[24]

To explain the comprehensibility or discursive justifiability of pragmatically responsible actions, on the other hand, or to challenge an entrenched pattern of pragmatic responsibility—as Thomson attacks the assumption that women are generally obliged to complete their pregnancies—we must recognize the ethical formation of the relevant evaluative concepts (including our general notion of "decency" in action). Once we are talking about our actions we are in the frame of ethics, just as we are in the technical-teleological frame of pragmatics.

In going back and forth between the two responsibility perspectives, we may experience confusing mixtures in the type of stringency we are subject to, as Thomson's discussion shows. How is it that *it would be indecent* to deny easily granted, vitally needed help, while at the same time the recipient of the help *has no right* to it? The operational difference, as Thomson frames things, is that the objection to "indecency" cannot be enforced; an onlooker would have neither a duty nor a right to interfere with the indecent unplugger. A background principle that makes sense of this is that the demands of pragmatic responsibility must be specified on the spot by the agent who is in his or her own arena, in touch with its particular pressures as no one

---

24. On infants, see Sarah Hrdy, *Mothers and Others: The Evolutionary Origins of Mutual Understanding* (Cambridge, MA: Harvard University Press, 2009), chap. 4. On nonhuman animals, see Dale Peterson, *The Moral Lives of Animals* (London: Bloomsbury, 2011), chaps. 10–11.

else can be. We can hope to influence the agent, but all influence must be directed to the agent's mind upstream from his or her decisions—getting the agent to notice or remember certain things, for example—rather than insisting on a decision, grabbing the rudder of his or her life, on the basis of common principles. Sometimes we do insist; we think that agents do not have latitude to cheat, for example. But in cases where we are not directly threatened with the breakdown of our system of practice we defer to the autonomy of others. Perhaps the strongest direction we can give is in such terms as these: "*I* can't imagine that action being the responsible action!" Though we cannot invoke the strictly shared subjecthood of ethical responsibility, we are not being passively indulgent either; we are sharing responsible subjecthood in a pragmatic way, refraining from pragmatic trespass.

The large task of arranging for a fully responsible sharing of historical, pragmatic, and ethical responsibilities, constraining what is properly constrained and allowing what is properly allowed in all of these perspectives, on the basis of explicitly discussed and rationalized collective agreement, is *political*. Being responsible in attending to that task is one of the leading embodiments of political responsibility, a mixed form (so I shall argue) that is our next topic.

Chapter Three

Political Responsibility

What defines the political? Our conceptions are diverse. The concern of politics is justice, or group identity and loyalty, or conflict and coercion, or negotiation and accommodation, or a collective opportunity for free, creative, and historic action. It is a realm for fulfilling civic duties, or a set of managerial issues to be handled by professionals, or the push for a particular scheme of government such as monarchy, democracy, or anarchy—or, deeper in the social grain, patriarchy or racialism or their removals. It may be seen as an entrepreneurial matter, limited but not driven by responsible considerations, so that political issues call for your attention only if that's what you're excited about. How political responsibility is conceived is likely to be affected by which of these visions is held—whether the emphasis falls on government or group, on fact or reason, on submission or expression.

I suggest that responsibility theory take its cue from this disunity and designate the political as an inclusive genre of practical concern that is inevitably mixed conceptually and roiled by controversy since it has the overarching purpose of bringing together in some appropriate way individuals' and groups' diverse interests in how life is to be shared—those interests to be rivalrously contested, or harmonized to the extent possible, or studiously contemplated. If there is a generally accessible arena for negotiating such interests then a principal location of political activity (but not the only one) will be the "public sphere."[1] Because of the inclusiveness of political

---

1. Commonly, political interest is contrasted with private interest, and this contrast is assumed to place political intentions in the public sphere; for example, Andrew Barry and Lucy Kimbell write that "an act is political when it demonstrates that an issue that

concern one might even wish to designate politics our supreme interest, for reasons related to Aristotle's reasons for viewing politics as the supreme science[2]—although today we would probably think not so much of locating our natural fulfillment in the *polis* as of managing as responsibly as we can in our complicated world of free individuals, families, voluntary associations, businesses, nations, and the ecosphere. The point in any case is to make the best arrangements for our unavoidable togetherness, in the fullest possible awareness of how our togetherness is and may be constituted.

The literature of political theory attests to several ideally strong conceptions of political responsibility, great Attractors as we might call them. It is important to appreciate all of them and not commit exclusively to any of them. Political responsibility is thought to be defined by (1) the technical objective of maintaining power over group processes, (2) the ethical goal of justice, (3) the pragmatic goal of expediency in the sense of near-term success with shared actions in hand (hitherto least well understood as a mode of responsibility), and (4) the goal of protecting and enhancing a historic collective achievement. We can observe how each of these Attractors organizes the field in its own cogent way, capturing and adapting the concerns of the other perspectives.

Political Responsibility and Power Wielding: The Motivation Issue

The idea that politics is primarily about wielding power effectively is associated with Machiavelli, but perhaps misleadingly; for while it is true that Machiavelli's advice to rulers is based on a hard-headed analysis of political behavior and causation, it is also permeated by an interest in the moral excellences of true virtue and true glory.[3] An ultimate premise for

---

people are generally unaware of, or that is considered simply as a private matter, should be a matter of wider collective concern. When a shopper buys 'fair trade' coffee, this is a political act . . ." "Pindices [Personal Political Indices]," in *Making Things Public*, ed. Bruno Latour and Peter Weibel (Cambridge, MA: MIT Press, 2005), 872–73, 872. But there are politics in all sorts of associations.

2. Aristotle, *Nicomachean Ethics* 1094b.

3. About Agathocles of Syracuse: "It cannot be called skill to kill one's fellow citizens, to betray friends, to be without faith, without mercy, without religion; by these means one can acquire power but not glory." Niccolò Machiavelli, *The Prince*, in *The Portable Machiavelli*, trans. Peter Bondanella and Mark Musa (London: Penguin, 1979), 104.

his theorizing (as for Hobbes) is that the alternative to powerful rule is a frightful disorder that no sane person would prefer.[4] So his position rests on spiritual principles.

To sip from a purer font of power politics we may turn to the Athenian sophist Thrasymachus as he is represented in Plato's *Republic*. Thrasymachus espouses a brutal realism that defines rightness or justice as "the advantage of the stronger" (339d). The standards of justice require the weaker to forego stealing, lying, and so forth so that the stronger may enjoy the selfish advantages of being unjust—stealing, lying, and so forth when expedient, with immunity from coercion (343–44). The ruler is interested in justice strictly as a tool for domination. The political meaning of justice from the ruler's perspective is related to morality—for that is the mode in which the ruled accept the ruler's demands as legitimate—but it is not a genuinely moral meaning since it does not constrain all members of the community.

Thrasymachus's view is realist because it purports to describe what does happen, whenever rulers are successful; it is a normative view too insofar as it tells rulers what constitutes full success on their part. Socrates responds in his own normative vein that if we are talking about genuine rulers, then the art of ruling (analogous to doctoring or piloting) must be understood by the benefit it confers on the ruled, which requires intelligent concern for the good of the ruled (341). Socrates' conception of ruling allows for a strong, normal-seeming sense of political responsibility, whereas in the world as Thrasymachus sees it, those who feel responsible are the victims of manipulation and those who act with the greatest power can be considered responsible only in a surprisingly skewed way; they presumably care about the efficacy of their own actions—otherwise they could not enjoy and admire themselves so much—but they do not care to be accountable to their fellow beings.

There are other realist positions that are not so adverse to responsibility or meaningful justification, but before we look away from Thrasymachus we might note what is arguably correct and helpful in his view. We do see rulers using the coercive machinery of government to exploit the ruled for their own gain and impose on them an unreciprocated responsibility.

---

4. "In order to recognize the ability of an Italian spirit, it was necessary that Italy be reduced to her present condition and that she be more enslaved than the Hebrews [before Moses], more servile than the Persians [before Cyrus], more scattered than the Athenians [before Theseus]; without a leader, without organization, beaten, despoiled, ripped apart, overrun, and prey to every sort of catastrophe" (Machiavelli, 162). "This barbarian dominion stinks to everyone!" (166).

Political realism should have the sober virtue of reminding us that political systems work in this way, commonly if not necessarily, which may limit what can meaningfully be realized as responsible conduct by a political agent and which may suggest abstaining from or disrupting politics as the most responsible conduct. More constructively, the spectacle of exploitative politics may serve as an enduring prompt for responsible political action: the theme of politics would be our engagement with that problem, either responsibly trying to mitigate it or irresponsibly perpetuating it.

Thrasymachus does not admit this, but his selfish power wielders are bound to be in chronic and often violent conflict with each other for lack of an accepted moral restraint on themselves. One cannot assume that there will always be a single dominant boss or gang. But this problem too suggests important realist theses: that political life has the character of power struggle and that responsible political action must engage in that struggle in the most defensible manner. A politically responsible stance will always be competitive, and will be stronger for being more competitive.

Thrasymachus forces us also to confront a problem in the understanding of "power," which for him means the ability to compel others to act in one's own interest. A plausible political realism will need a more socially viable model of power than this, even if it does not reach all the way to the spiritually charged Arendtian conception of power as a function of voluntarily concerted collective action.[5] It seems unarguable that at least one major theme of political concern and action is the wielding of power, which has to do with certain factors being intentionally made to prevail in the shaping of action sharing in a collective; and that any action that could count as politically satisfactory would involve a practically sustainable and (trans)subjectively acceptable coherent pattern in that prevailing-in-shaping. Dynastic continuity in a legitimate monarchy might fulfill this ideal, but so might a turbulent struggle among parties in a modern democracy. In a family, a "firm but fair" style of command by a head of household might seem to fulfill the ideal, but so too might a much looser, less predictable sequence of persons alternating in the roles of guide and guided.

Thrasymachus's definition of justice is not simply a mistake. Anyone seeking to accomplish something politically would be bound to profess allegiance to a standard for a collectively acceptable arrangement, some version of "justice"; at the same time, anyone intending to *prevail* in the exercise of power in a collective, and thus to *impose* a putatively acceptable arrange-

---

5. Hannah Arendt, *The Human Condition* (Chicago: University of Chicago Press, 1958), chap. 5.

ment, would probably use a political standard of justice different from any ideal that would be approved by a purely ethical reflection. (I say "probably," not "necessarily," because Platonic justice is conceived as an ethical ideal of each agent performing their own naturally complementary function in the community, this ideal being forcibly imposed by the well-educated Guardian rulers performing *their* proper function. Justifications of monarchy and caste privilege have often run along these lines. But this view would be unlikely to find favor in contemporary ethical discussions, as it seems unfairly to disempower many individuals.) Thus a realist can argue that a politically satisfactory action is something different in principle from an ethically satisfactory action; and this point places political responsibility at least partly on a different intentional wavelength than ethical responsibility.

In this perspective we might say that "justice" in the political context is optimally a posit of realistic political responsibility. That is, responsible political agents do appeal to and claim to fulfill a standard of collective acceptability, *and* they candidly admit this standard to be subject to the exigencies of imposing solutions on power wielding problems, so that political justice is distinct in principle from an ethical standard. That is not to say it is disconnected from ethics.

Turning to the relation between political and pragmatic forms of responsibility, we might also look for a distinctively political posit of "expediency." Responsible political agents should be sincerely interested in facilitating satisfactions of pragmatic responsibility so far as they can. But their own view of expediency will be adapted to their priority of prevailing in the shaping of shared action and maintaining the power structure that enables them to continue to prevail. It is sad but not shocking, therefore, to learn of personal betrayals and the sacrifice of various interests incurred in politically successful actions. There is some incongruity but no real contradiction if politically responsible agents support politically irresponsible allies on occasion, given the exigencies of power holding and political victory or survival.

That power holders seek to perpetuate their power is, in one aspect, quite innocent and healthy—the political version of the general self-regarding concern of responsible agents to develop and preserve a competency to do all that is desirable for them to do—but in another aspect poses one of the greatest essential problems of political life. Monarchy and democracy have both been regarded as fundamental solutions of the problem. The legitimate monarch and his or her heirs are supposed to be secure from fighting for power (internally) and have nothing material to wish for, so their rule can be disinterested. Democracy supports interested, striving parties on all hands but relies on elections for fluidity in power holding and on checks and balances at any given moment to maintain a healthy distribution of powers among agencies. Each approach has seemed at times to work well enough.

The politically responsible agent can proceed on the basis of a primary realization about power wielding as a fundamental issue in action sharing. This could be a Machiavellian realization about the way to prevent foreign enslavement: that there must be a skillfully manipulative ruler, ruthless when need be, to hold a national community together. Or it could be a Hobbesian realization about the way to prevent anarchy: that there must be a government sufficiently empowered to enforce agreements. Or it could be a Spinozan realization about the maximizing of human power in political association as the basis of the greatest intrinsic felicity, which consists of living rationally (*Ethics* IV). Or it could be an ecofeminist realization about the hopelessness of correcting cultural sexism with anything less than an intently amplified biophilia.[6] In any case the power will probably be best wielded by those who have a vocation for politics. We can discriminate better from worse power wielders politically by the purity of their focus on effectiveness in helping the polity. We can tell that this version of political responsibility has been lost when the ruler turns to self-gratification, as in the scenario Thrasymachus unwisely evokes, or when the ruler is overtaken by personal passions, as happened to Creon in *Antigone*.

The Relation between Political Responsibility and Ethical Responsibility: The "Obligation" Issue

From the start of our lives we have been fitfully yet persistently sharing with other agents a profound concern for proper practical relations. The concern has been articulated and its general standards set by moral and ethical discourse, which figures us as choosers among better and worse types of action.

The principle of fairness plays a central role in ethical discourse because it crystallizes our general interest in putting practical relations in an acceptable order. Saying "That's fair" evokes an encounter of bargainers who posit a continuing mutual support that all of their deals will be con-

---

6. As in Mary Daly, *Gyn/Ecology: The Metaethics of Radical Feminism*, rev. ed. (Boston: Beacon, 1990), a text notable for its effort to express the force of its realizations with vivid language.

sistent with. It is both a ratification of the present deal and a freshening of the basic deal.

Fairness is an important standard in modern politics with its orientation to voluntary subscription. When we act politically, we are concerned with ideal fairness in the measure that we are ethically responsible. The same can be said about the standard of justice: it has ethical meaning in the measure that we invoke it with ethical intent. But we may not be invoking justice with purely ethical intent; we may be invoking a more general sense of rightness that awaits ethical or other kinds of specification, or we may be invoking a nonethical specification of rightness—perhaps a sense of "fairness" in a specific arrangement that could not be defended as ideally fair but *has* been accepted and can be implemented with its own consistency. Justice is actually a hinge or bridge notion for us as it can express a comprehensive rightness in a practical system from various points of view. It can stand for a rightness of political practicability, including the integrity of a legal order.[7] It can serve as the conceptual venue for the dialectic of a "political ethic."[8]

The political moralist John Rawls affirms justice as the definitive political goal and in *A Theory of Justice* (1971) gives priority to the ethical conception of justice as fairness, thus subordinating political to ethical responsibility.[9] Later he moves to separate the political ideal of justice as fairness from any ethical doctrine, as his political liberalism cannot be based on any principles that citizens can reasonably disagree about. In *Justice as Fairness* (2001) Rawls derives the rightness of justice from our most basic

---

7. On the conceptual history of justice see Otto A. Bird, *The Idea of Justice* (New York: Frederick Praeger, 1967).

8. In *Political Responsibility* (New York: Columbia University Press, 2016), Antonio Vázquez-Arroyo adopts a "dialectical" conception of "political ethic"—that is, of the guidance for political practice—which involves refusing the exclusion of ethics from politics but also refusing to impose ethical categories on political life (218–19). Despite intending a neo-Weberian critique of political moralism, Vázquez-Arroyo conceives the difference between the political and the ethical as the difference between issues of principled right conduct for collectives and for individuals, that is, between two branches of ethics; thus his dialectic and its implied conception of justice are too narrowly ethical, in my view, although he turns partway toward the pragmatic and historical forms of responsibility in his theoretical recognition that "political ideals . . . are thoroughly mediated by particular predicaments of power in their historical unfolding" (xiii).

9. John Rawls, *A Theory of Justice* (Cambridge, MA: Harvard University Press, 1971).

interest in responsible cooperation and well-ordered association, characterizing this interest as "moral" in the broadest sense.[10] In effect he is appealing to our broadest sense of responsibility, hoping to show that it has a primal political implication. However, in moving from generic responsibility to political life he continues to conceive the practical ideal as a controlling general principle of rightness generated by agreement in an abstracted Original Position; and so Rawlsian politics, even with its socially and historically realistic inflections and its contingent public rather than a priori justification, remains an ethics predicated on constant universal compliance. As an ethics of fair reciprocity applied to basic political issues it is of great political significance, but it misses some other relevant forms of justification and thus some other considerations for political guidance and legitimacy.[11]

Political realists hold that political agents do not, either in fact or in principle, have the implementation of any ethical standard as their top priority.[12] The realist point is not that political action is immoral or amoral but rather that it has its own distinct agenda geared to prevailing in the struggle for control of the political community and in the competition among political communities. My own principal realist claim is that political agents have a distinctive *pragmatic* responsibility *to* politically collaborating agents and *for* politically successful results subject to the exigencies of their operative collaborative arrangements. (Analogously, we think of businesspeople being pragmatically responsible to their collaborating workers and investors for business success.)[13]

---

10. John Rawls, *Justice as Fairness: A Restatement*, ed. Erin Kelly (Cambridge, MA: Harvard University Press, 2001), 14. See also "The Idea of Public Reason" in *Collected Papers*, ed. Samuel Freeman (Cambridge, MA: Harvard University Press, 2001).

11. Formulating political rightness as a general principle of conduct is a necessary strategy in political philosophy as Rawls conceives that task—the theory of political rightness *in principle* (*Justice as Fairness* 3). If my thesis is correct that political responsibility is an unstable compound form, the political-principle approach cannot encompass all of the sources of political responsibility and legitimacy (except by restrictive definitions of the relevant values).

12. For contemporary realist arguments against political moralism see Enzo Rossi and Matt Sleat, "Realism in Normative Political Theory," *Philosophy Compass* 9/10 (2014) 689–701, and Matt Sleat, ed., *Politics Recovered: Realist Thought in Theory and Practice* (New York: Columbia University Press, 2018).

13. See Hans Morgenthau's sixth principle of political realism: "Intellectually, the political realist maintains the autonomy of the political sphere, as the economist, the lawyer, the moralist maintain theirs. He thinks in terms of interest defined as power, as the economist thinks in terms of interest defined as wealth; the lawyer, of the conformity of

A political moralist can reply that for agents who *are* ethically responsible the satisfaction of ethical demands is *always* the overriding priority. When we deliberate on action sharing, ethics is always on the highest ground. There could not be an approvable implementation of an action sharing scheme that violated constant ethical standards of honesty and equity. There is also a long-range ethical goal of fully implemented respect for human rights that could not approvably be trumped by any other sort of collective goal. The vital political goal of fending off anarchy is compulsory because it defends human rights, an ethical requirement. Political power cannot be a supreme good in itself; as Locke insisted against Hobbes, a powerful government can be worse for us than no government at all.[14]

But the moralist line of thinking fails to distinguish between the broader sensitivity of being a spiritual agent concerned to rectify mutually supporting relations—the field of all responsibility—and a narrower normativity in the ethical determination of approvable types of action in principle. Even Rawls, who comes to think that he must make such a distinction, fails to sustain it due to his commitment to the ethical ideal of fairness. Consequently, moralism cannot do much to elucidate the obvious differences between normal assumptions of political and ethical responsibility. We may consider two forms of political responsibility that become puzzle cases when political responsibility is interpreted as a branch of ethical responsibility. The puzzles can be solved by showing the footing of political responsibility in pragmatic responsibility.

Political "Obligation" to the State

Is there a basic, universally stringent requirement to uphold the institutions, laws, and lawful orders of the country in which one is living? Thinking teleologically it seems there is good reason to uphold the arrangements of one's state in order to maximize the welfare of the residents in one's state-level community; and yet situations often arise in which an individual's or

---

action with legal rules; the moralist, of the conformity of action with moral principles. The economist asks: 'How does this policy affect the wealth of society, or a segment of it?' The lawyer asks: 'Is this policy in accord with the rules of law?' The moralist asks: 'Is this policy in accord with moral principles?' And the political realist asks: 'How does this policy affect the power of the nation?' (Or of the federal government, of Congress, of the party, of agriculture, as the case may be.)" Hans J. Morgenthau, *Politics among Nations: The Struggle for Power and Peace* (New York: McGraw-Hill, 1993), 13.

14. John Locke, Second Treatise on Civil Government, §§90–91.

group's welfare can be improved by disobeying the state. As for deontological considerations, even with the state positioned as a necessary enforcer of ethical standards one might conscientiously disagree with some of its policies or actions; it is hardly an unknown circumstance that a state makes its constituents victims or unwilling coperpetrators of injustice. It seems, then, that the political requirement or commitment is easily overridden, even if it is basic in the sense of being an inescapable issue for political beings. Is this where we are? Does nothing bind us to the political arrangements under which we live except fear of losing whatever prudential or ethical help we think we are getting from them at a given time?

The question has been taken up in recent philosophy under the rubric of "political obligation." But the discussion repeatedly hits a pair of significant snags in the concept of obligation.

The first problem is lack of agreement as to whether obligation as such, or the kind of obligation that is requisite for political life, is necessarily ethical. To hold that political obligation is ethical (as many philosophers do) implies that citizens are bound to support a state just insofar as the state's demands qualify as ethical requirements; but this ideal constraint seems too weak *politically* because it fails to bind citizens to *all* of a state's demands, and it also fails to bind them exclusively or preeminently to *their own* state's demands (the "particularity problem").[15] If, however, political obligation is held to be nonethical or (with that sense) nonmoral, the objection arises that the demand cannot be considered a true *obligation*.[16] It is better thought of as a defeasible practical hypothesis.

The second problem is lack of agreement as to whether obligation must be voluntarily incurred. For some writers the terms "obligation" and "duty" are interchangeable, so that "obligation" could refer to any strong normative requirement; but others hold that obligation obtains only with agreement or as the result of a promise.[17] On the more restrictive view it

---

15. See A. John Simmons, *Moral Principles and Political Obligations* (Princeton: Princeton University Press, 1979), 31, 191–201.

16. A leading nonmoralist is Thomas McPherson in *Political Obligation* (London: Routledge & Kegan Paul, 1967), and for that objection see, for example, Simmons, *Moral Principles and Political Obligations*, 4.

17. John Rawls, *A Theory of Justice*, 96–100. See also Gilbert's discussion of agreement theories of political obligation in *A Theory of Political Obligation* (Oxford: Oxford University Press, 2006), 55–90, and Simmons, "Associative Political Obligations," *Ethics* 106 (January 1996): 247–73.

may be impossible to allow for obligation to be *found* in an already-ongoing practical relationship lacking a point of voluntary entry where it might have been *assumed*. Natural duties can be taken as given, but not obligations.

I suggest that we reframe this question as one of political responsibility, which will admit a mixture of pragmatic and ethical considerations and allow us to resolve the unsettled concept of obligation.

A likely starting point for any modern discussion of political obligation is social contract theory, which boldly applies the ethical model of agreement keeping to an arrangement to which most agents have never agreed and in which it is usually not feasible to ask for agreement. In its most plausible form, the theory claims that if one thinks about which general arrangements for social collaboration reasonable agents *would* agree to, the principles of the political scheme we actually live in might be found to coincide with the ideal, making due allowance for real-world exigencies. Whether the scheme in which we are living comes reasonably close to coinciding with the ideal determines whether it is just; if the existing scheme is just, we have an *obligation* to obey it, for in our ideal anticipation we agreed we would.

Now, even if it is admitted that relatively few people can freely agree to be subject to their state, it can still be argued that we all have good reason to idealize our political position as one of voluntarily assumed obligation inasmuch as we are bound to want our government to deal with us on this premise. If we are not being treated honorably as reciprocating agreement keepers, then we are, in actuality, being herded like sheep; and a sheep-herding political model is hardly viable for modern democracy, however appealing the "good shepherd" ideal may have been in an era of despotic monarchy. Citizens in a democracy must be able to criticize laws, practices, and proposals that seem to them inconsistent with a voluntarily undertaken obligation, and this prerogative implies the touchstone of a fair deal, justice, that would have made it reasonable to undertake that obligation.

Hobbesians might point out that the democratic idealization of the situation actually opens the door to anarchy quite dangerously. For everyone will have their own idea of the conditions under which their agreements must be kept, and their ideas of honor will be heavily influenced by their material interests, their rivalries, and their philosophical preferences. The state will fail if obedience is voluntary to that extent. Fortunately, most states *are* functional because obedience in them is *not* so voluntary. But this argument seems to be a way of emphasizing the sheep-herding aspect of political life; it does not establish political *obligation*. The Hobbesian attempt to provide for voluntariness in an original agreement to submit to a government must resolve either into sheep psychology—the original bargainers being simply overpowered by their fear of anarchy so that they clump together under a shepherd, any shepherd, giving up their powers of talking back—or into a genuinely ethicized social contract that allows for the anarchy of constant conscientious quarrel.

A less voluntary version of obligation that might fit the political situation better has been called "associative" by Ronald Dworkin and others.[18] This approach calls attention to the two great facts that we are fundamentally dependent on the communities we live in and that we feel solidarity with our consociates. These facts must be a major part of the explanation of why political structures exist and work. There is a normative implication: given that I can recognize and reason about my profound interdependence with a certain ensemble of others, many temptations and uncertainties about my conduct are most satisfactorily resolved by reaffirming my participation in this shared action. Practically this means fulfilling received familial and political roles.

A political ethicizer will want to insist that the normatively overriding question about an existing collaboration is what we might freely decide to do about it in light of our general ethical commitments, especially when the collaboration is ethically problematic.[19] For example, the family I have grown up in might be a crime family, or the state of which I am a citizen or official might be prosecuting an unjust war. My true obligations snap into focus just when I ethically evaluate the roles that are offered me. But this ethicizing conclusion has been conceptually guaranteed by identifying all obligation with moral or ethical obligation. We have not yet recognized a requirement that obtains just in living in a particular community—and this is one of the main things a political theory has to account for.[20]

Margaret Gilbert has developed another branch of thought about associative obligation that is more oriented to single undertakings in the present and thus to the immediately apparent conditions of pragmatic responsibil-

---

18. Ronald Dworkin, *Law's Empire* (Cambridge, MA: Harvard University Press, 1986), 195–216; John Horton, *Political Obligation*, 2nd ed. (New York: Palgrave Macmillan, 2010).

19. Simmons, "Associative Political Obligations."

20. Simmons, *Moral Principles and Political Obligations*, 31; John Horton, *Political Obligation*, 10.

ity.²¹ On her view we incur obligation whenever we enter into an actively shared action. For example, if I start walking and talking with you—even without any earlier promise, like "Yes, let's go downtown," that would have implied a specific obligation—just by virtue of sharing this action with you (in Gilbert's language, forming a plural subject of the action) I acquire a significant reason not to abandon or change it in a way that would be unwelcome to you. It is a reason that may be overruled by other reasons, but not properly by a merely selfish reason; that is why, according to Gilbert, we can say that an obligation obtains.²² This sort of constraint is appreciable even in the hard cases of ethically unacceptable shared action: a criminal has *a* compelling reason to continue playing his or her part in a shared criminal activity, and is a better agent (mindful, diligent, faithful) in doing so than in acting merely selfishly, even though the criminal action ought not to be done.²³

Gilbert says that by "obligation" she means nothing other than an ideal requirement to act in a certain way.²⁴ She does not debate with those who view obligation as a distinctive normative category. But her model of action sharing implies a politically relevant form of normative requirement—a requirement that can be *found* as obtaining in a situation without any previous agreeing and yet can be thought of as *incurred* by the activity in that situation. The "found" aspect is more suggestive of natural duty than

---

21. Margaret Gilbert, *On Social Facts* (Princeton: Princeton University Press, 1989) and *A Theory of Political Obligation*.

22. The *teleological sense* of a joint endeavor (and in that sense the *reason* for it) is normally determined by my own plan of action as it overlaps and entwines with the plans of others on such occasions. See Michael Bratman, *Shared Agency: A Planning Theory of Acting Together* (Oxford: Oxford University Press, 2014), 129. But the instrumental obligations that are generated by the overlap and interdependence of plans of action are not of the same order as the present pragmatic obligation to be supportive of an active collaborator.

23. Richard Vernon objects that we do not think that fulfilling one's responsibility in a criminal enterprise has any *moral* weight, because if it did, keeping a promise to murder someone would mitigate the murder. "Obligation by Association? A Reply to John Horton," *Political Studies* 55 (2007): 865–79, 865–66. But this seems an excellent example for showing (a) how evaluations anchored in pragmatic responsibility can differ from evaluations anchored in ethical responsibility, and (b) how ethical responsibility can override pragmatic responsibility—even shout it down very loudly—without completely erasing it.

24. Gilbert, *A Theory of Political Obligation*, 26–27.

of obligation. The "incurred" aspect, however, places us in the neighborhood of obligations.

Prying apart the pragmatic and ethical modes of responsibility gives us an opportunity to sharpen the concept of obligation. I could simply make a move similar to Gilbert's and define an obligation as any of the items in a job description for some sort of responsible agency. Thus I could say that as an ethical communicator I have an obligation always to be truthful, and as a pragmatically trusty piano mover I have an obligation not to drop the piano if I can help it. But while these assertions of obligation do not sound strange, neither do we need the term *obligation* to say them. I can just as well say that I have a responsibility to be truthful and not to drop the piano. If obligations are equated with responsibilities we are missing one of the ways a claim of obligation gets distinctive pragmatic traction, namely, in how it is characteristically generated by a promise or a helpful action looking forward from a particular situation rather than being simply given in a role or situation. Obligation only needs to be mentioned in the piano-moving case if I have to justify to someone else my going there as promised—"and so (*because of what happened earlier*) I have an obligation (*to my friend*)"—or in a grateful coda to the action from my friend, "I'm much obliged (*to you, because of that*)." The point is the commitment to follow-up. Thinking that shared action is going to be a longer haul than what we are doing right now, we not only stand ready to apply any ethical standards that may be relevant, we adopt larger structures of pragmatic loyalty that apply specifically to situations we can foresee being in with the same collaborators. My promise *to you* will be kept in due course and my helping *you* will be reciprocated by you helping me, perhaps with our associates involved, as appropriate occasions arise, hopefully tending toward a fair allocation of effort and sacrifice overall. Seen at this angle, the concept of obligation is an extension of pragmatic responsibility into the future and a bridge to ethical responsibility insofar as consistent promise keeping and reciprocation of help will require commitment on the basis of general types of action, not only the pressure of present action.[25] Once I have a definite

---

25. For example, Thomas Scanlon's principle F, an ethical a priori of fidelity distilled from many variations of pragmatic responsibility: "If (1) A voluntarily and intentionally leads B to expect that A will do X (unless B consents to A's not doing so); (2) A knows that B wants to be assured of this; (3) A acts with the aim of providing this assurance, and has good reason to believe that he or she has done so; (4) B knows that A has the beliefs and intentions just described; (5) A intends for B to know this, and knows that B does know it; and (6) B knows that A has this knowledge and intent; then, in the

obligation, I understand that it is the kind of demand that an honorable person fulfills; once I am thoughtfully operating in an ethical dimension, I see that some obligations must trump others. But there is an insistent pragmatic pressure when obligation begins. It is something *I* and *you* feel is appropriately posited between us.

For this reason I agree that obligations cannot simply come with membership in a nonvoluntary association, or with passive acceptance of what that association is doing, but must be voluntarily undertaken.[26] Accordingly, I reject the notion of political obligation as applied generally and strictly to subjects of a state.[27] This move protects the distinctive significance of specific political obligations that may indeed be pragmatically generated, such as the obligation of party members to support their party's nominees, and of proposals that certain political obligations be accepted by all, as when a leader calls on the citizenry to assume an obligation to uphold a standard of health care. What I do affirm generally is the political *responsibility* of all permanent residents of a state to support state-related causes, based on the facts of their present interdependency in sustaining their state combined with an ethically requisite general concern for reasonable conduct in political matters. The sense of this responsibility is well displayed by the reasons that have been given in favor of "associative obligation" and that ideally support a normatively charged conception of membership in a group.

---

absence of special justification, A must do X unless B consents to X's not being done." *What We Owe to Each Other* (Cambridge, MA: Harvard University Press, 1998), 304.

26. Massimo Renzo argues that associations of political interest are "quasi-voluntary"—we did not choose to join them, but we can choose to withhold our endorsement of them. "Associative Responsibilities and Political Obligation," *The Philosophical Quarterly* 62 (January 2012): 106–27. I think that to make "quasi-voluntary" association a scene of obligation we must suppose a choice not to withhold endorsement, that is, an *assuming* of endorsement, where withholding endorsement is a feasible option with distinctive consequences; but that is to make the quasi-voluntary fully voluntary. Anyway this seems to be the reply required by the conception of obligation I am recommending.

27. I say "generally and strictly" because I do not wish to deny the political relevance of the *thought* of shared obligations rooted in consciously undertaken shared action on the scale of the whole state—a thought that is powerfully evoked in the US, for example, by the Declaration of Independence. Americans are regularly encouraged to identify with the Founders and other notable contributors to a unified national endeavor, and their sense of a political obligation being generated by an inclusive collaboration among Americans may continually be nourished by their own political experience. But to see this is not to see that all Americans (let alone all citizens of all states) have an obligation to uphold their state.

Political responsibility prompts a variety of actions, some of respectful care for one's country as it is and some promoting better policies and practices. To act unpatriotically or to be "apolitical" is not to violate an agreement—*pace* Socrates,[28] few would say that they entered an agreement with their country just by growing up in it—but it is nevertheless letting one's compatriots down.

POLITICAL VERSUS CIVIC RESPONSIBILITY

Two kinds of political engagement can be projected directly from ethical responsibility. One is the critical stance epitomized by Thoreau's essay "Civil Disobedience," which requires individuals to challenge anything in the constitution or operation of the state of which they morally disapprove. The other centers on the supportive ideal of "civic responsibility." Assuming that human well-being depends on a well-functioning state and that the health of the state depends on the good conduct of its subjects, we have a general responsibility to uphold whatever state system we happen to be living in for the sake of respecting our fellow beings, in some situations helping them using the instrumentalities of the state. What this support consists of will depend on how citizens are situated, but normally there will be a strict duty to obey laws and lawful orders. In a democracy it will aspirationally include participating in elections by studying and communicating about major issues and by voting.

The significant point here is that the ideal of civic responsibility does not necessarily coincide with the ideal of political responsibility, though the phrases are often used interchangeably. On the contrary, the two forms of responsibility can make sharply contrasting demands and can attack each other's authority—in the extreme case, pitting the conscientiously law-abiding citizen against the conscientious terrorist. To explain this disunity in responsibility merely by saying that different civic-political agents have made different rankings of values is not essentially wrong, it is correct in values-speak, but it misses how different genres of responsibility are shaping the practical scene.

The adjectives *civic* and *political* refer to the same practical contexts but do not presume on action in those contexts in the same way. (I allow for contexts other than the state because I take it that we can speak non-

---

28. Plato, *Crito* 49e–52.

metaphorically of being "a good citizen" in the workplace or entering into "the politics" of a group of friends.) The ethical presumption is compulsory and universal; the political presumption is elective and partisan. It is normal to urge every citizen to vote; it is not normal to urge every citizen to run for office or to do campaign work. The voters exiting the polls can claim to have fulfilled a *constant* responsibility; campaign workers waving signs nearby would claim to be fulfilling a *present* responsibility to promote the best election result for the community. These latter might or might not say they feel a requirement to do this—it would depend on how seriously they construed the stakes of the situation.

Civic ideals presuppose an established scheme and civic action's noble cause is always the health of that scheme, whereas the identification of political ideals and goals is much freer. Political philosophy is concerned with the intentionally shared actions of the collaborative We—on the scale of the state, "we the people"—who may or may not subject themselves to a particular scheme or be adequately served by a particular scheme. One can even be a political anarchist. There is no such freedom in civic reckoning.[29] Political thinking is chronically uncertain about who is effectively acting as, or for, the collaborative We, and is free to make new proposals about who constitutes the We, whereas for civic reckoning the criteria of citizenship are normally quite clear. (Part of political responsibility is reflecting on this issue with due diligence.)

The freedom in political reckoning allows for revolution, the archetypal divergence between civic and political responsibility. Revolution is almost impossible to justify civically because it strikes at the framework that makes civic responsibility possible. Certainly there are forms of civil disobedience that can be given an ethical justification, as when life in the state has become so deeply problematic ethically that one can recognize a

---

29. Wayne Leys approaches this point by deriving types of responsibility from degrees of agreement: "The decision-making machinery of society has several gears. In high gear, when there is substantial agreement on the ends of action, the nonpolitical conception of responsibility [i.e., oriented to the merits, to ideal values] is relevant. In second gear, when there is disagreement on the end to be achieved but agreement on procedure, the legal conception of responsibility (respect for due process) is appropriate. In low gear, when there is disagreement on the ends and no clear agreement on procedure (beyond the avoidance of civil war), the [Machiavellian] political conception of responsibility takes over." Wayne A. R. Leys, "Platonic, Pragmatic, and Political Responsibility," in Friedrich, ed., 71–83, 80.

natural duty to disobey an existing government. This sort of realization could justify illegal efforts to rescue Jews from the Nazi regime, for example. But a plot to overthrow the Nazi regime would be a direct attack on the state and could only be justified pragmatically-politically.[30]

Typically when we avow ethical responsibility we mean to keep faith with constantly applicable standards. We refrain from acting unethically even if we could get away with it and even if, in refraining, we forgo a desirable outcome. We say about an unethical action, "That is not who we are," with a view to maintaining our bona fides in the universal assembly of possible collaborators. We treat a problematic action as a question of the survival of our ideal character. In contrast, the primary concern of political responsibility, reflecting its component of pragmatic responsibility centered in a conscious sifting of existence, is to be responsive to near-term practical need, especially urgent need; and the benchmark case of urgency, and so the clearest case of obligation, is one in which survival is at stake—the survival of others to or for whom the agent is responsible. Thus at the same time that the American government ethically renounces torture (the president says, "That is not who we are"),[31] the fictional hero Jack Bauer resorts to torturing a terrorist to get information in a "ticking time bomb" situation to save American lives.[32] Bauer is, we stipulate, not callous or sadistic, but he is able to respond to the crisis.

From an ethical point of view it is reasonable to say that ethical requirements should never be overridden. Often enough there is no reason even to think seriously about an override. Many shared endeavors can just as well be allowed to fail, and criminal shared actions really ought to fail. When political responsibility makes a cogent claim it is not automatically as compelling as

---

30. Such a plotter could construe the revolution as an emergency defense of the *true* German state from the ethically intolerable usurpers who had lately taken it over, and in that light could claim to be fulfilling a civic responsibility. But that ethical idealization of the situation would be pragmatically suspect in the absence of an actually functioning true German state that needs defending. It would be more honest (though not necessarily more effective) to claim political responsibility in acting on behalf of a more acceptable state.

31. "That's not who we are"—Barack Obama in a 2014 *Telemundo* interview. "Obama: That's Not Who We Are," apnews.com, December 9, 2014, accessed October 20, 2021, https://apnews.com/article/637247cb92a7471293b076ddc5aa54eb.

32. The television show *24* was criticized for normalizing torture scenarios. See "Critical Reaction to *24*," accessed October 20, 2021, https://en.wikipedia.org/wiki/Critical_reaction_to_24#Torture.

ethical responsibility. Yet it can be said from a political point of view that in survival emergencies ethical standards must be adapted to the pragmatic demand. One of the supreme exercises of political responsibility is to define and enforce a standard for the action in hand that is in the least total conflict with expectations rooted in ethical and pragmatic responsibility (and other forms). A powerful definition of the political vocation is to seek such solutions.

The supreme survival emergency for a collective is war, and the corresponding strong form of political responsibility is war patriotism, which compels firm support of one's compatriots and ruthless attack on the enemy's war capability. The head of British air raids on Germany took the ethically abhorrent position that "the whole of the remaining cities of Germany [are not] worth the bones of one British Grenadier."[33] Even in 1945, with the outcome of the war no longer in doubt, Bomber Harris's pragmatic-political responsibility to his war colleagues was paramount. (Of course his position, even though ideally meaningful politically, could also be criticized politically, as Churchill and others did criticize it, with other modes and scales of collaboration in view.)

It will be claimed from an ethical perspective that civically responsible action is immune from error, whereas politically responsible action as such depends on pragmatic judgments that can always be second-guessed. High-stakes politically responsible action is liable to tragic failure. For example, Indira Gandhi's Sikh bodyguards killed her to fulfill a responsibility they felt to the Sikh community, which had recently been attacked by the Indian Army—and the assassination caused yet more suffering for the Sikhs. Had they simply voted against Gandhi in the next election, they would have been irreproachable. But even if civically responsible action is invariably justified on its own terms, it is not always justified, all things considered. When a state has been taken over by a bloody tyrant or a viciously discriminatory organization, law-abiding civic responsibility can be tragically irresponsible. The Sikh assassins thought—nay, *realized*—that they were in just such a situation.[34] They felt required to kill in that situation, though others may judge either ethically or pragmatically that they were required not to.

---

33. Sir Arthur Harris, letter to Sir Norman Bottomley (March 29, 1945), quoted in Dudley Saward, *Bomber Harris* (New York: Doubleday, 1985), 294. The "bones of one grenadier" phrase is borrowed from Bismarck, who had said that the whole of the Balkans were not worth the bones of one Pomeranian grenadier.

34. See the court statement by assassin Satwant Singh, accessed October 20, 2021, http://panthic.org/articles/2275.

To the degree that political agents maintain an ethical focus, they will think of political power and political expedience as tools of virtue and justice. But to the degree that they are politically responsible, they will recognize the possible division between ethical and pragmatic obligations and try to minimize the conflict between them.

The Relation between Political Responsibility and Pragmatic Responsibility: The Organization Issue

The pragmatic responsibility of present collaborators to each other is an essential ingredient of political responsibility. A schemer or would-be leader whose plans have nothing to do with helping collaborators succeed in their own efforts, who is dedicated only to domination, would be completely irresponsible politically and thus would not even qualify as a political agent in a socially normal sense. (Socrates used a version of this premise in his critique of Thrasymachean realism.) On the other hand, a schemer or would-be leader with a purely ethical agenda of ideal justice (possibly Socrates or Plato) whose plans make no supportive contact with what a community is presently doing would not be acceptably political either.

The most natural way for political activity to arise is for participants in a shared effort to entertain ideas about how to organize their effort for better results. Say a small farming community meets as usual in their common field at the beginning of the planting season. They are about to disperse to the areas of the field that their families have traditionally worked. But someone proposes an idea for a more efficient work scheme. There is disagreement. Alliances come into play, determining whose view prevails. Henceforth the farmers live under the intentionally negotiated regime of either the new idea or a counteridea. Such an idea originally gets traction because it serves the action in which these agents are engaged—it seems to be the intelligent version of that action. (It is like one piano mover astutely saying to another, "No, grip it *there*.") It is pragmatically responsible because it responds supportively to what collaborators are trying to do. But the idea carries additional freight. It is a scheme for all similar actions in the future—the first version of a political ideology. It is a taking of precedence by the authors and promoters of the idea, possibly a continuing precedence—the first version of a political party and power structure. It becomes a satisfaction or an incitement of ambition to rule—

the first corruption of responsible concern for competence by desire for dominance and preeminence.

In claiming pragmatic responsibility, political agents emphasize the aspects of situations that activate the priorities of that genre, the opportunities and emergencies that must not be neglected. The "cause" of collective action and the "interests" of collaborators are conceived in their present sensitivity to being fostered or hindered. "Justice" will be touted in the form of a fairer deal now—an immediate rectification.

Pragmatic responsibility will always pull on political life to address the endemic problem of inflexible ideologies and power structures. There is a technical problem in an inflexible order that cannot admit new information or change for the better, and there is a spiritual problem in an inflexible order that will not respect collaborators for what they are and do beyond what the order has prefigured. Political inflexibility occasions costly sacrifices of opportunities and horrendous sacrifices of people and relationships. Appeals for a corrective "pragmatism" usually refer to the technical problem but can also express concern for the spiritual problem if pragmatism is conceived as involving pragmatic responsibility. This is a strong appeal for leaders who position themselves as moderates or centrists.

The problems will not be solved by refraining from organizing; even if that were a real option, the costs of not organizing would be very great. One might argue that the material benefits we would give up in a minimally organized life would be more than outweighed by avoidance of the spiritual evil—oppression, alienation, mass violence—caused by our developed political schemes. It is doubtful, though, that those evils would be absent in the organizationally simplest human community. Human beings impose and contest schemes for action in groups of any sort, including small families, hunting groups, and gathering groups. If the development of political organization makes oppression, alienation, and violence worse in some ways, it also enables more protections and more opportunities for rewarding collaboration.

I don't suppose that we can resolve any of the variously framed debates on the optimal state of human society solely on the basis of a theory of responsibility, but I think it can at least be said that a position on this question will be less meaningful if it is not a politically responsible position, meaning by this that the position takes into account not only statecraft and ethics but also the pragmatic demands of present collaborations of all kinds. And I'm sure we will continue to see a large portion of political behavior calculated to reassure the community that the schemers and leaders intend to be supportive of their constituents' pragmatic actuality.

The Relation between Political Responsibility and Historical Responsibility: The Collective Identity Issue

A political initiative aims to shape the scheme of action sharing for a collective. We can imagine an unhistorical collective that is immediately and wholly defined by a single short-term action they have undertaken, say, a pickup group of piano movers; this group's political need can be met simply by being the one who says "Heave!" in the right rhythm. However, the moment the group's unity is no longer assured by the very action on which they all have their hands, as when one of them gets a call demanding that he return to his regular workplace, it becomes necessary to relate the present to the past. How did we come to this collaboration such that we now have this set of practical possibilities and issues? Our present sense of what makes us a team, our active sharing of an action, needs support from a sense of what has made us a team, the already-shared action in the past that will continue to grow or be modified or terminated. The legitimacy of our present team's practices will probably depend on beliefs about how the team has functioned previously. A historical reckoning is needed. A historically responsible reckoning will be conscientiously affirming of relations with past actors.

At the level of our most enduring and inclusive platforms for shared endeavor, such as church and state, the collective's historically funded identity becomes no less relevant politically than its issues of organization. In these contexts the time scale of political thinking must reach far beyond the ordinary pragmatic time range between an initiation of action still in the agent's own memory and a foreseeable completion. Some of the greatest communal "actions in hand" require ceremonious memorialization (as opposed to ordinary remembering) of the initiation of action—*This is how we left Egypt*—and declared hope (as opposed to ordinary foreseeing) of success—*This is how we shall return to Jerusalem*. Every enduring collective has some sense of a career of building and defending itself.

Responsible political leaders very often guide large collectives by invoking standards of rightness that are historical as well as ethical. They speak of long continuities of virtues of the collective, of long-running friendships between groups, of historic opportunities to solve shared problems, of an enduring collective interest and conception of justice. They may also speak of shared experiences, reflecting and enriching the group's identity as *we to whom these things have happened, we who cannot but know these things*, but the clinching assertion of identity for a politically capable group will be more actively practical: *we who have this power, this trajectory, this proper task*. For the sake of maintaining consensus and the best motivational state, leaders will espouse ideals of collective destiny. For example, an American leader who could not speak effectively on the theme of the US as "the world's best hope" (in Jefferson's phrase) would be, under present circumstances, politically impaired. Such a leader would seem to be representing American interests without an adequate notion of what those interests are. Even now the adequate political notion of America is of a 1776 vintage.

Historical awareness informs me that I am a member of a historical ensemble of agents, but am I responsible to or for that ensemble in such a way that I am required to submit to any of the political schemes that are proposed to defend or extend the achievements of that ensemble? A scheme may seem essential, as the constitutional republic of the US seems essential to sustaining the American historical venture. Here a historical responsibility and political responsibility support each other strongly. But most schemes will seem debatable from historically responsible points of view, even the long-enshrined US scheme of political parties (except from inside the parties' own histories), while most interpretations of the group's history will be debatable from the various points of view of political responsibility. A continuing crossfire of responsible arguments should be expected in a normally communicative society.

The leaders of ambitious political causes will want to be able to leverage their constituents' identification with the political community. They will want their constituents to stay convinced that individual life success is inseparable from group success. That conviction can be maintained by purely prudential, instrumental reasoning, or in the mode of the naive enthusiasm that sports fans have for their teams, or in modes of responsibility. The meaning of "group identity" will differ accordingly.

Even if I am ensconced in a politically constraining group identity, additional practical realizations may complicate it. I may discover that my ethnic or national identity is crossed by my membership in an exploited working class who are continuing to reinforce the conditions of each others' oppression. Crossing my class identity, I may realize that I am contributing along with workers and capitalists alike to an industrial economy that produces a general increase of wealth but also life-threatening pollution. Ideologues will try to strengthen my sense of the reality and actuality of such identities.

A rhetorical advantage of group-identity historical support for politics is that a compelling story can be told about forebears and heroes of the collective cause and its classic episodes. Such stories are historically revelatory and activating of historical responsibility when taught to children or members of insular smaller groups. But they are historically problematic in that they can be very resistant to any correction that would threaten a desired image of coherence in shared life. What these stories provide may be called "heritage," an intentional, politically guided reduction of history that is not necessarily vicious but must always be regarded with suspicion by anyone whose sense of responsible relatedness to past actors is more inclusive than the imagined nation or class. "Heritage" and heritage-based group identities are at best halfway houses in the development of historical responsibility.

It seems fair to say, on the other hand, that history in the sense of the whole true story of shared action is far too complex and lacking in definite practical implications to be treated as a constraint on politically responsible actions—that history only becomes actionable when it is "heritage." This is true even when a group's official history is subjected to a stern correction, as the American heritage taught in schools now includes slavery and genocide as well as the planting of a Western-style society in a New World. If a push for national reparations for American slavery succeeds, it will be based on an agreed idea of a national heritage of injustice. This heritage, though historically simplistic like any heritage, is arguably superior to rival conceptions in its own time because it better facilitates variously responsible relations with past and present collaborators.

Historical responsibility differs from historical passion in opening up to better approximations of the true whole story of how action has been shared. A remarkable example of this kind of opening up is seen in military communities after a war has ended and animosities have subsided; the direct military experience of the sharing of war action prompts a more disinterested and inclusive inquiry into what happened and how it happened. This genuine historical inquiry can be in tension with popular mythmaking about the heroes and villains of the war, and in that way can be politically disruptive.[35]

---

35. Edward Curtis had gotten from Crow eyewitnesses a different account of the mythified battle of Little Big Horn, "Custer's Last Stand," but Theodore Roosevelt asked him not to include that information in his book *The North American Indian*, arguing that

In summary, I contend that the four Attractors of political responsibility are like Permanent Members of political responsibility's Security Council, each a major power in political life and each with the power to veto any proposal about political life that goes too much against its own interests. An ideally adequate political stance will have to balance the technical, ethical, pragmatic, and historical concerns that appeal to politically responsible agents.

How does an agent prepare to find that balance in actuality? By contemplating other agents who have managed it, I will suggest.

Touchstones of Political Responsibility: Heroes and Cautionary Examples

Because of the complexity of political responsibility—a complexity guaranteed by the plurality of modes of responsibility that are involved in it and by the changeful array of actions we have in hand—an agent cannot design a sovereign best stance or find one by observation and calculation. Yet a politically responsible agent wants to be well oriented and ready to play an appropriate part in shared action subject to its various claims. The most persuasive realists about political responsibility, including Max Weber and Benedetto Croce in my reading, have been pluralists about the responsibility itself, rejecting both the dominance of ethical considerations as espoused by political moralists and the dominance of technical political considerations as espoused by realists.[36] Such pluralism seems to admit only the precarious solution of *equilibrium* among claims at a given moment. One must strive

---

American youth needed Custer as a hero. Herman J. Viola, *Little Bighorn Remembered* (New York: Crown, 1999), 161–62.

36. Not by Machiavelli himself; his *Discourses on Livy* make his ethical concerns clear. For Weber, see "Politics as a Vocation," in H. H. Gerth and C. Wright Mills, eds., *From Max Weber: Essays in Sociology* (New York: Oxford University Press, 1948), 77–128; for Croce, *Politics and Morals*, trans. Salvatore J. Castiglione (New York: Philosophical Library, 1945). The phrase "political moralist" must not be taken in the sense rejected by Kant: "I can actually think of a *moral politician*, i.e., one who so interprets the principles of political prudence that they can be coherent with morality, but I cannot think of a *political moralist*, i.e., one who forges a morality to suit the statesman's advantage." Immanuel Kant, "To Perpetual Peace," in *Perpetual Peace and Other Essays*, trans. Ted Humphrey (Indianapolis: Hackett, 1983), 107–43, AA 8:372.

to rectify relations with one's fellow agents in multiple ways, giving the least possible offense to each way while satisfying the others as best one can. The answer for each agent has both a continuing aspect that can be reconsidered at leisure—a political philosophy—and an ever-new pragmatic aspect that must be resolved at each juncture of action.

Arriving at equilibrium may produce a sense of relief without a sense of conviction. But conscientious political agents will probably be realizers who have taken the data of the responsible life to heart in a particular orienting and mobilizing way, proceeding on the "Here I stand; I can do no other" basis that Weber so admired.[37] In the absence of a rational recipe, concrete exemplars can give them crucial guidance toward finding equilibrium and may also serve as foci of realizing. For example, two culture heroes of the American South are widely considered classic guides in civic and political responsibility because they wrestled articulately with harmonizing the two and seemed to resolve that struggle in their personalities: Robert E. Lee and Martin Luther King Jr. (whose birthdays are still uncomfortably observed on the same day in Alabama and Mississippi). Both Lee and King violated applicable law to meet what they saw as urgent needs of their communities; both project serenity and effectiveness. Most Americans think of Lee as fighting for a bad cause and King for a good one on the national scale. But Lee is notable not only as a general on the pro-slavery side but as a civic-minded statesman who criticized Southern animosity toward the federal government after the Civil War, and King is notable not only as a champion of constitutional rights for all citizens but as a controversial critic of the Vietnam War and capitalism, deeply at odds with the national government. These two leaders would probably not agree with each other on any but the most innocuous political questions, yet both were conspicuously conscientious in arriving at their positions.

Because Lee and King were explicitly political agents with great power on the national stage, they are among the boldest types of political respon-

---

37. "It is immensely moving when a *mature* man—no matter whether old or young in years—is aware of a responsibility for the consequences of his conduct and really feels such responsibility with heart and soul. He then acts by following an ethic of responsibility and somewhere he reaches the point where he says: 'Here I stand; I can do no other.' That is something genuinely human and moving. And every one of us who is not spiritually dead must realize the possibility of finding himself at some time in that position. In so far as this is true, an ethic of ultimate ends and an ethic of responsibility are not absolute contrasts but rather supplements, which only in unison constitute a genuine man . . ." Weber, 127.

sibility that are appreciable by Americans collectively. King, moreover, is connected to one of the strongest examples one could give of a responsible collective action providing national leadership, the Civil Rights Movement. But political responsibility is not the exclusive burden of public leaders, and public models of political responsibility are not the most relevant models for many of us. Political action sharing is underway constantly for all of us in closer-to-home frames of reference, whether we are trying to provide the needed leadership or to rightly follow it. Each of us acts on the basis of negotiated determinations of our various shared actions, the schemes in which they take place, and their prioritization. Each of us has grown up deeply impressed by (even if not always clearly understanding) how our parents and other vividly present authorities provided technical, ethical, pragmatic, and historically mindful direction for action sharing. As adults, most of us continue to give high priority to our responsibilities for close personal relationships just as our seniors did, but now we do so for the compelling reason that we realize that our individual actions have the greatest effect on the state of personal relationships, whereas the effect of joining or declining to join a large-scale political action is for most of us comparatively tiny.

An agent whom we mark out as distinctively political is one who, thanks to talent and accidents of collaboration, has come to a position where his or her actions do have appreciable effects on the state of large-scale action sharing. But this does not mean that public political responsibility is left entirely to that sort of agent. It cannot be correct to assert that I, a private citizen living in the US, do *not* have a practical relationship with people in China and (more to the issue of the political) do *not* intentionally address the state of that relationship. It would of course be unreasonable to say that I relate to the Chinese in the very same way that I relate to my family or my professional colleagues who depend on my actions on a daily basis. But it would also be unreasonable to say that I have no responsibility to the Chinese at all with regard to modes of energy use that affect the global climate, or patterns of consumption that affect the global economy, or hygienic practices that affect global health. The very least one should expect of me as a citizen in a democracy is for me to communicate my concerns about these matters to leaders and candidates and to bear their positions in mind when I vote.

Individual discernments of political responsibility can produce very different results: I might play the acceptable part of an ordinary stay-informed-and-vote citizen while my neighbor might just as acceptably be devoted to political activism for one or more causes. We could not decide to be so different where our civic responsibility is concerned.[38] But this does not mean that there are no general standards of political responsibility. I was able to point to factors that qualify Lee and King as exemplars, and typical failings in responsibility are pictured in classic cautionary stories: the paranoid Creon in *Antigone*, who can no longer distinguish between threats to the state and challenges to his personal prerogatives; the extremist Pyotr Verkhovensky in Dostoevsky's *Demons*, who stokes up the excitement of revolution into a purely violent anarchism; the distracted Mrs. Jellyby in Dickens' *Bleak House*, campaigning for African missions while neglecting her own family. In all of these problem cases an important part of the virtue shown to be lacking is political.

The Pursuit of Collective Political Realization

To attain a maximum of fair inclusion, collaborative synergy, and historical coherence at a given level of concerted action—from the household to the workplace to the nation-state to the envisioned world community—an approvable political order will need the technical advantage of a scheme that works well and the good fortune of not being derailed by poverty, plague, or excessive conflict. Shared understanding of the scheme and commitment to uphold it will be needed as well.

It is an inspiring (though not new) idea of the Enlightenment that a freshly stated principle for a political scheme can itself become one of the strongest motivations of a polity's constituents. The beneficent "invisible hand" in Adam Smith's free-market economics is a great example of this: defenders of capitalism *believe in* the invisible hand.[39] Socialists, for

---

38. It can be argued that political activism is generally necessary for fuller personal self-realization and for realizing justice goals. "Having and exercising the opportunity to participate in making collective decisions that affect one's actions or the conditions of one's actions fosters the development of capacities for thinking about one's own needs in relation to the needs of others, taking an interest in the relation of others to social institutions, reasoning and being articulate and persuasive, and so on. Only such participation, moreover, can give persons a sense of active relation to social institutions and processes, a sense that social relations are not natural but subject to invention and change. The virtues of citizenship are best cultivated through the exercise of citizenship." Iris Marion Young, *Justice and the Politics of Difference* (Princeton: Princeton University Press, 1990), 92.

39. Adam Smith, *The Wealth of Nations* (New York: Random House, 1994), 485.

their part, have argued that instituting collective ownership of the means of production will cure the fever of competitive greed and the social ills it produces: socialists *believe in* collective ownership. These shared convictions produce landscapes of political responsibility. Much like a jungle guide who does a good job by keeping his party on the trail, leaders in a capitalist society are much more likely to be able to explain their proposals and retain their followers' trust if they consistently reference free-market principles, and so too with socialist leaders and collectivist principles.

Before signing on to the proposition that shared political conviction is part of the recipe for the best political situation, we should pause to note, first, that conviction can worsen the conflicts in a "polarized" society to such an extent that wiser heads will plead for relief from it; and, second, that a broadly shared conviction can reinforce an oppressive complacency in an all-too-unified society with very unpleasant consequences for anyone regarded as deviant. Conceding these perils, politically responsible agents must still be in search of a political solution for polarization or majoritarian complacency, or for anything else that ails the collective, and can hope to implement a solution lastingly only if enough commitment is shared by enough collaborators.

Looking ahead to how education and political discourse will work on such a foundation, we may write a constitution for a republic dedicated to the rationally attractive principles of, say:

> *liberty*—the right of all to noninterference with thought and practice as consistent with the liberty of others and basic collective security;
>
> *equality*—the right of all to equal treatment by the government (and perhaps also by society generally);
>
> *solidarity*—the right of all to humane consideration, especially with regard to basic vital needs; and
>
> *participation*—the right of all to effective communication with the government's decision makers.

If the constitution is well written, key political realizations will come to be commonly shared and a sense of collective identity will incorporate them, determining for the future what will qualify as authentic approaches to problems facing the collective. Filling in this landscape of responsibility, further realizations can obtain with regard to more specific issues by a direct-seeming derivation from inarguable principles; for example, US politics are constrained by a broadly shared realization of a need for church-state separation, a policy derived by applying the liberty and equality principles to religions, and may yet be constrained by a realization of a right to health care, if a prior commitment to solidarity proves strong enough.

Liberals may wish to argue that a political society should not base itself on collective realization. We can acknowledge and honor particular shared realizations, but we should not posit a profound society-wide conviction that would disallow a natural and desirable free variation in individual thoughts and actions. It might also encourage disingenuous maneuvering under cover of "the general will." Those collectives that are designed to maintain a deep unanimity in realization, like an army or a church, are not good models for the larger, more diversely motivated, and involuntarily enrolled society governed by the state. The preferable basis of concord in an appropriately liberal larger society is an "overlapping consensus" among diverse loyalties and pursuits of diverse goods.[40] The political leadership of a liberal society has no right to impose a policy deduced from any one apprehension of what it takes to live an acceptable life; what is right politically is to foster an accommodating partial harmony among competing approaches.

The realizationist can point out, however, that liberal practice itself is sustained by a realization, a liberal one: the rightness of the approach strikes us and enlists us insofar as we recognize that collaboration among agents invested in diverse life-guidance systems requires liberal accommodation.[41] Associated procedural realizations support the strong rights of free speech and political representation that liberalism embraces. These are understood to enable a fair political process that will unfold in a measure of freedom from anyone's concrete realizing. Nevertheless, when participants contemplate the outcomes of the process, they will tend to arrive

---

40. See John Rawls, *Political Liberalism*, expanded ed. (New York: Columbia University Press, 2005).

41. Rawls's approach here is more (as he puts it) "moral," characterizing the basis of agreement as a normative reciprocity and direct respect of fellow citizens in a spirit of "civic friendship." See "The Idea of Public Reason Revisited" in *Political Liberalism*, 446–47.

at a realization—perhaps a somewhat bemused realization—that although no one individual or party is in a position to realize concretely that the collective way taken is necessarily the one satisfactory or best way, the taking of that way is right nevertheless. Those whose own more concrete realization regarding an issue fortunately coincides with the realization implied by liberal accommodation may have a deceptive nonliberal sense of the society as collectively realizing what they themselves realize, since congenial results of the process cannot but vindicate their sense of reality. For example, secularists could take American religious pluralism as confirmation of their conviction that religion is politically irrelevant. Thus we can say that a liberal accommodation, as such, is a nonrealization—its content is not determined by any actual subject's insight or conviction—which nevertheless, under politically optimal circumstances, is approved by a shared liberal realization. The pursuit of a liberal solution could turn out to be the midwifing of a realization, as we have seen in the popular American affirmation of religious liberty emerging from accommodations of rival religious and nonreligious parties. Politically responsible discourse in this society will reinforce the liberal pluralist realization while avoiding more concrete realization-based claims on public policy.

An ambitious world leader or cosmopolitical optimist might see a similar potential for beneficial shared realization of the principles articulated in the UN Universal Declaration of Human Rights, or simply in current trends of discourse on human rights. The UN Declaration itself is the result of an arduous discussion of how comprehensive and specific a list of universal human rights can be while being sufficiently convincing in the global arena.[42] Will the Declaration prove to be a long-term political success despite not being enforceable by an international authority? Can enough political agents become committed to respecting those rights universally? Will human rights lose credibility as the result of entrenched or recurrent practices around the world that disregard them?[43] Is there any other promising way of "thinking globally" that would be conducive to a beneficial globally shared political realization? We will consider these issues in the next chapter.

---

42. See Mary Ann Glendon, *A World Made New: Eleanor Roosevelt and the Universal Declaration of Human Rights* (New York: Random House, 2001).

43. Eric A. Posner, *The Twilight of Human Rights Law* (Oxford: Oxford University Press, 2014).

Political responsibility is not the only important political motivation, obviously. But is it necessarily the most important political motivation—more important than political creativity, say, or the ambition to expand government power? From a responsible point of view it will be asserted that the desire for a greater polity can be among the greatest motivations only if it is ruled by responsible sensitivity to fellow constituents of the polity. Otherwise one is merely some sort of glory hound—if successful, merely some sort of conqueror. On the other hand, political responsibility could not be a great *political* motivation if it were not actuated by desire to establish a great polity of some sort.

The most politically ambitious choices and actions are not necessarily the politically best choices and actions, but the most politically responsible choices and actions are not necessarily the best either. We can say that they are generally likelier to be politically successful insofar as they reduce the chances of alienating allies and being blindsided by neglected factors; there must be some teleological wisdom in conceiving the standards of responsibility as we do. But political endeavor is always a struggle and involves alienation and blindsiding despite the best plans, as well as surprising openings for success.

On the plane of thought and communication, a politically responsible person is likelier to *become* a more *mature* political thinker—a holder of views and preferences that match more closely the optimal blend of realism and humane optimism that we would expect to preside over the most politically advanced shared life. For someone like me who does not have the vocation of handling the levers of government power, the project of coming to think more maturely about political issues (which includes recognizing the entailments of political judgment for my own conduct) is the politically compelling part of responsible life.

Anyone hoping to get direction from an articulated ideal of political responsibility will be disappointed to find that all the hard problems in relating power wielding to ethical, pragmatic, and historical concerns are loaded into the responsible mind and become its dilemmas. When responsibility becomes complex it becomes essential to it—and paradoxically self-weakening—that the agent cannot state conclusive justifications. This makes the impressive political leaders, and more broadly the more fully responsible agents, all the more impressive, when responsibly beheld.

This chapter's exposition of political responsibility's complexity is but the first phase in discovering the meaning of being politically responsible. The second phase, undertaken in the next chapter, is to trace the lines of more satisfactory and less satisfactory responses to a representative selection of contemporary political challenges.

Chapter Four

Challenges in Four Spheres of Political Responsibility

Agents who are disposed to be responsible realize that they are called on, with or without an express summons, to act for the rectification of relationships with their fellow beings. They have found that their own prospects for affirmable existence—the conditions under which they can live with themselves—are inseparable from affirmable conditions of existence for others. Thinking in the format of responsibility, they realize that the claims of relationship are not hopelessly indeterminate but can be addressed in practical schemes involving reasonably defined roles and tasks. *Politically* responsible agents realize that part of the needed rectification of relationships must come about through acting intentionally on the apparatus and strategy of collective action sharing, that is, in schemes of government (in a broad sense). An ethically responsible agent may come to political responsibility in taking thought for the fuller implementation of ethical ideals; a pragmatically responsible agent may come to political responsibility in taking thought for the best provisions for inclusive collaborative success in the present; a historically responsible agent may come to political responsibility in taking thought for the total success of long-term shared action. The richest political ambition we can conceive of is moved by all these kinds of concern to seek more comprehensively satisfactory political approaches.

Political responsibility so understood is not simply a virtue of good politicians. It takes a wide range of forms that all responsible agents should be acquainted with. Let us begin to survey that range by distinguishing four spheres of responsibility pertaining to humanly essential collaborative ensembles on structurally different scales of action.

1. Political action on the smallest scale is found in the face-to-face collaborations of family and friends whenever it is a question whether the group's affairs are being conducted in an acceptable way. In the family's typical way of doing things there is a hierarchical premise, with deference owed to one's seniors and oversight owed to one's juniors, while friendship, in contrast, is conducted in a refreshingly egalitarian style; however, we may also find equality in families and deference and duty among friends. Among family and friends there is an intimate dependence for pragmatic support and personal recognition. Their affairs are plainly not satisfactory when they do not meet these needs, and agents are often doing something about this, often responsibly.

2. The collaborative ensembles we call "organizations" are deliberately constructed to serve purposes in which agents from diverse personal backgrounds will have a common stake. An organization's way of doing things is usually explicit—it must be explained to every new member who comes on board, and may be frequently reviewed by its leaders—and so is a constant target of political evaluation, even if the organizational culture is rigidly hierarchical and resistant to change. The "family" ideal of personal solidarity is often invoked in organizations but cannot be assumed to be in force.

3. The consistently relevant large ensemble is called "the community." The community includes everyone we rely on directly for meeting our needs (perhaps not the car maker but probably the car dealer), so that it *seems* self-sufficient. It is diverse and sprawling enough that it has a "public sphere" and needs a dedicated agency to govern it, but it is well enough unified by a communication system and legal order that all its constituents can be allowed to participate in its direction. To the extent that this approach is safe at all, it is safe at community level to institute the use of coercive means for the protection of life and property. In our current political era the state has become the dominant community, but we are still debating whether state assumptions of power are justifiable and whether states can be adequately responsive to the needs and interests of their constituents or adequately respectful of human rights generally.

4. The largest ensemble of all is conceived as maximally inclusive—global, cosmic, historical, or eternal. We speak now of "the global community" in our easily surveilled world even though the normal conditions for a community are not fully met and may never be, given the unquenchable rivalries among functional communities at state level. Despite these rivalries,

the fact that humans have no choice but to share their planet has significant cosmopolitan import (as Kant pointed out),[1] as does the extensive actual interdependence among human societies.

Political responsibility is an ideal and a variable on each of these scales. The iconic traditional figures of Father, Lord, and God embody the ideal in the family, community, and cosmos, respectively. Such figures remain fascinating because they are supposed to offer the fullest satisfaction of our need for politically responsible leadership—with implications for how we think of ruling, authority, and government—in each frame of reference.

In the following sections we will consider what political responsibility can mean in family, community, and global affairs under the pressure of some major contemporary problems. Based on our earlier discussion, the following elements of political responsibility will be taken as axiomatic:

1. Political responsibility is a stance both cooperative and competitive; a politically responsible agent is always concerned to build up productive coalitions and to overcome opposition.

2. Political responsibility has a mixed and unstable base in diverse forms of responsibility, including ethical, pragmatic, and historical responsibility.

3. Political responsibility should include seriousness about satisfying ethical requirements in actual practice to the greatest possible extent, although political choices are not defensible solely as fulfillments of general ethical prescriptions.

4. Political responsibility should include pragmatic seriousness about successfully concluding shared actions in hand. This interest extends to seizing all opportunities for more productive and inclusive collaboration and for improving or better securing the governing scheme.

5. Political responsibility should include historical seriousness about promoting better states of shared action recognized or envisioned as an accomplished whole.

---

1. This point is cited by Immanuel Kant in "To Perpetual Peace," in *Perpetual Peace and Other Essays on Politics, History, and Morals*, trans. Ted. Humphrey (Indianapolis: Hackett, 1983), 107–43, AA 7:358, and *The Metaphysical Elements of Justice*, trans. John Ladd (Indianapolis: Bobbs-Merrill, 1965), AA 6:352. The theme is taken up by Seyla Benhabib in *The Rights of Others* (Cambridge, UK: Cambridge University Press, 2004).

Family Responsibility and Abortion

The abortion decision is well recognized now as a site of complex, difficult-to-resolve responsibility. Its political significance on the scale of family affairs is less well recognized, partly because the political character of family affairs is obscured by modern individualism.

Let us duly appreciate that the family is a unit of survival, a biologically common (though varied) scheme for successfully raising young that is often supported by proto-moral instincts of parental, filial, and conjugal solidarity.[2] Humans long ago added another political layer to their primate family scheme by forming clans and tribes with their own procreation agendas and by adopting exogamy rules to reduce inbreeding and support intergroup alliances. Thus kinship became a standard for collective identity and mutual help—a standard that serves as a focus for realizations of duty, as when Arjuna anguishes about fighting his relatives in the Kurukshetra War (Bhagavad Gita 1). When humans settled down to agriculture and wealth production, the family became a primary structure for allocating and managing material resources: "The family, as a person, has its external reality in *property*; and only in the latter, in the shape of *resources*, does its substantial personality have its existence" (Hegel).[3] At the same time the dynastic principle became a structure for allotting political power and professional privileges. In the patriarchal family format the Father functions as the chief political agent and governor. On all these levels family is a structure of cooperation that is all the more important for being deployed in a field of unrelenting competition, including biological competition for the survival of a form of life into the future, economic competition for the means of surviving and flourishing, and political competition for status and authority.

The state is obliged to coordinate the agendas of the families that are rich and influential enough to force political changes when they are dissatisfied. The state also makes families generally an object of policy as the site of population replenishment and birth control.

In a modern society of wide opportunity, high mobility, and equality under the law, it is easy for many people to remain unaware of the

---

2. On variations in human family structure and the variable relationship between kinship and household schemes, a useful critical review of research is Sylvia Yanagisako, "Family and Households: The Analysis of Domestic Groups," *Annual Review of Anthropology* 8 (1979): 161–205.

3. G. W. F. Hegel, *Elements of the Philosophy of Right*, trans. H. B. Nisbet, ed. Allen W. Wood (Cambridge, UK: Cambridge University Press, 1991), 208.

family-based competitiveness of human life. Either because one is already comfortably advantaged ("college graduate" is a conventional marker of this condition in the US) or because one is not even within hailing distance of social advantages ("high school dropout"), one may not see that one's life chances depend directly on the success of one's family in controlling property and maintaining respectability—so that, in the positive case, making a respectable living would be easy, and in the negative case, staying out of prison would be difficult. It may seem as though one has been released into the ocean to fend for oneself like a sea turtle. And it may seem that meeting another sea turtle and forming a personal liaison has nothing whatever to do with preserving a family's economic and political foothold in the world.

Human behavior massively belies this unconsciousness of family interest, even in modernized societies, yet liberal theory is resolutely individualist. A discourse of rights knows how to attach rights to individuals but not to collectives.[4] Collectives are valued only for their instrumental significance for the well-being of individuals. This is how liberal theory seems to be confirmed in a socially comfortable sort of case: two individuals leave the family homes in which they grew up, move to an interesting city and secure good-paying jobs, feel grateful to their parents and siblings for the good life they have had so far, come to feel that they would like to play the parental role in a similar experience in the future, meet each other and discover their shared interest, marry, and then successfully raise children, staying in close friendly touch with their relatives all the while. They know of no binding reason why their children should make all the same choices later on, but they go to all necessary trouble and expense to make sure their children have an upbringing as helpful as their own; this seems a duty owed to their children individually on account of having brought them into the world. And then their children move on to land good jobs and form their own families. Meanwhile the grandparents have been able to fund their own retirement and end-of-life health care, so no one has financial or logistical worries on that front.

As I add in more and more of these convenient features, the portrait applies to fewer and fewer families even in my own relatively affluent and individualistic society. Most families experience a heavier interdependence, partly on grounds of sentiment (living too much apart from one's closest relatives is emotionally uncomfortable) and partly for coping with the

---

4. Miodrag A. Jovanović discusses the challenges helpfully in "Recognizing Minority Identities through Collective Rights," *Human Rights Quarterly* 27/2 (May 2005): 625–51.

various practical challenges that buffet individuals throughout life (losing a job, needing help with child care, having a health crisis).

Martha Nussbaum, among others, has argued that common human needs for care require a major modification of liberal individualism.[5] Dependence is normal. The point applies most consequentially to individuals in two categories: those who unavoidably fall short of independence in needing care, and those who lose freedom and life opportunities unfairly by being assigned undervalued roles as caregivers, often considered a woman's role.[6] Although hospitals, schools, and other public agencies provide a great deal of needed care, families remain the primary structure of caregiving; for most people during most of their lives, the household and close-kin communications make up the venue of intimately living together in which the requirements of care are impossible to ignore.

Our shared understanding of norms for family and household could change, of course. We might come to a collective realization that individuals are too vulnerable to deprivation and abuse when placed at the mercy of persons in the spouse or parent role—roles that are fraught with destructive psychological tensions and historically conscripted for social oppression.[7] Or we might embrace the administrative advantages of Plato's ideal republic or Huxley's brave new world. Then possibly the only remaining small ensemble type of great interest would be friendship in roughly the same form that we know it now, with its lighter burden of care responsibility. (Do we not observe, however, that friendship becomes more family-like to meet the needs of individuals who cannot draw on family help?)

For purposes of the present discussion I will assume that for the foreseeable human future there will be continuing widespread commitment to a type of small ensemble, the family, dedicated to successful procreation (keeping up or expanding the number of close kin) and meeting its members' needs for care. One could predict this for purely biological or sociological reasons, some of which would be crucial to understanding the competitive position of a family, but I predict it in consideration of the spiritual satisfaction in maintaining a community of the strongest practicable interpersonal solidarity, what is sometimes idealized as "unconditional love." It is a

---

5. Martha Nussbaum, *Frontiers of Justice* (Cambridge, MA: Harvard University Press, 2006).

6. See Susan Moller Okin, *Justice, Gender, and the Family* (New York: Basic Books, 1989).

7. Shulamith Firestone vigorously developed this sort of critique of the family in *The Dialectic of Sex* (New York: William Morrow, 1970). While Firestone's psychological and sociological premises are questionable, a similarly inspired critique could be very pertinent.

reasonable assumption that human beings will find their quality of existence deeply affected by how the affairs of such an ensemble are conducted.

Now two political questions are sure to arise about the family scheme for action sharing, as they arise about any scheme: how the scheme can work best, and which initiatives bearing on the conduct of affairs in such a scheme are best. For a relatively simple first illustration of what can count as a good answer in the realm of family, I offer two answers that are widely accepted in a liberal society: marriage should be revocable for any serious reason of incompatibility, and divorce should be as amicable as circumstances permit. Thus it looks like responsible legislation to allow divorce; it looks like responsible leadership for one spouse to propose to the other, "Look, we can't go on this way, we're unhappy—our needs aren't being met"; and it looks like responsible conduct for both spouses to try significant life adjustments or undergo counseling to give the marriage its best chance of surviving. In comparison, a husband unilaterally divorcing a wife by saying "I divorce you" three times seems irresponsible, and so at the other extreme does a church or state absolutely forbidding divorce to its members.

These answers are popular,[8] but so far as I have given them they do not face up to two difficulties. The lesser of the two difficulties in most situations will be the undermining of alliance between groups that were bound together by the marriage. This is not a consideration only for Henry VIII divorcing Catherine of Aragon; many commoners will be materially affected by losing the resources and privileges they had obtained by joining their erstwhile spouses' families. (Or they may end up in a materially improved position, depending on later developments.)

The greater difficulty has to do with protecting the rights and assuring proper care of any children involved. A conspicuous weakness of the revocable marriage scheme is that once the parents want to separate, they then become conscientiously bound to provide for their children as best they can separately, while the children continue to belong to both. Bitter fights over custody and property are common and may or may not be settled by a judge's mediation.

---

8. I do not want to conceal an important complexity in the "popularity" of liberal divorce law. Some take this view on the basis of a belief or realization that the freedom of the individual trumps all other considerations; some on the basis of a belief or realization that marriage cannot properly exist in the absence of a certain grade of love; and some without much conviction, merely reaching an equilibrium result from weighing the evils of broken promises and broken homes against the evils of personal unhappiness and vulnerability to abuse.

Some will not want to allow that these "personal" choices, acts, and results are "political." In my view, that reaction irresponsibly overlooks or conceals the political character of our formation of schemes of action sharing as well as the political issues specific to the family scheme.[9] Others will seize the opportunity to assert that the personal is the political, especially in gender relations. But that claim is problematic, too, in that it often retains the assumption that political issues are by definition action sharing issues for the whole community—the "political" qualification coming from the fact that husbands, wives, and parents, as such, participate in preserving or changing community-scale gender patterns of authority, privilege, and conduct. My present claim is different. It is that family affairs, no less than affairs of state, constitute an arena for intentional action with respect to the existing conditions of action sharing, and that in this arena too the most approvable agents are responsible *to* their collaborators (primarily) and *to* everyone who will be affected *for* their impact on those conditions *under* relevant standards of best practice in that context. In the happiest family, all members act on the basis of a shared political realization (with cheerful compliance by those below the age of reason) that the way in which they are actually helping, guiding, and deferring to each other is their best feasible way. But even the happiest family, as a political arena, is a site of disagreement and power struggle.

I propose that we examine a family issue that does not have an agreed-on answer in my society: the issue of under what circumstances abortion is approvable. The lack of agreement about abortion places significant spiritual strain on families and on the larger body politic.[10] At the level of community politics, the issue is under what circumstances abortion should be allowed by law, and pro-choice advocates on that issue appeal not only to the civic

---

9. For an effective critique of the tradition of placing the family beyond political justice calculations, see Okin, chap. 2.

10. A 2021 Gallup poll reports that 58 percent of Americans favor upholding the Roe v. Wade ruling that abortion should be at a woman's discretion until the last trimester of pregnancy. Lydia Saad, "Americans Still Oppose Overturning *Roe v. Wade*," Gallup News, accessed October 20, 2021, https://news.gallup.com/poll/350804/americans-opposed-overturning-roe-wade.aspx. But for a variety of reasons this figure could be misleading about what Americans think about abortion. An explicit priority for one of the two major American parties is to tighten restrictions on abortion. A fascinating study of a long-running social ambivalence about abortion in Japan, with important comparative observations, is William R. LaFleur's *Liquid Life: Abortion and Buddhism in Japan* (Princeton: Princeton University Press, 1992).

liberty of women but also to the responsibility of the individual woman to decide whether to go forward with a pregnancy, while pro-life advocates take a more restrictive line on legal allowance in accord with their more restrictive view of what *could* be a responsible abortion decision. For many on both sides of the issue the ethics and legality of abortion line up squarely, but some feel constrained to distinguish their legal judgment from their ethical judgment, which reveals different forms of responsibility at work: some on the pro-choice side regard some kinds of abortion as morally objectionable but also think it would be pragmatically irresponsible to impose a general requirement on women to give birth, while some on the pro-life side view all abortion as morally objectionable but find it pragmatically irresponsible not to allow exceptions for violently imposed pregnancies.

On either side, a judgment of historical responsibility may enter in as well—perhaps to preserve a traditional way of handling family affairs, perhaps to advance the civil emancipation of women.

I would like to attend to the individual pregnant woman's responsibility which, though rarely framed as a political responsibility (except by those who see her in solidarity with other women in large-scale politics), deserves recognition as political on the small scale.[11] We already saw in revisiting Judith Jarvis Thomson's classic abortion argument that pragmatic responsibility is a distinct variable in abortion decisions that might or might not align smoothly with ethical responsibility.[12] The immediate political challenge for the abortion chooser is to bring about a satisfactory total fulfillment of responsibilities by making the best use or adjustment of the collaborative structure in which an abortion decision is seen through. At the center of this structure is the parents-and-child family that a woman problematically belongs to by virtue of being pregnant, a nascent family embedded in families already extant.[13] She has the political power to enable or to terminate this small coalition of agents, thus imposing certain consequences on larger coalitions. Disturbing a patriarchal ethos, she displaces the authority of the Father over such matters.

---

11. This is not a foreign concept in anthropology—see Yanagisako (note 2, 106).

12. See above, 62–67.

13. I am not making the contentious claim that the pregnant woman's inseminator and embryo or fetus are already properly her "mate" and her "child," so that she already has all applicable responsibilities to persons in those categories; I am referring to the prospects that her choice refers to, namely, whether to have that mate and child, and whether to assume those responsibilities.

Some of the reasoning of political responsibility is articulated by the subjects in Carol Gilligan's 1982 study of women's thinking about abortion.[14] Gilligan sought to illuminate a female-associated "ethic of care" centered on norms of responsiveness in particular relationships, an ethic that prioritizes helping and not hurting individuals over observing general rules of justice. Because Gilligan and her respondents are continually generalizing ethical norms from their feelings of responsibility, pragmatic and political forms of responsibility tend to be disguised; however, reading some of the women's thoughts at a different angle from that of ethical theory can bring these data to the fore.

A pragmatic reason that Gilligan characterizes as "pre-moral" and documents in the earliest stage of considering abortion is the felt necessity of self-preservation. "I really didn't think anything except that I didn't want it . . . I didn't want it, and I wasn't ready for it" (75). The abortion chooser who expresses herself in this way might feel as though she is cut off from responsible relationships, but no matter how she understands her position she is deciding against fulfilling the family relationships initiated by her pregnancy, so that she is *seceding* from at least one ensemble project of which she is aware. Her choice is political in addressing the viability of a practical scheme.

The respondent who says she "wasn't ready for it" may be claiming that she is too young, that she has not yet crossed the threshold into the possibility of taking responsible initiatives with respect to family. But she may have positive intent about family life in principle and wish to protect her capacity to enter into it in the right way, thinking of herself as a future collaborator with a different child and possibly a different mate. She may be thinking in the vein of pragmatic responsibility, though not to the exclusion of self-interest, when she decides against bringing a child into the world under circumstances in which she cannot be a good parent ("I am sure I did the right thing. It would have been hell for that poor kid and for me too" [120]); and she may consciously want to perform

---

14. Gilligan's book, *In a Different Voice* (Cambridge, MA: Harvard University Press, 1982), is framed as a study of moral reasoning. A more recent and cross-cultural study, lacking Gilligan's interpretive depth but not without interest for this discussion, is Maggie Kirkman et al., "Reasons Women Give for Abortion: A Review of the Literature," *Archives of Women's Mental Health* 12 (December 2009): 365–78. See also M. Antonia Biggs, Heather Gould, and Diana Greene Foster, "Women Seek Abortions for a Variety of Complex Reasons," In *Abortion*, ed. Tamara Thompson (Greenhaven: Farmington Hills, 2015), 34–53.

this action for the benefit of the scheme itself, "family" in the senses most relevant to her.

The abortion chooser may see abortion as the best resolution of particular relationships with her prospective mate and child, and consequently she may be torn between a pragmatic sense of rightness and a moral sense of wrongness in terminating human life. "I am saying that abortion is morally wrong, but the situation is right, and I am going to do it. . . . I would have to change morally wrong to morally right. (*How?*) I have no idea" (86). The standard ethicization of rightness has not prevented her from saying "the situation is right," but it makes the rightness harder for her to explain. The need to explain has an obvious personal aspect in the desire to reduce emotional and cognitive dissonance, but it also has a political aspect in taking up the task of resolving for her family the conflict between the moral and pragmatic claims of the situation.

One woman who had considered the alternative of bearing her child for adoption said, "I don't think it would be fair to give life to a child if it couldn't have its own mother" (112). Here the ethical view of what is generally fair can be read at the same time as a political realization about justice in the operational scheme for family formation; she herself had been put up for adoption and was disturbed about apparently having been "unwanted" (111), which made her critical of that way of dealing with a pregnancy. In *her* family the affair will not have been managed that way, averting unfairness and pragmatic dissatisfaction.

Do we get any additional spiritual traction in viewing the abortion decision as a venue of political responsibility? Are there telltale signs of greater or lesser responsibility of a political kind when an abortion decision is made in one way versus another? Claims about what constitutes the more responsible choice will proceed from different views of the individuals involved and of unborn life, children, family life, women's and men's roles, human rights, and the status of the national or global population. One key to the question is the family power the pregnant woman is able to exercise in that situation; she exercises political responsibility in consciously making the best use of that leverage. At the same time, her situation is unavoidably informed by the postures already taken by groups, for she cannot be ethically mindful without applying communally approved ethical standards such as respect for human life, and she cannot choose a pragmatically responsible approach without reckoning with how her preexisting family and the larger political community are willing to work with her. But if she takes all these considerations seriously, she is more politically responsible for that reason.

Thus asking about the political aspects of her choice is a way of illuminating its spiritual complexity as well as calling attention to its power wielding significance.

Possibly the most important political variable that is specific to the abortion chooser's situation is her relationship with the prospective father, whose child that child would irrevocably be if it were born, or with anyone else who would serve as another parent of the child. Whether or not she is considering upholding a general ideal of family, or of individual or female freedom, she is definitely considering whether or not to enter into a certain parental alliance that could be warm or fraught, hopeful or dangerous. If her co-conceiver or her close relatives want the child, she must make the determination whether her present relations with them can be successfully modulated into that family. She is more responsible *to* them and *for* that if she weighs this possibility seriously, and if her reasons for accepting or rejecting it are not merely selfish. If there is conflict, she shows herself more responsible for the result and to the supporters of that result if she exerts herself to overcome the opposition to that result.

In this scene, qualifying a choice as more responsible obviously does not guarantee that it is the best choice, all things considered. Nevertheless the more responsible choice is spiritually preferable in its moment. And a politically responsible choice can be more responsible, because it can be more comprehensively responsible, than a choice that is responsible in any simpler mode. Conscientious abortion choosers sense this magnitude of responsibility; pro-choice arguments may register it supportively, while pro-life arguments may pay tribute to it in political disagreement about the family scheme.

Organizational Responsibility and "Good Jobs"

Few people could write their responsibility memoirs without taking account of their experience as members of organizations, and many would give organizations major credit for enabling their responsible agency. But organizations also create major responsibility problems. One can be caught in a tug-of-war among the prima facie valid claims of one's employer ("Complete the work!"), one's union ("Strike for a living wage!"), one's religion ("Keep the Sabbath!"), and one's neighborhood association ("Stop the pollution!"). Standing above the political challenges that arise within each of our organizations is the great challenge of responsibly coordinating all of our organization-based responsibility fulfillments. A society with a rich array of complementary organizations is spiritually "advanced" in an important way, but if it causes paralyzing conflict between undeclinable responsibilities—as when an aggressively secularist regime oppresses religiously devout citizens, for example—it has a profound political problem.[15] On the other hand, an authoritarian society that forcibly imposes a harmony of all such responsibilities is in deep political trouble, too, in preventing the free negotiation of competing concerns; its harmony is unreal.

Membership in an organization normally involves responsibility for helping the organization to fulfill its purpose by fulfilling one's assigned role. There might be something wrong with the organization's purpose (as in a criminal gang) that prevents us from accepting any claims of responsibility to it or for it. Assuming a defensible purpose, there might yet be a problem with the organization's methods and structure, including the roles it allows its members (as in imposing greater demands or reduced protections in employees' contracts).

An organizational role that draws interest from all major political parties and business leaders in liberal societies is that of a "good job." Good jobs should be available to all who seriously seek them. Leaders on the right would rely on free enterprise to create enough good jobs while leaders on the left would rely more on government action, but the value and high priority of the goal would not be in dispute. As the health of the national economy is continually measured by its "jobs reports," there is a mostly unexpressed, mostly unpursuable hope that the jobs that count as positions of employment also provide decent livings for their holders and, best of all, are good jobs.

In the simplest political calculation, a good job is a job someone would be happy to have. Can we say what a good job is substantially? The Good Jobs Institute publishes a list of standards that sum up contemporary common sense on this subject: a good job is secure and safe, is reasonably compensated and scheduled, offers a path of career advancement—this much falls in with the popular political goal of "building the middle class"—and furthermore is challenging and develops agent capabilities, is inherently meaningful, supports team pride and collegial respect, and affords

---

15. A good survey of the "moral" benefits and perils of organizations is Garrath Williams, "'Infrastructures of Responsibility': The Moral Tasks of Institutions," *Journal of Applied Philosophy*, 23 (2006): 207–21. He emphasizes the positive aspect of the challenge of reconciling organization-based responsibilities as "training in moral pluralism."

recognition of significant achievement from within the organization and from clients and customers.[16]

Oddly, most of these "higher human needs" standards of a good job contradict the very idea of a "job." Except for basic safety and minimally adequate pay, any of these features in a job would be grounds for saying "It's not just a job." In my own work experience as a professor it has been my good fortune to have realized all of the listed benefits, and for that reason it seems horrendously unappreciative to describe my work as a job, even a good one, although I must grant the baseline importance for me, as for anyone else, of "having a job" and getting a paycheck, which helps to keep my family afloat economically.

A "job" is a piece of work, conceived from the point of view of the person who wants the work done. It is inherently meaningful at least because, from some point of view, it *needs* to be done; it has the dignity of embodying our relationship with practical necessity. From that same point of view it will have been "good" if it succeeds in meeting the need. (From the worker's point of view the job will have been "good" in the sense of "well done" if it satisfies professional standards.) A job is not a collaborative proposition, except in the basic sense in which everything people do together is collaboration. On the contrary, the point of configuring work as a job is to minimize our practical entanglement: you will do just this thing for me (as I do not plan on doing it myself), and I will give you just this payment in return. We are not teammates. We do have responsibilities to each other for dealing fairly and humanely, and the need to complete our bargain properly is now added to the need for the work to be done as a condition for our self-realization as agents dealing with needs; but the "job" format of responsibility is one of the best illustrations of the spirit of limitation in a responsibility system. This limitation is essential to the obtainability and affordability of the work, for the customer, and to the freedom and availability of the worker.

Some of the most awful "full-time jobs" are expedient or necessary expansions of particular tasks. An awful job can be a valid specimen of responsibility. "Your job is to screw in these widgets on the assembly line" is an appalling prospect for full-time work, but not because it is not a significant role. (Compare: "Your job is to keep loading shells into this gun during battle.") A job *must* embody responsibility insofar as it is freely

---

16. My paraphrase of "What Is a Good Job?," Good Jobs Institute, accessed October 20, 2021, https://goodjobsinstitute.org/what-is-a-good-job/.

assumed; slaves under the whip cannot be said to be "doing their job" while performing like pieces of machinery. On the other hand, the freely assumed character of job work is compromised by every element of a given job that a responsibly disposed free worker would reject (for example, being required to build with shoddy materials).

Self-employed agents do various jobs for various customers; their line of work is not a job but an occupation or profession. Suppose that the family living in Crumbling Mansion, having brought in a plumber once to fix a sink, once to fix a toilet, and once to fix a leaking pipe outside, now decides it is time to advertise a "full-time job" of staff plumber. They want the help to be available all the time and for who knows what will go wrong next. That is what makes it a good kind of hire for them. To achieve this, they may have to offer some guarantees and benefits beyond a weekly salary, but they are not asking the plumber to live onsite and they are not envisioning the plumber as part of their family. It is still a sharply limited proposition of responsibility.

Meanwhile an applicant for the Crumbling Mansion position may perceive more security or reward in this single big job than in the many jobs a typical plumber takes on. The job is still a transaction more than it is an instituted collaboration. It is in one clear sense a good job if it is steady and well paid, and if the employers turn out to be reasonable.

Not inevitably, but very naturally, the reciprocal responsibilities in this arrangement could ratchet up, the transactional employer-employee relationship turning into a more fully invested collaboration. The family starts to think of their employee as one of the Crumbling Mansion team; their sense of the integrity of the project of maintaining the Mansion becomes inseparable from their sense of the requirements for the doability of the plumber's job and then for the livability of the plumber's life. They are thinking and functioning now more properly as a work organization, a "company." Meanwhile the employee thinks of the work as "taking care of the Mansion" and by that means taking care of the family and supporting the whole work effort. Dedication to doing the job well becomes inseparable from a broader sense of the family's needs.

You see where this is going. As the parties become more considerate of each other, the role of the staff plumber expands into something more like a superintendent, the family helps the plumber in a widening range of ways, and the job more and more acquires the profile of a "good job" by losing some (not all) of its "job" limitations with increases in pragmatic responsibility. The notion of the Crumbling Mansion Team becomes a reality. Belonging to that Team is not necessarily the very best employment for the plumber; in being so much determined by the changeable interests and actions of just a few individuals the situation will always have certain disadvantages in comparison with larger organizations. But it is a positive development. (If we told a story about dealienation in a larger organization, growth in pragmatic responsibility would be at the heart of that story as well.)

The purpose of my sketch of how a job becomes a good job is to contrast the transactional premise of a job as such with the responsible premise of a good job. The transactional premise is supportive of the more powerful bargainers in the marketplace fully leveraging their advantages to give away as little as they can—but also of the freedom of the less powerful to walk away, whenever they can afford to. This is a massive but not absolute advantage of capital over labor.

Not everyone wants the greater commitment of a good job; not everyone thinks that work is one of the most important venues of humanly fulfilling responsibility. There is an ethical requirement that dignity be preserved in work, but responsible work is not a recognized human right in the US or in the Universal Declaration of Human Rights.[17] To set particular requirements for "meaningful work" is a violation of liberal neutrality toward agent preferences.[18] National leaders in my country do consistently talk as though work is a crucial venue of responsibility—as they must, since our system depends on families supporting themselves and paying taxes—but they do not actually support good jobs, and this is mainly because for the low-paid categories of employment employers do not want to sponsor good jobs.[19] The dominant large-business goal of maximizing money profits

---

17. Article 23 of the UDHR asserts the right to work by free choice, with dignity, and with a living wage.

18. See Ruth Yeoman's discussion of this barrier in "Conceptualising Meaningful Work as a Fundamental Human Need," *Journal of Business Ethics* 125 (2014): 235–51. Yeoman appeals to "values" of freedom, autonomy, and dignity in work that deserve recognition as "objective" and as human needs; taking a "liberal perfectionist" approach to setting work standards, she argues, can do more than liberal neutralism to require the removal of obstacles to human flourishing while still allowing much meaningful choice among work experiences (242–43). She conceives "meaningful work" as "appropriating the values" that are accessible in work; see her *Meaningful Work and Workplace Democracy* (Houndsmill: Palgrave, 2014), 34–36, 61–64.

19. It is possible to sponsor a "good job" mentality in the absence of the actuality; this is the art of managing low-wage employees, which can be practiced with sincerity. A heartbreaking story of one such manager is told in the movie *Support the Girls* (dir. Andrew Bujalski, 2018).

requires minimized investment in employees at lower levels; convergently, the dominant consumer goals of convenience and lowest cost require that workers' demands be minimized. Thus most of the jobs in our economy are not good and arguably are blocked from developing into good jobs—blocked to some extent by economically undeclinable advantages of certain divisions of labor.[20] Whoever has a good job, as I have had, is considered lucky.

If I do have a good job, and management arbitrarily changes some feature of it so that I unwillingly become less responsible in my work activity, my collaborative position has been worsened and there is reason to charge management with pragmatic irresponsibility. It is a question of ethical irresponsibility only if I have been subjected to work conditions inconsistent with human dignity—conditions that are generally realized to be intolerable, not merely unlucky—or if I am the victim of distributive unfairness. In the classic dilemma of Taylorism, responsibility for direction of work is drastically shifted from workers to managers advised by efficiency experts, impairing the dignity of workers while responding pragmatically to the economic interests of other shareholders in the business.

Scarcity of good jobs is not an ethical tragedy—but is it a social tragedy nonetheless? The argument for this view of things is not often made in political discussion. I would make it, because (1) I view work responsibility as high on the scale of human fulfillments, (2) I recognize that work organizations shape our experience of work responsibility, and (3) I see how possible laws, regulations, and consumer actions could constrain work organizations in a way that would shift our economy toward enlarged worker responsibility.[21] We can regard work organizations as agencies of collective responsibility for that kind of fulfillment of our citizens. But a not-strictly-ethical point about responsibility, however solid, does not automatically generate normative conclusions or charter agencies. Political leaders oriented to this priority must figure out how to build on the contemporary rhetoric of good work and draw enough attention to our pragmatic and ethical discontents in work to move our society in that direction.

---

20. One indication that the majority of US jobs are not good is an October 2019 Gallup poll in which only 40 percent of respondents characterized their jobs as good. See Niv Elis, "Fewer than Half of Workers in 'Good' Jobs," thehill.com, October 23, 2019, accessed October 20, 2021, https://thehill.com/policy/finance/467126-fewer-than-half-of-workers-in-good-jobs-survey.

21. For the "economic democracy" program, see, for example, David Schweickart, *After Capitalism*, 2nd ed. (Lanham: Rowman & Littlefield, 2011).

Community Responsibility and Immigration

Relations among families must be coordinated; individuals must be enabled to cooperate with individuals from other families in various fields; common economic and security needs must be addressed for the population of a territory. Thus a more inclusive government than that of the family must be devised and maintained, and "political responsibility" in its now-prevalent sense will be much concerned with the government of the state. The devisers and maintainers are the "we" of "we the people" (the ones who "ordain and establish" the government in the US Constitution), the social partners who are capable of taking political initiatives and accepting political duties together. The phrase "the people" when claimed by the speaking "we" refers pointedly, yet with strategic vagueness, to those who are politically active in a cooperating community together with whoever else might be persuaded or allowed to join them; it does not automatically include everyone in the community, let alone everyone who might be affected by the community's collective action. In principle it includes everyone who is eligible and who intends to share in running a particular society.

The state may not be the optimal large-scale political community, but for present purposes I will assume that community politics are sited in the state and set up the discussion to illuminate a prominent problem today in state politics, the status of immigrants.

Since I am a democrat, I cannot accept a political leadership that writes off part of a community's population as incapable of sharing in political responsibility, treating some as sheep and others as enemies. I grant that a leader could conscientiously exercise political responsibility in this style and achieve meaningful political goals in a particular situation. But I cannot grant that the authoritarian stance could be as politically satisfactory as the expansive, inclusive responsibility assumed in democratic politics. In democratic perspective, the most necessary political *work* is the explicit negotiation of terms of action sharing in the community for which the obviously best vehicle is an ongoing conversation to which anyone can contribute. In a spiritually healthy community, members are always able to speak to other members about matters of shared interest, benefiting from the standard of civility and the dignity of citizen status.[22] Given modern societies' attainments in literacy and communication, it is not reasonable

---

22. R. G. Collingwood, *The New Leviathan* (Oxford: Oxford University Press, 1992), 303.

not to accept that important political issues are most meaningfully dealt with in the most socially inclusive conversation.

Even granting a democratic presumption of inclusiveness, however, the question of eligibility for membership does not answer itself. Is membership in the community family-like, centrally determined by descent and kinship, necessarily full and irrevocable, with the special duties and advantages of assured helpfulness and loyalty that the family paradigm implies? Or does it pragmatically depend on actual or feasible collaborations (or betrayals) at a given juncture? Is it based strictly on the sharing of living space? Should we grant different kinds of membership depending on modes of action sharing—one kind to a native-born citizen, another to a guest worker?[23] How, as a matter of citizenship policy, do we acknowledge that a new collaborator is eventually no longer an adventitious fellow traveler but a colleague for a full range of purposes—like someone who has lived and worked with a family so long and intimately that he or she shares the family life as much as any of them do (or *can* share it equally by avowing loyalty)?

Despite the feasibility of nearly unrestricted inclusion of citizens in the state-level political process, some citizens will choose not to participate and will either comply with the existing scheme like sheep or else menace it like wolves. They will be separated from the plural subject "We the people" across a fuzzy border of decreasing social sympathy and political understanding. Nevertheless they, along with all other citizens, will benefit from the advantages and bear the burdens that are inherent in the scheme. There will not be an injustice in subjecting everyone, sheep and wolves included, to the coercive power of the government, so long as no one is barred from participating in the democratic community's self-ruling.

So far I have been describing a society without acknowledging foreign visitors or immigrants, but this omission is unrealistic.

The politically active leaders of a society may believe that denying rights to foreigners and minimizing immigration are necessary to preserve their society's economy and cultural cohesion (although they may of course believe the opposite, that immigration is economically and culturally invigorating). In implementing such policies they can claim to be exercising a sovereign right of self-determination supported by a larger legal order or in the court of public opinion. Their land is *theirs* to rule, theirs not in the sense of owned property—for property owning is established only

---

23. Michael Walzer articulates this approach in *Spheres of Justice* (New York: Basic Books, 1983), chap. 2.

within states, by their varying laws and customs—but in the sense of a self-appointed and not-effectually-challenged jurisdiction, the *realm* of that collective's political project.[24] Since the basis of governmental authority is not ownership, a government cannot order anyone away from "its property" as an individual or corporation might (and as a king in former times might expel someone). A government can order people around only on the basis of its laws, and how the state's laws treat people is determined by its political process.

The jurisdictional authority of a state cannot be absolute, as it is easy to think of grotesque implications of that premise: *We have the right to breed people as slaves. We have the right to destroy all wildlife in our territory.* So there are some constraints on the acceptability of a regime that any reasonable evaluator would insist on. Protection of basic human rights seems to be one such constraint, and access to political participation in a community seems to be one such right. But assuring political access for new immigrants is less straightforward than for the native-born, who seemingly *must* be counted as members if the state is to be sustained through generations.[25]

We could think of every agent as ideally a sharer in whatever governmental work is necessary wherever he or she is, on whatever scale he or she shares action with others. If, for instance, people from diverse homelands find themselves on a ship, the politically responsible among them will take some share in maintaining the scheme by which the ship is run, at least by obeying the ship's rules. If the ship sinks and they find themselves on a lifeboat, they will form and maintain a consensual scheme for managing the affairs of the boat. If their boat washes ashore in a country that refuses to help them leave but also refuses to allow them to participate in managing that country's affairs, or ever to qualify for participation, then we can see that something is wrong—partly because we know that their disenfranchisement makes them more vulnerable to unjust treatment and partly in support of their being able to exercise political responsibility to whatever end, purely as a human fulfillment.

---

24. I follow Anna Stilz in preferring a Kant-inspired jurisdiction account against a Lockean property-owning account, for which she argues in "Why Do States Have Territorial Rights?" *International Theory* 1 (2009): 185–213. See also Thomas Hobbes, *Leviathan* (New York: E. P. Dutton, 1950), 210.

25. One may imagine a skill-based policy by which a state grants citizenship to the best-qualified workers with no guarantees for anyone else, native-born or not. But such a scheme would be highly impractical: few would be willing to settle in a place where their children might be denied citizenship.

We may be thinking of the shipwreck survivors as helpless refugees and blank slates of political responsibility, but persons of recent foreign provenance usually do have older political affiliations that could generate competing claims. The host community has to be concerned about possible threats to its well-being. What norms will these new arrivals respect? To whom do they figure to be loyal in case of war? With whom will they be allied in economic competition? (A native interest group may ask: Will they drive us out of our livelihood?)

When a community deliberates on whether to admit or grant fuller privileges to those of recent foreign provenance, the focus of political responsibility as far as those persons are concerned is at first a responsibility-for: we are ethically obliged to give anyone hospitable treatment while they are in distress, for example, and we may be obliged for security reasons to monitor their whereabouts. But if we have been collaborating with them—if they have been a significant presence in our economy for years—then a point arrives at which responsible insiders feel political responsibility *to* these others (even if other insiders prefer to make a political caste distinction that blocks that possibility), such that their political standing in our community, not merely their basic welfare, claims our respect.[26] An argument can then be made that their political privileges in our society should not be out of line with their economic participation.

The welfare of *our own people* is always a top priority for a political community conceived as a particular people's vehicle for flourishing, and a people's flourishing is always competitive (as well as cooperative) with the flourishing of other peoples. *Our* government is set up to be responsible for *our* welfare. However, our political leadership might realize an ethical or pragmatic responsibility to noncitizen immigrants that calls for expanding the *we*.

Resistance to immigration might be able to give plausible reasons: that it worsens average wages for workers, that it overburdens social services, that it sparks a regressive politics of xenophobia and resentment, or even that it reduces the livability of the immigrants' country of origin. Any of these claims might or might not stand up when rival views of the situation are weighed for the seriousness and cognizance of their responsibility. But sometimes a purportedly responsible opposition to granting citizenship to immigrants assumes a conception of "us" or "the people" (as the primary

---

26. I am in tune here with Walzer's discussion of the situation of Turkish guest workers in Germany in *Spheres of Justice*, 56–61.

reference of responsibility-to and responsibility-for in the community) that is arbitrarily frozen in the condition that preceded the advent of the latest immigrants. The new immigrants and their advocates can reasonably plead: Why not accept that we belong to "the people" *now* since we are *here*, sharing in the life of *this* community? Unless there is a definite prospect of harm to persons or the legal order in accepting them, mere adherence to a particular vision of the composition of the community—a call perhaps to defend its "cultural integrity" based on its "heritage"—will lack the substance of political responsibility. For loyalty to a culture is not the same thing as loyalty to a political community; the membership of a culture is never necessarily coextensive with the membership of a political community, and their histories are never the same.[27] The same point can be made about the membership of a political community in relation to the membership of a particular family or group of families: even if a political apparatus was first set up in defense of certain families, the apparatus now serves a collaborative community, not certain families. In this way the ideal of political responsibility is friendly to immigrants.

Global Responsibility and the Displacement of Persons

> We are at a point in political evolution when the unitary model of citizenship, which bundled together residency upon a single territory with the subjection to a single administration of a people perceived to be a more or less cohesive entity, is at an end.
>
> —Seyla Benhabib[28]

Those who are concerned about doing justice to immigrants, or to refugees from unlivable situations in their home countries, may also be prompted

---

27. As Ryan Pevnick points out, a position that treats the government as the instrument of a culturally unified community is really loyal to *that* community, which may live in various countries, rather than to the particular government; the proprietors of that government's political project are the bearers of assigned rights and responsibilities under that government, not members of a culture. Ryan Pevnick, *Immigration and the Constraints of Justice* (Cambridge, UK: Cambridge University Press, 2011). See also Richard W. Miller, *Globalizing Justice: The Ethics of Poverty and Power* (Oxford: Oxford University Press, 2010), chap. 2, classing political discrimination in favor of a cultural group with nepotism.
28. *The Rights of Others* (Cambridge, UK: Cambridge University Press, 2004), 178.

by a sense of political responsibility in a global frame of reference. But global political responsibility is especially hard to figure because its referent in shared action is vast and anarchic. The states of the world improvise schemes of relationship with each other without the stabilizing assurance of an empowered authority over them—only recognizing that for the moment they have to deal with each other and that humanity must in any case continue to share the planet, subject to the perennial urging of reason to come to fair terms rather than fight.[29] Although "regimes" of international agreements are in place, sometimes supported by an agency like a High Court, to guide the actions of governments with regard to human rights, and although operative global "governance" enables easy movement and cooperation around the world for many, implementation of norms is always at the discretion of actual governments and is sorely inconsistent.[30]

Not only state governments but transnational economic, religious, and activist organizations should be recognized as important political factors in everyone's globalizing life inasmuch as they powerfully coordinate agents and resources on a global scale. But they too are improvising political community—or insisting on an ideally defined global polity, as in the case of would-be revivers of the Islamic Caliphate—in the absence of a really established global political authority. An ordinary citizen clearly has a politically significant choice whether to support Oxfam and Amnesty International, or whether to support internationalist candidates for office, but has no politically authorized way of allying with citizens in other states or resolving disagreements with them. Citizens can indeed think of themselves as members of global society and undertake "global citizenship" initiatives on the premise that a global political community is "emerging."[31] Negatively

---

29. Haskell Fain offers an optimistic view of the ungoverned plurality of nations. "I contend that the world political community, though it does not have a central government, is not an anarchy because as members of an egalitarian world political community, nations possess equal political powers of various kinds over one another. It is the existence of these political powers . . . that make it conceptually possible for nations to enter into *binding* treaties with one another. . . . the world has been drawn together in such a way that the attainment of the good life within the single state is inextricably bound to its attainment in all others." Haskell Fain, *Normative Politics and the Community of Nations* (Philadelphia: Temple University Press, 1987), 15. But the problem of the lack of an enforcer remains.

30. James N. Rosenau, "Governance, Order, and Change in World Politics," in Rosenau and Ernst-Otto Czempiel, eds., *Governance without Government* (Cambridge, UK: Cambridge University Press, 1992), 1–29.

31. Ron Israel, *Global Citizenship* (CreateSpace, 2012).

they can think of themselves as *not* nationals, detaching in principle from key claims of the state. But they have no vote in the global arena and no other legally sanctioned role.

Despite their lack of a defined role, people anywhere can be put in the position of *intending to be* citizens of the world by a technical-political consideration, an ethical consideration, a pragmatic consideration, or a historical consideration. We can examine each of these types of consideration using the practical focus of the displaced persons problem.

1. My discussion of this point must be brief, as I know no more than any other newspaper reader about the merits of specific claims made in this dimension; but the movements of large numbers of displaced people evidently create political challenges in the countries they leave, the countries they travel through, and the countries they land in. A certain kind of regime, like Assad's in Syria, may judge that its own survival, which it believes serves its country better than any of the available alternatives, requires that citizens who cannot be reconciled to the regime must be destroyed or driven away, or only readmitted with very restrictive vetting. Another kind of regime, like Orbán's in Hungary, may judge that the survival of its country's government requires that displaced persons be prevented from entering. Yet another kind of regime, like Merkel's in Germany, may judge that its political integrity requires putting forth a major effort of hospitality for displaced persons.

The Merkelian judgment may seem to you, as it does to me, more fully responsible; it is certainly more affirming of global collaboration. But all three judgments are responses to global conditions, all three can claim to play an appropriate role in implementing an optimal scheme for the protection of human rights, and all three are politically debatable. Assad and Orbán might have been right that their unfriendly policies were needed to prevent political disasters for their countries. Merkel might have wrongly risked a political disaster for her country. That she did not cause such a disaster (as seems to be the case at the time of writing) is not a complete vindication, as she might have been reckless and lucky, but it does tend to support a view of her judgment as responsible; that Assad did cause a national disaster (which is hard to dispute at this point) counts against his judgment, even if he was careful and unlucky. That Merkel's judgment looks better counts in favor of an internationally responsible stance, subject to necessary caveats about constraints in the societies in which these leaders operate.

Merkel's judgment may seem a bad specimen of power wielding responsibility because of its dependence on an ethical appeal. But the political success of a regime like Merkel's depends on its perceived ethical sensibility. Ethics plays also as political power.[32] Further, when Merkel adopted the slogan "We can do this," positioning Germany as responsibly committed to and competent for the massive hospitality effort, she was advertising and asking for reinforcement for the power of Germany under her regime to accomplish historically great things.[33]

2. For the ethical activation of political responsibility to and for displaced persons, the leading appeal in our world is for respect for human rights. The concept of universal human rights appears to be our one usable basis for articulating standards of global justice otherwise than by projecting the justice norms of one political community or ideological sect onto others.[34] Lack of freedom of expression is a justice problem in a country whether or not it is a liberal democracy; lack of personal security is a justice problem in a country whether or not it is a security state. "Reasonable" persons realize that certain forms of freedom and support must be granted to human agents in any "decent" society (Rawls).[35] Global ethical realizations are evoked by arguments that turn on basic reciprocity—"Don't you see that your own life

---

32. I don't know what the Ottoman ruler Bayezid II risked by welcoming displaced Spanish Jews in 1492, but that could have been a power win for him quite apart from the humanitarian aspect.

33. On negative political consequences of that slogan, see Janosch Delcker, "The Phrase that Haunts Angela Merkel," politico.eu, August 19, 2016, accessed October 20, 2021, https://www.politico.eu/article/the-phrase-that-haunts-angela-merkel/.

34. The concept of universal human rights has a very different significance in international politics than it has in bioethics, where questions about the right-bearing personhood of unborn or impaired humans are important. For this reason I will not respond to arguments like those of Douglas Husak in "Why There Are No Human Rights," *Social Theory and Practice* 10 (1984): 125–41.

35. In *The Law of Peoples* (Cambridge, MA: Harvard University Press, 1999), John Rawls argues for fairness as the principle of global justice and derives a short list of universal human rights from fairness (65). He also gives the concept of human rights the historic post–World War II role of constraining state autonomy by forbidding states to go to war (except in self-defense) or to abuse their own citizens (79). Rawls distinguishes the more basic "moral" realization of the requirement for fairness, which should not be controversial, from the commitments of "ethical" doctrines, which inevitably will be. For my comment on that distinction see chap. 3, 75–76.

would be unbearable if you were treated that way?"—or on basic compassion, as in Peter Singer's argument that any morally sensitive person would accept a minor inconvenience to prevent someone else's serious suffering.[36]

Building on a post–World War II collective realization of the vulnerability of human beings deprived of state protection, the Universal Declaration of Human Rights endorsed by the United Nations in 1948 is a remarkably full list of rights asserted from diverse points of view. As with any list, the UDHR can be criticized for privileging certain people's preferences—in this case, liberal Western preferences for unrestricted political participation and sexual equality.[37] And the uneven implementation of UDHR standards by the world's states remains a serious limitation of its practical meaningfulness. But the existence of the UDHR even as a problematic thesis on standards of global justice provides a universally accessible venue for political activism. It is impossible now to shrug off the notion of human rights without shrugging off the relevance of justice thinking altogether.

A discussion of justice on the premise of universal human rights must be open to the claim that anyone has the right to flee abuse. This right seems practically entailed by having a right not to be abused in the first place, combined with the real possibility of a state failing to perform its proper protective function. Accordingly the UDHR asserts rights to leave one's country and also to seek asylum from persecution (articles 13 and 14). There is an awkward dangler on the arrival side, however: the person who must be allowed to leave country A, even fleeing persecution, does not therein have a right to live in country B. Does a refugee have the right to live in *some* safer country? Article 28 of the UDHR says that "everyone is entitled to a social and international order in which the rights and freedoms set forth in this Declaration can be fully realized," which implies that the "international community" must provide for arrival sites for people who are entitled to emigrate. Sometimes, as has been seen recently in the European Union, serious efforts are made at state level to improvise an international solution for refugees. But the political responsibility to address the needs

---

36. Peter Singer, "Famine, Affluence, and Morality," *Philosophy and Public Affairs* 1 (Spring 1972): 229–43.

37. This view of the Declaration overlooks the serious cultural pluralism of the drafting discussions and underestimates the extent to which Western political ideologies were checked. See Mary Ann Glendon, *A World Made New: Eleanor Roosevelt and the Universal Declaration of Human Rights* (New York: Random House, 2001), and Hans Ingvar Roth, *P. C. Chang and the Universal Declaration of Human Rights* (Philadelphia: University of Pennsylvania Press, 2016).

of the refugees is challenged in each state with political impunity, and the policies and procedures adopted by the states that do accept this responsibility are unstable.

Article 29 of the UDHR states a consideration owed to communities: "Everyone has duties to the community in which alone the free and full development of his personality is possible." Such duties might be in tension with an individual's right to live in a safe place. A particular state might take the position that its viability has certain cultural and technical conditions; for instance, a popular political position in the US now is that only English speakers with desirable job skills should be allowed to reside here. There may be good pragmatic reasons to disagree with this position but there may not be a compelling ethical reason, if the position is not arbitrarily discriminatory. Against the prima facie rightness of allowing free passage to anyone we must weigh various rights realizations concerning elective association, property owning, and security. For example: you *should* let a stranger into your house *if* there is a terrible storm outside and *if* there is no definite reason to worry that the stranger intends to abuse your family . . . and a refugee is like a stranger in distress, a community is like a house, and the community's preexisting population is like a family in some relevant respects.[38]

Pushing harder for the ethical priority of community, it might be argued that the most suitable premise for global justice thinking is a civic requirement that individuals help however possible to maintain their community's social harmony as defined by its authorized leadership. This ethical alternative would not apply one set of standards universally, as human rights thinking does, but would be varyingly specific to communities. The supreme norm at the global level would be noninterference between communities. Communities would be confirmed in their right of "self-determination" regarding all their policies, including their immigration and asylum policies however restrictive.[39]

This kind of communalist position seems a nonstarter, however, because one of the main points of ethical reflection and discussion, as we now under-

---

38. For an open borders argument see Joseph Carens, *The Ethics of Immigration* (Oxford: Oxford University Press, 2013), chaps. 11–12, and Phillip Cole's portions of Christopher Heath Wellman and Phillip Cole, *Debating the Ethics of Immigration: Is There a Right to Exclude?* (Oxford: Oxford University Press, 2011). The political meaningfulness of the argument depends on the functioning of a global political apparatus.

39. This argument has been made against the human rights regime by Asian leaders. See Joanne R. Bauer and Daniel Bell, *The East Asian Challenge for Human Rights* (Cambridge, UK: Cambridge University Press, 1999).

stand ethics, is to detect and denounce the various abuses of individuals and smaller groups that would be licensed by deferring in this way to the alleged needs of larger groups. We would be abdicating from ethics if we could not object to discrimination and coercive exploitation. Human rights discourse is a direct expression of the ethical interest in fairness in human affairs—an inherently global interest that is solicitous of individuals and human projects on all scales, wherever they may be encountered. A totalitarian or caste society could justify itself ethically only if it could plausibly argue that its approach is best for serving *all* its citizens; it could impose great inequalities and sacrifices on its citizens, but it could not deny any of them respectful treatment.[40] A society closed to immigrants could justify itself ethically only with the unlikely argument that its approach really is best for everyone or with the suspect claim that it has special needs compared with other states.

Another communalist position on global justice is ecologically oriented and nonanthropocentric and would figure to be unresponsive to claims of immigrant or refugee rights. It contends that the requirements for the health of the whole Earth community are paramount; when we fixate on "human rights" we are distracted from our duties with respect to nonhuman beings and to the functional integrity of the biosphere.[41] But a nonanthropocentric position has difficulty establishing itself as a binding ethical priority as opposed to an optional aesthetic preference, given the anthropocentric conditions of ethical justification—namely, the presumptions for a reasonably communicating and collaborating "we" that undergird the ethical kind of evaluation. It seems obvious that a position that subordinates human rights to ecological needs will get sufficient political traction only in a widely recognized human survival emergency. Thus the most important inspiration for an ecologically responsible policy on migrants—not necessarily a policy that will encourage or protect them—will be found not in ethical discussion but in recognizing near-term human accommodations that are necessary to avert ecological disaster.

---

40. Social deviants may be regarded as having forfeited their claim to respectful treatment, and harsh treatment of deviants may seem to more liberal minds a human rights violation. But an ethical justification of that treatment must take the human rights idea seriously.

41. On the Deep Ecology critique of "human rights" see George Sessions, "Shallow and Deep Ecology: Review of the Philosophical Literature," in Robert C. Shultz, ed., *Ecological Consciousness* (Washington: University Press of America, 1981), 391–462. For a practical defense of the concept of human rights in the context of ecological concern see William Aiken, "Human Rights in an Ecological Era," *Environmental Values* 1 (Autumn 1992): 191–203.

The human rights principle is generally supportive of migrants' rights, even if not conclusively so in every situation. It is in a strong position in global political discussion not so much because human beings around the world all possess valuable human properties (although no serious discussant would deny that human lives are precious) but because we have realized practically that we share the world with everyone and are, in principle, in conversation with everyone and thus subject to a universal basic reciprocity. This seems the best understanding of a relevant moral constraint on states in global society. It combines the Lockean sense (revived by Rawls) that we encounter each other as colleagues in "civil society" with the Hobbesian recognition that we have to accept a deal with assurance of enforcement to serve our most important shared interests effectively.

3. We can be positioned as "global citizens" also by pragmatic considerations. There may be a momentous threat or opportunity relating to an action currently in the hands of a global community, a near-term practical prospect sufficiently concrete and urgent that it makes us project the political requirements for a global course correction. Thus we realize that if we all keep using energy and plastic in our current pattern (or keep rapidly growing our population, or keep arming for nuclear conflict) the world could soon become unlivable. Or we may realize that there is insurance against human extinction in a space colonization program that is now feasible but requires international cooperation. (Or a nationalist may realize as a matter of strategy that to fend off global-political claims one must discredit all ideas of global threat or opportunity.) Leaders of states who are not willing to work with other states on addressing such issues, especially the clear and present dangers, and citizens who fail to press their governments to address such issues are pragmatically-politically irresponsible.

Massive displacement of persons is a present global challenge, part of a larger challenge posed by the incompetence of states. Citizens in numerous states lack basic protections due to various mixtures of governmental incapacity and bad conduct. Some of these states can no longer be considered homelands but are instead hellish places that anyone would flee who could. Migrants under these conditions have not come in response to work opportunities or to help relatives—familiar circumstances that allow for relatively easy integration. Instead they are arriving without those practical connections and perhaps in large numbers, straining the social fabrics of the receiving country.

The pragmatically responsible question that arises immediately for citizens of the receiving country is, how best may we deal with *these* people in light of the possible relations between their project of finding a safe haven and our project of running our society productively and safely? The question should be informed from the start by awareness of the burdens on government and the citizenry and how these might be adjusted in new scenarios. It is certainly informed by ethical assumptions: shooting the migrants down or forcefully driving them away would violate human rights, and setting up quasi-permanent refugee camps on the border would be patently unfair since no one would want to be stuck in such a camp. Then the question should become further informed by pragmatic insights into the state of the present world by addressing the broader question, what altogether is happening, and why? Who is doing what, such that this unacceptable situation results? This broader question brings the "failing states" phenomenon into view and imposes an agenda for international action. The global citizen perspective asserts itself in calling for a more accurate and fair understanding of the displaced persons issue and for action toward resolving it with the least possible damage to actions in hand.

The pragmatic requirement of recognizing and respecting a perspective other than one's own becomes even more important in global communication than in ordinary political communication within a state framework. For the established political apparatus that allows vigorous partisanship within a well-ordered state is missing on the global stage, which means that the prevailing of one party is not an episodic victory in an ongoing game but rather a conquest and suppression that may be hard to overcome for a long time. This is why an ideal portrayal of global citizenship emphasizes conscientious communication.

> Almost every global issue has multiple ethnic, social, political, and economic perspectives attached to it. It is the responsibility of global citizens to understand these different perspectives and promote problem-solving consensus among the different perspectives and the building of common ground solutions. A global citizen should avoid taking sides with one particular point of view, and instead search for ways to bring all sides together. (The Global Citizens Initiative)[42]

---

42. Ron Israel, "The Rights and Responsibilities of Global Citizenship," accessed October 20, 2021, https://www.theglobalcitizensinitiative.org/index.php/the-rights-and-responsibilities-of-global-citizenship/.

New pragmatic challenges can never be dealt with in isolation; they jostle with other challenges that agents are already occupied with, forcing a search for a new total solution. What if you admit that a displaced population ought to be given hospitality by a comparatively wealthy and stable country, but you also believe that the country next door is wealthier and more stable than your own? Shouldn't the migrants go *there*? Mightn't this be a politically conscientious position, not merely selfish, considering the economic and political vulnerability of your own country in competition with its peers? To override a reasonable fear of imminent damage to one's state, one would need to obtain a firm global commitment based on a definite prospect of momentous success or failure for the global community.

Many new pragmatic challenges are evaded because they seem to involve unpleasant complications. A state can decline the challenge of displaced persons by closing its border: then those people will have to go somewhere else and we will not have to figure out how to accommodate them and possibly become less secure and less prosperous with them in our midst. In the present world of increasing international movement, however, "those people" become harder to compartmentalize politically in one's mind; it becomes a more common experience that one runs into "those people" in the grocery store, and thus one comes nearer the perception of a normally diverse community from which it would be illogical to demand that anyone of a supposed foreign type be expelled. At the same time, the contemporary upsurge of nativism shows that there can be a powerful counterrealization that a culturally coherent and satisfying way of life is unsustainable if *we* who share *this* life are forced into extensive cooperation with *them* partly on *their* terms. Nativists may have a strategic realization that they need to reverse the normalizing of diversity, lest their political assertion of in-group priority be overwhelmed by a realization of global belonging. But the cultural community they rejoice in is not the same thing as the community they live in.

4. Although not everyone contemplates the historical thickness of shared action in this connection, a historical sense of responsibility for displaced persons would affect one's political judgments.

One might have a progressive conviction that humanity (or a particular collective or coalition acting as the vanguard of humanity) has an opportunity to reduce the intergroup violence and governmental abuses that have historically produced the displacement of persons. On this basis, a historically conscientious way to act is to lend one's efforts to the strengthening of global governance to help that improvement come about. Alternatively, one might have become convinced that the violent and corrupt causes of displacement will never be removed, and that conscientious agents in any era can expect nothing more than to have occasional opportunities to alleviate some of the suffering of the displaced. How best to go about that must be judged pragmatically; a careful prioritization of national well-being might be indicated, on the analogy of the well-kept ship that is better able to take care of shipwreck victims.

Each of these historically responsible stances has decided by implication what counts as historical irresponsibility—neglecting opportunities to advance the protection of humans through global governance, from the progressive point of view, and neglecting to keep communities in the best possible working order, from the conservative point of view. Agents and ensembles who are not yet equipped to think about the historical dimension of the issue cannot be faulted as historically irresponsible, but their actions, policies, and habits can be so characterized.

The most fully responsible agents politically are responsive to all four of these factors. They are not utopians, not absentminded about the present requirements of shared action, not naive about economic and cultural competition between groups and the power struggle among political agents and factions; but neither are they cynical or indifferent about justice. They are interested in maximizing practical respect for human rights, but they have tempered expectations for cooperation where government enforcement is lacking. They do not lock themselves into a congenial set of historical beliefs, yet they try not to be out of touch with important long-term developments.

I think we have impressive living role models for global political responsibility in Mikhail Gorbachev, Barack Obama, and Angela Merkel. One need not agree with all of their policies and actions to see them as exemplary in this way and thus to have a strong reason to seek out, support, or try to become leaders with their orientation. Many who disagree with me on global politics would nominate different role models. But some might not, since the question of who best exemplifies responsibility is not the same as the question of who provides the best leadership in a particular juncture, everything considered.

※

The conceptual clarification I have proposed for political responsibility does not strictly entail any normative conclusions, yet it is directively suggestive.

In each of our four cases a nonobvious responsible stance is made accessible by thinking out a politically fully responsible approach to the issue.

1. The abortion chooser can be responsible in a family scheme (or not) in making either choice—abortion can be chosen for reasons not selfish and can be declined for responsible reasons not ethical. The chooser acts on and by means of a family government and in so doing can intend to achieve the most fully acceptable outcome.

2. Work organizations can and should support responsibility fulfillment in work by enlarging the responsibilities of their members, going beyond the "job" model of normal employment and the ethical standard of dignity in work—although the mutual commitment of organizations and workers requisite for more responsible work is in tension with high-ranked values of corporate and worker freedom to limit work relationships. The ideal of meaningful work is supported but not fully demanded by the ethical standard of dignity in work.

3. Citizens facing new immigrants can be responsible *to* them, while also being responsible *to* their fellow citizens, in the state scheme—ethically, in respecting their self-presentation as bearers of human rights, but also pragmatically, respecting the actuality of present collaboration with them; historically, with the intent of fostering humane progress in the practical remit of states to meet human needs; and politically, pursuing the most comprehensively acceptable policy.

4. Would-be "global citizens" cannot be responsible in a civic way, since there is not a functioning global government, but they can be politically responsible, supporting global cooperation in quest of the most fully acceptable arrangements for displaced persons.

Political responsibility is the fruit of extra thought and requires extra effort, so it is realized very unevenly in a community. Possibly our everyday life would be under too much strain if everyone were politically aware and activist; there could be an attentional tug-of-war among too many agendas about too many issues (like being trapped in the satirical portrait of a tumultuously "woke" high school or college), or there could be an unfortunate self-confirming unanimity of the like-minded operating like a political militia. Nevertheless the democratic ideal of full political participation calls for promoting political responsibility in all citizens. Given the modern expansion of literate communication, this program is not unrealistic. Given the strong appeal of stubbornly simpler forms of responsibility—from high-minded politics of principle to conniving with one's gang—the most humanely sensitive version of this program is needed to mitigate responsibility-fueled conflicts.

Chapter Five

Full Responsibility

> I'm an American citizen. In America, everybody is responsible for everything.
>
> —Mr. Pulaski in *The Talk of the Town*[1]

Limiting and Maximizing Approaches to Full Responsibility

It is a given that we have, or might have, various responsibilities. We must assume that role expectations can be feasible and that agents can be sincerely committed to fulfilling them. We cannot assume that all role expectations *are* feasible as currently defined, that the scheme of expectations rests on a fair consensus and will be upheld by the community, that agents are always sincerely committed to fulfilling roles, that agents will be held responsible strictly in good faith, or that attempts to fulfill roles will be harmonious with each other, but we will certainly hope for these felicities if we are serious about responsible action. Some version of a *fully responsible life* is an irresistible ideal for us. It would mean that everything that needs to be attended to is being attended to and that everyone's agency is fully engaged materially and socially. (It also must mean that we have not fallen into a nightmare of surveillance and persecution—a *1984* version of full responsibility, or the extreme of litigiousness or moral policing.) The most persuasive total ideal for developing and exercising our agency will surely

---

1. *The Talk of the Town* (Columbia Pictures, 1942), screenplay by Dale van Every, Irwin Shaw, and Sidney Buchman.

include escapes from responsibility—for relaxation, selfish enjoyment, some crazy risk-taking, perhaps a little mischief—but we will stipulate that our nonresponsible activity will not keep us from fulfilling our responsibilities by the end of the day.

It was a classical vision of politics, and in a chastened way it is still a widely shared idea, that the point of political endeavor is to maintain a social system in which the greatest compossibility of goods can be realized. This is provable from the negative: anyone indifferent to the degree to which, say, honest commerce or artistic creativity or moral virtue or religious devotion is structurally allowed to flourish in their society evidently falls short, to that extent, of an ideally politically responsible attitude, supposing it is knowable that the scheme for action sharing *could* be made more accommodating. A society's political leadership can be expected to advance a comprehensive political concern proactively, or a governmental system can be asked to correct for any disservice of a matter of responsible concern. No nonpolitical agent or agency is held to so inclusive an expectation. In this way there is a convergence between political responsibility and the full responsibility ideal.

Although we are generally pro-responsibility, it would be very unusual for an individual to want or try to become the most fully responsible person possible. That might be self-defeatingly unilateral, a kind of domination project. Moreover, it might be impossible for a free agent to cut off forever any personal escape routes from responsibility. But at least one good thing about an ambition to be most fully responsible—for an agent who can see the complexity of responsibility—is that it would prevent one from claiming to be a maximally responsible agent, and on that basis unchallengeably authoritative, merely by virtue of having assumed a single responsibility regarded as supreme, as a dogged functionary or religious fanatic might have done.

For many agents in many situations, the ideal of being fully responsible is met by conduct that is *satisfactory*, so that one is comfortable in self-examination and roundly approvable in one's community. That is very different from the pedal-to-the-metal ideal of *fullest* responsibility that asks for the greatest possible seriousness in some role, as, for example, the way ardent lovers and leaders challenge themselves to respond to others more profoundly and serve them more effectively, adjusting the terms of engagement as needed. Supporting this ardor there may be a thought, possibly a justified belief, that all parties have a chance to grow in sensitivity, understanding, and skill through the most intensely responsible engagement, changing the baseline of what they can expect from each other. Lovers feel that their assumption of deep responsibility in their relationship is a great spiritual adventure; political leaders seek to arouse a similar optimism and excitement in the movements they lead; so do the conductors and directors of artistic collaborations.

In practice, an agent's degrees of ethical and historical responsibility are measured only at times of relative crisis when our assumptions about ourselves and each other come into question. In contrast, pragmatic responsibility is measured as often as jobs are undertaken. It is part of the nervous system of collaboration. Falling short, letting others down, causes a kind of pain.

For a particular job, in a particular collaborative setup, the pragmatic hope is for pitching in wholeheartedly and capably, and the expectation is that the agent will be reliably functional. Points could be added for going further than expected, but points could be deducted for overstepping one's role. For example, if I ask you to help me move a piano into my house, you might:

1. Show up wearing nice clothes, unwilling to get sweaty.

2. Show up wearing work clothes and ready to shove. That is quite satisfactory.

3. Show up with a dolly that you thought to borrow from another friend. Under the circumstances, that is an excellent example of full responsibility taking, without taking away from anyone else's sharing of responsibility for the task.

4. Show up announcing that you've blocked out the whole afternoon, you've printed out advice from websites, you've made a map of the property.... This is too much! You have taken charge of the job that I should be in charge of. You are distorting more than fulfilling our pragmatic encounter. The other piano movers may now decline to share responsibility for the activity and blame you alone for anything that goes wrong.

That is the small, granular scale of responsibility fulfillment. There are larger situations of pressing need, such as in wartime, where there might be a strong interest in asking agents to take the fullest responsibility. On the scale of a whole life, however, agents will most often have latitude to view the standard of full responsibility either in a more limiting way—fulfilling responsibility by *only* taking care of certain assigned matters *within* normal human competence, in a scheme of properly balanced complementary roles—or in a maximizing way, pressing toward the most serious intention and engagement.

Models of Full Responsibility

Conscientious agents have a variety of models of full responsibility to choose from. I think there is value in identifying these and sounding each one out, even before we ask why the range is as it appears to be: we see more of the extensive innervation of our practical life by responsibility considerations.

The Full Portfolio of Responsibilities

In any culture, various specific responsibilities have been found to be important for members of the group. Full responsibility seems appropriately specified by compiling the list of those responsibilities: faithful child, parent, worker, citizen, club member, church member, and so on. It is better still if one is thoughtful about balancing all these engagements, grasping them as a system. There is a passage in the *Nicomachean Ethics* that clearly views full responsibility in this way, although it is written in the idiom of social duties and honors.

> It is quite clear therefore that all people have not the same claim upon us, and that even a father's claim is not unlimited, just as Zeus does not have all the sacrifices. Since the claims of parents and brothers, comrades and benefactors, are different, we ought to render to each that which is proper and suitable to each. This is in fact the principle on which men are observed to act. They invite their relatives to a wedding, because they are members of the family, and therefore concerned in the family's affairs; also it is thought to be specially incumbent on relations to attend funerals, for the same reason. It would be felt that our parents have the first claim on us for maintenance, since we owe it to them as a debt, and to support the authors of our being stands before self-preservation in moral nobility. Honor also is due to parents, as it is to the gods, though not indiscriminate honor: one does not owe to one's father the same honor as to one's

mother, nor yet the honor due to a great philosopher or general, but one owes to one's father the honor appropriate to a father, and to one's mother that appropriate to her. Again, we should pay to all our seniors the honor due to their age, by rising when they enter, offering them a seat, and so on. Towards comrades and brothers on the other hand we should use frankness of speech, and share all our possessions with them. Kinsmen also, fellow-tribesmen, fellow-citizens, and the rest—to all we must always endeavor to render their due, comparing their several claims in respect of relationship and of virtue or utility. Between persons of the same kind discrimination is comparatively easy; but it is a harder matter when they are differently related to us. Nevertheless we must not shirk the task on that account, but must decide their claims as well as we are able.[2]

The responsible life is not entirely straightforward—"Zeus does not have all the sacrifices"—but "we must not shirk the task" of fulfilling our many given responsibilities in the best possible way. The task is fascinating in its complexity and meritorious for the agent in its magnitude.

One of the ideals for a government, coordinate with its function of making decisions, is oversight of all responsibilities—actually holding the full portfolio, even if all the specific executive responsibilities are delegated.

The Full Range of Basic Modes of Responsibility

Max Weber pointed out the phenomenon of multimodal responsibility: "an ethic of ultimate ends and an ethic of responsibility are not absolute contrasts but rather supplements, which only in unison constitute a genuine man."[3] Weber's scenario is conceived with two modes, ethical (the ethic of ultimate ends) and political (the ethic of responsibility). There are more. It is easier to illustrate them in their absence, through our all-too-common disappointments, than in their subtly and unevenly mixed presence. For instance, imagine a terrible bandleader who (1) is capricious and musically heavy-handed in directing the band; (2) does not treat band members fairly in matters of pay and scheduling; (3) has no interest in the history of the

---

2. Aristotle, *Nicomachean Ethics* IX.2 (1165a), trans. Harris Rackham.
3. Max Weber, "Politics as a Vocation," in H. H. Gerth and C. Wright Mills, eds., *From Max Weber: Essays in Sociology* (New York: Oxford University Press, 1948), 77–128, 127.

music the band plays or the history of relations between such bands, their employers, and their public; and (4) is reflexively hostile to a musicians' strike. Not only that: the bandleader does not keep track of the band's finances, does not take care of instruments, is a romantic heartbreaker, casually sneers at religious beliefs . . .

Now, it is unlikely that any bandleader would have consciously set out to be pragmatically *and* ethically *and* historically *and* politically responsible in every way. But a responsibly oriented person would be sensitive to various indications of need and dissatisfaction and thus would probably evolve toward that desired fullness. The terrible bandleader is a contrarian (to use a polite word) who has evolved in the opposite direction.

For a positive type, the opposite of the terrible bandleader, we can turn to the wonderful stalwart of a family, brimming with strength, ingenuity, concern for justice, and zeal to solve everyone's shorter- and longer-term problems that Eudora Welty imagined in the character of Jack Renfro in *Losing Battles*. Jack's psychology is not quite realistic, for he seems primarily defined as the hope of the family that wants to rely on him; he is a mythic son, husband, citizen, and patriarch-in-the-making, yet at the same time it is believable that being the rod and the staff of the family could inspire a young fellow. Jack holds no public office (in contrast to his inferior rival Curly Stovall), but his political disposition and talent are conspicuous.

Full Dedication to Responsibility

Like Aristotle, Kongzi as we encounter him in the *Lunyu* (*Analects*) wants to survey correct behaviors across the full human range and to distill their rational form. But the responsible role he prides himself on is not that of an expert lecturer on ethics but that of a perpetually engaged learner: "In a hamlet of ten families, there may be found someone as honorable and sincere as I am, but none so fond of learning" (5.27).[4] "He who aims to be a man of complete virtue . . . frequents the company of men of principle that he may be rectified—such a person may be said indeed to love to learn" (1.14). "I have been the whole day without eating, and the whole night without sleeping, occupied with thinking. It was of no use. It is better to learn" (15.30). "If some years were added to my life, I could give fifty

---

4. All Kongzi quotations are taken from *The Analects of Confucius*, trans. James Legge, accessed October 20, 2021, http://oaks.nvg.org/analects-legge.html.

to study; then I might come to be without great faults" (7.16).[5] "Learn as if you could not reach your object, and were always fearing also lest you should lose it" (8.17). He told Ran Qiu that no one can complain that his program is too demanding until they actually collapse in pursuing it (6.12).

Kongzi's dedication means more than staying busy. The supreme object of learning is proper comportment, with the serious address of other persons at its core.

> The Master said, "The filial piety of nowadays means the support of one's parents. But dogs and horses likewise are able to do something in the way of support—without reverence, what is there to distinguish the one support given from the other?" (2.7)

> He sacrificed to the dead, as if they were present. He sacrificed to the spirits, as if the spirits were present. The Master said, "I consider my not being present at the sacrifice, as if I did not sacrifice." (3.12)

It may sound at times as though Kongzi wants to simplify the responsible life by boiling it down to a principle.

> Zi Gong asked, saying, "Is there one word which may serve as a rule of practice for all one's life?" The Master said, "Is not 'reciprocity' such a word? What you do not want done to yourself, do not do to others." (15.24)

But his aim is to shift the main challenge from specifying correct actions to being fully in earnest. When agents are earnestly prosocial, acting in the true spirit of reciprocity, everything in their shared life will fall out in the right way, as symbolized by the sage-king Shun who ruled a Chinese golden age merely by reverently facing south (15.4). Full coverage of human responsibilities will be assured by full dedication to living responsibly. The classic Confucian portfolio of the Five Relationships of parent/child, ruler/minister, husband/wife, older/younger, and friend/friend (*Mengzi* 3A.4) points out the prime venues for earnestness as its preferred way of displaying the structure of humane life.

---

5. I have slightly amended this passage in line with Waley's interpretation. *The Analects of Confucius*, trans. Arthur Waley (New York: Vintage, 1938).

Despite the modern tendency to take up Confucian discourse as ethical, its orientation to actual encounters is pragmatic and its guiding vision of an inclusive scheme of responsibility fulfillment is political.

Another model of full dedication is the "infinite responsibility to and for the Other"[6] that Levinas affirms as a principle of human subjectivity, an impractical "obsession" and "hostage condition" that orients all humane comportment.[7] But "responsibility" is a misleading term for this prosocial passion. Responsibility more properly comes onstage in a Levinasian account only when the subject is constrained by the third party to face the ethical and political question of how rightly to order a multiplicity of interpersonal relations.[8] Humane life is then understood as a complex of self-centeredness, obsessive availability, and (in a more normal sense) assumable and fulfillable responsibility.

Full Attention to the Responsible Direction of Life

The Kantian approach to responsible life is similar to the Confucian in being centered by a principle of reciprocity and a sovereign attitude of respect for propriety. But its requirements reach further because of the implications of the concept of universal law, as we see in Kant's complementary formulations of the ethical imperative in the *Groundwork*.[9] To be an agent of pure practical reason requires universalizing one's maxims of action (according to Kant's first formula for the imperative, "universal law") so that they are appropriately binding and feasible for all agents; they must also be consistent with approvable workings of the whole world-system (second formula, "law of nature"), which imposes ideal constraint on every consequential move one makes, not just one's conduct in certain important

---

6. Emmanuel Levinas, "Transcendence and Height," in Adriaan T. Peperzak et al., eds., *Emmanuel Levinas: Basic Philosophical Writings* (Bloomington: Indiana University Press, 1996), 11–32, 18–19.

7. These are themes in Levinas's *Otherwise than Being or Beyond Essence*, trans. Alfonso Lingis (The Hague: Martinus Nijhoff, 1981). See also Jacques Derrida's responsible openness to the full rectification that is to come as articulated in "Faith and Knowledge: The Two Sources of 'Religion' at the Limits of Reason Alone," trans. Samuel Weber, in Jacques Derrida and Gianni Vattimo, *Religion* (Stanford: Stanford University Press, 1998), 1–78.

8. These elements are well balanced in Levinas, "The Ego and the Totality" [1954], in *Collected Papers*, trans. Alfonso Lingis (The Hague: Martinus Nijhoff, 1987), 25–45.

9. Immanuel Kant, *Groundwork of the Metaphysic of Morals*, AA 4:420–34.

relationships.[10] To determine whether a maxim is a good law tenable for all agents, it is necessary to be collegial with all other agents, fully instructed by them on what can constitute a contradiction in the form or willing of a policy; thus conscientious agents must imagine themselves members of a body of lawmakers deliberating on all policies in a Kingdom of Ends (fifth formula).[11] In this perfection of ethical scruple we arrive at the fullest possible extension of the scope and standards for responsibility: except in your most trivial actions there is nothing you are not responsible for and no one you are not responsible to.

This maximally demanding reading of Kant is controversial; many interpreters of Kant and normative Kantians would resist it.[12] One might also wish to resist the takeover of all kinds of responsibility by a maximized ethical responsibility: if one has a nonethical responsibility to, say, laugh at a friend's jokes, then even maximized ethical responsibility cannot by itself be the fullest total responsibility. Nevertheless we can see here a Kantian path to a version of the fullest conceivable responsibility, rivaled in ethical theory only by the utilitarian demand to act always to maximize value—another principle of maximal conscientious attention to choices and actions.

Kant's Kingdom of Ends ideal can also be read as a return to the political ground from which his ethical principle of universal law is derived—a political responsibility that is more fully tasked than any other human responsibility could be. For the "kingdom" is the frame of everything we do, from making our homes and our livings to forming relations with supernatural entities. The government of the kingdom must make provision for every responsible agenda: we set that standard for it, inspired perhaps by the image of an all-seeing benevolent ruler but not passively hoping that a ruler will solve all our problems for us.

---

10. There may be a hint of an unlimited practical reach of Confucian principle when the *Lunyu* surprisingly includes the information that Kongzi fished with a line but not with a net (7.27).

11. I have added an active discussion among agents that is not specified by Kant but I think solves problems with his account. If agents do not need to consult with each other, why even imagine a legislative assembly? And in the absence of personal communication, in what sense are agents respected for their own sakes rather than merely as interchangeable sites of reason?

12. On the issue of the demandingness of Kantian ethics see Marcel van Ackeren and Martin Sticker, "Kant and Moral Demandingness," *Ethical Theory and Moral Practice* 18 (2015): 75–89.

Fully Extended Responsibility

Either as the direct result of an attempt to conceive the most perfect responsibility, or as the accumulation of new realizations and competencies, the ideal of full responsibility pushes outward to a universal sharing of being responsible to and for all beings. If we stay within the lines of the traditional concern for "social justice," responsibility can be assigned to all agents for everyone in the world who is unfairly disadvantaged, as in Iris Marion Young's global social connection model of shared responsibility for structural injustice.[13] But the full extension of responsibility can also press on to become multigenerational, multispecies or holistically biotic, or (if this is thinkable) eternal. A religious model of extended responsibility is the great savior Avalokiteshvara, also known as Guanyin or Kannon, who with many organs of perception hears all cries.[14]

As an ideal for living humans, fully extended responsibility seems to dissolve into impracticability and go against the spirit of limitation in a responsibility system. Yet the agenda of responsible agents could evolve in this direction; in fact, we are now in the midst of a struggle to expand the circle of moral and political consideration.[15] Olaf Stapledon made a remarkable attempt to project such an evolution fully in his 1930 novel *Last and First Men*.[16] Billions of years in the future, as the universe is finally winding down, the seventeenth species-successor to homo sapiens has telepathic insight into the personal existence of everyone who has ever lived and can enter into constructive mental relation with all. (Never mind the time-travel paradoxes; the story is a parable for issues *we* should be attuned to *now* if we are fully responsible.) For the Last Men, with their advanced capability, this kind of superambitious mission of mercy is the doable thing that is most compelling.

The full extension emphasis is problematic in presupposing a very strong competency and commensurate wisdom without providing for either

---

13. Iris Marion Young, *Responsibility for Justice* (New York: Oxford University Press, 2011).

14. See appendix 3, 198–200.

15. Peter Singer, *Expanding the Circle: Ethics and Sociobiology* (New York: Farrar, Straus & Giroux, 1981); Bruno Latour, *Reassembling the Social* (Oxford: Oxford University Press, 2005); *Making Things Public: Atmospheres of Democracy*, ed. Bruno Latour and Peter Weibel (Cambridge, MA: MIT, 2005); Steven G. Smith, "The Structure of Unlimited Action Sharing," *Philosophical Frontiers* 4 (July–December 2009): 57–71.

16. I discuss Stapledon's conception in "What We Have Time For: Historical Responsibility on the Largest Scale," *Journal of the Philosophy of History* 13 (June 2019): 163–82.

of these things. It is hard to argue with the ideal of a bodhisattva who liberates people from suffering, but Stapledon's Last Men are trying to heal, to "fix," all lives in all respects; they seem dangerous meddlers who could not be qualified to provide such overbearing service to others—unless they are angels of an infinitely wise deity. There is a warning here for social justice campaigners: if their objectives are not clearly delimited, they might seem intolerably presumptuous.[17]

A differently aimed ideal of full extension can reduce if not remove this risk. That is the ideal of a fully extended collegial sharing of responsibility, as seen, for example, in the mentality of scientists who constantly reference and check each other's work within an inclusive collaborative network of knowledge producers, and also in the mentality of many cultural and religious ecumenists—for instance, serious students of scriptural guidance who weigh what other interpreters of a scripture have said across the generations and across sectarian lines.

Full Sensitivity to Concerns for Responsibility (the Mahatma Ideal)

Mohandas Gandhi, popularly designated a Mahatma or "great soul," felt responsible and tried to fulfill responsibility to many fellow beings for many shared concerns; and he distinguished himself further as a practical leader in creating structures for responsible action in his ashrams and his civil disobedience campaigns. He was a diligent student of ethics, history, politics, and spirituality and liked to present himself as a perpetual learner, though he did not specialize in learning and teaching to the extent that Kongzi did. He likewise exemplified full attention to the direction of life in a responsible manner and under the aegis of a unifying principle—that principle being ahimsa or creative nonviolence—but rather than systematizing like a philosopher, he emphasized his experimentalism. He is especially notable for extending responsible consideration to marginalized fellow agents, women and untouchables, and (what went against the grain in Hindu circles) to Indian Muslims; but he did not press for a full extension of responsibility in the manner of a bodhisattva or utilitarian. In fact, he is a disappointment from an animal rights or welfare perspective, for though he expressed

---

17. Young discusses several counterclaims that full responsibility for social injustice must overcome—that conditions force us to act as we do, that we are not connected with those people, that immediate demands take precedence, and "it's not my job"—but not skepticism about engineering the best world (*Responsibility for Justice*, chap. 6).

dismay at animal sacrificing he did not campaign against it. After seeing sheep slaughtered at the Kali temple in Calcutta he said, "I hold that, the more helpless a creature, the more entitled it is to protection by man from the cruelty of man." But then he said: "It is my constant prayer that there may be born on earth some great spirit, man or woman, fired with divine pity, who will deliver us from this heinous sin, save the lives of the innocent creatures, and purify the temple."[18]

Because Gandhi *was* the Mahatma, one may remonstrate with him: Mr. Gandhi, why would you, of all people, wait for a great spirit to be born? Who could have been fired with divine pity more than you? Why did you not shoulder that vocation? How could you say: on this issue, someone else needs to be the Mahatma, whose great soul cannot tolerate an abuse?

Of course, Gandhi the political leader had other and arguably proper human priorities. If he had seriously campaigned for the protection of animals he would have come into conflict not only with animal sacrificers but with meat-eating Muslims and Christians all over India. (The political realities of his India in this respect are not so different from those of my own country, where it is still inconceivable that any major party candidate would run against the meat industry, or against sport hunting, or even against unnecessary animal experimentation.)

But the power of the Mahatma ideal is seen in Gandhi's provoking my complaint. Because of his openness to responsibility and his candid imperfection he is a door opener to new visions of fuller responsibility that anyone may have. Meanwhile, because of his historically well-informed imagination of practical possibilities and his disciplined restraint in picking his priority areas for activism, he is a strong type of political responsibility.

THE HEADQUARTERS VIEW

Using philosophy to define responsible life is likely to produce a comprehensive program. Aristotle, Kongzi, and Kant all institute a rule of reason, Kant going the furthest in conceiving rational principle in such a way that it overridingly constrains all of our practice in a systematically unified way. The rationalist approach positions the ordinary agent at Headquarters, so to speak, where determinations of right goals, right strategy, and right practices

---

18. Mohandas Gandhi, *An Autobiography. The Story of My Experiments with Truth* (Boston: Beacon, 1957), 235–36.

are made for a field of action sharing. In this scene the individual agent, awakened and empowered by philosophy, possesses the discerning power and ideal authority of reason as much as anyone else does, and deserves absolute respect (though not uncritical deference) accordingly. But agents making headquarters-level decisions are called on to be fully competent, understanding what is to be done, and fully considerate, aware of the needs and wants of fellow beings. Thus the responsibility they are given by reason is enfolded by political responsibility.

One of Kant's formulations of the ethical principle highlights the autonomy of the individual agent (the fourth formula). The only authentic enactment of law is one's own. The ethical agent does not take ethical orders from anyone else. But autonomy in this sense is not a permission to go one's own way, as a libertarian or hedonist might have inferred from the idea that rational agents are "ends in themselves" (third formula); rather it places one on a seat in reason's Parliament, where one's authorizing rationality functions as a "supreme limiting condition" on subjective ends so that all selfish interest is filtered out.[19] (This version of a Headquarters View is adapted from Rousseau's theory of the general will.)[20]

In practice, agents occupy roles that are responsible without being at Supreme Headquarters level. Indeed, the point of a distributed responsibilities scheme is that there can be multiple headquarters for multiple fields of action and that not every actor has to be positioned at a headquarters, other than the personal headquarters of one's own intelligent agency. In the role of soldier, for example, one is expected to take orders from superiors in a hierarchy of command; the soldier role exists for the sake of implementing centralized decision-making on a large scale, so that battles may be won. With the subordinate role comes a limitation of responsibility. It is not the soldier's job to decide when to drill or when to attack. (Meanwhile, it is not a general's job to clean the latrines; there are limitations of responsibility at every level to make the various jobs doable by human beings.) But the conscientious soldier understands it as his or her responsibility to await and to obey lawful orders. If a soldier protests an unlawful order, he or she speaks not from the military headquarters point of view (second-guessing the military commanders), but from civic headquarters, as an ordinary supporter of the law, or from ethical headquarters. Though not constantly speaking out in this way, the responsible soldier does constantly evaluate situations.

---

19. Kant, *Groundwork*, AA 4:431.

20. Jean-Jacques Rousseau, *The Social Contract* II.3.

Ideally, soldiers and commanders are equally vigilant legally and ethically, and are supported in their vigilance by published standards.

Religious agents who posit a maximum of responsibility in a transcendent deity will think of headquarters, too, as transcendent. But human agents would actually be prevented from being fully responsible if they were required to take orders from a headquarters they cannot question. The scripture premise solves this difficulty in a way, for a text's figurations of deity and divine guidance *can* be conscientiously questioned.[21] By that means humans do share in or approximate to headquarters-level understanding to the extent that they are capable of it. That is one reason that scripturalism (not necessarily in a literalist or *sola scriptura* version) can be understood as a superior, even unsurpassable form of responsibility.

ETERNAL RESPONSIBILITY

The idea of a divinely unlimited responsibility for how things are, how things progress, and how everything will end up calls for a supporting idea of an ultimate concatenation of all things, "eternity." (The Western term *eternity* has analogues elsewhere, such as "Heaven" for Kongzi.) Any eternity-minded agent can adopt this perspective, though probably not with all the insight and executive power of a god. Believers in a Last Judgment can hold this perspective in fear and trembling, resigning their lives to eternal disposition, hoping for the best.

We actually have two kinds of conception of eternity, one blind and one that is supposed to see something. It is a blind conception that simply traces the greatest facts of our life to whatever their basis is. For example, if the supremely nonnegotiable consideration for us is that our people exist, then we think that our epic ancestor (Abraham, Aeneas) had an eternal destiny. We may dramatize this thought by telling a story in which a god gives our ancestor the great mission, but we do not pretend to know anything about the ultimate ground of history except that it seems fortunately to be in our favor. Another blind reference to the eternal is for the sake of designating the open horizon and bottomless question of what is Other—which is one meaning of Kierkegaard's "infinite qualitative difference between God

---

21. See Paul Ricoeur, "What Is a Text?," in *Hermeneutics and the Human Sciences*, ed. John B. Thompson (Cambridge, UK: Cambridge University Press, 1981), 145–64; *Interpretation Theory* (Fort Worth: TCU Press, 1976), 31; and Steven G. Smith, *Scriptures and the Guidance of Language* (Cambridge, UK: Cambridge University Press, 2018), 174.

and man"[22]—or to emphasize the unbounded importance of spiritual life, as the excess of meaningfulness in ethical encounter with the other person motivates Levinas to say that the other appears in the trace left by God.[23]

On the speculative side, we posit that the ground of our existence is an unconditional kind of life, even an agency, even a superlatively responsible agency. It possesses a controlling efficacy that is not limited by interactions and a wisdom that is not based on observations. God has "got the whole world in his hands" in such an original way as to provide for the fundamental possibility of there being a world and a world-God relation, and for the actualization of that possibility; God has a meaningful intention for the world in such an original way that there can be, and are, all the meanings and intentions that humans realize, with their historical frustrations and fulfillments.

There are at least two serious problems of thinkability in this thought. One is that eternity is a mode of being that transcends our ordinary means of comprehension. A being free of all temporal limitation is after all only emptily conceivable, just as the thought of unlimited power and wisdom that led our minds in that direction was merely a reach. (Yes, I can think of some items as time-free, such as mathematical forms, but that a triangle is always on hand in form-fashion does not mean that the triangle *is* eternally in the way that God is supposed to be; for God is the basis of existence as well as form, and of *all* existence and *all* form. And yes, I can *infer* a necessary basis of everything that exists; but beyond admitting the sheer unavoidability at the base of existence, there is no rational compulsion to attribute any agentic characteristics to a supposed eternal being.)[24]

The other problem is that a responsible God must be a historically active God. A God sited strictly in eternity cannot be in any sort of reciprocating relation with anyone else (although it can be blindly *said* that God is in changing relations with creatures from God's own supratemporal yet

---

22. Asserted in many of Kierkegaard's texts, including *Practice in Christianity*, trans. Howard V. Hong and Edna H. Hong (Princeton: Princeton University Press, 1991), 140.

23. Emmanuel Levinas, "The Trace of the Other," trans. Alfonso Lingis, in *Deconstruction in Context*, ed. Mark C. Taylor (Chicago: University of Chicago Press, 1986), 345–59, 359. This can be taken as a figure for the "extreme vigilance" of ethically aroused consciousness (*Totality and Infinity*, trans. Alfonso Lingis [Pittsburgh: Duquesne University Press, 1969], 285).

24. There is an impressive consensus on this point among the classic philosophical theologians of the Abrahamic traditions. See David Burrell, *Knowing the Unknowable God: Ibn Sina, Maimonides, Aquinas* (Notre Dame: University of Notre Dame Press, 1986).

not static base).²⁵ This creates a dilemma, if an adequately awesome divinity must have the ontological perfection of eternity but also must be the perfection of responsibility. Theology in the Israelite tradition can say that the revealed covenanting God is a historical emanation from eternity, which is a different relation to the eternal ground than the general dependence of everything that exists, but not inconsistent with that general dependence. God's responsibility for and to ourselves is designed in eternity because we, and God's relationship with us, are all envisioned eternally; the responsibility plays out in history along with our life-careers.

Perhaps it does not matter whether the divine version of full responsibility could possibly obtain; what matters is that it shows a direction in which our aspirations for fuller human responsibility can properly run, toward a sound rootedness and comprehensiveness. But it may also point out a pitfall: a human agent could take too much responsibility, assuming too much control and wisdom, with too little respect for the contingent responses of other agents. One of the reasons for a general presumption of limitation in a responsibility regime is to protect us from hubris and tyranny. In support of that spirit of limitation, the idea of a divine being that is uniquely fully responsible may free us from the inappropriate goal of assuming an overfull responsibility ourselves—or, disastrously overshooting, it may free us from responsibility altogether. Kongzi aimed for a strongly rooted yet properly balanced relationship with a highest responsible agency, affiliating himself with it while acknowledging its transcendence.

> The Master said, "I would prefer not speaking." Zi Gong said, "If you, Master, do not speak, what shall we, your disciples, have to record?" The Master said, "Does Heaven speak? The four seasons pursue their courses, and all things are continually being produced, but does Heaven say anything?" (*Lunyu* 17.19)

Another sayable, though only problematically thinkable, possibility is that *all* agents are eternal. Each agent's principle-of-a-life or "soul" resides at ontological headquarters with the world's other necessary elements, and on that basis—which includes the souls' eternal relations with each other and (for theists) with God, with varying degrees of responsiveness (in the sense of one's plan for life being determined partly by others' plans) and

---

25. I allude to such proposals as those of Alan G. Padgett in *God, Eternity, and the Nature of Time* (New York: St. Martin's, 1992) and Garrett J. DeWeese in *God and the Nature of Time* (Aldershot: Ashgate, 2004).

consistency across those relations—they sponsor their variously responsible and irresponsible actions in time, thus manifesting the grounds for their eternally deserved praise or blame. This Neoplatonic conception, revived in Leibniz's monadology, still informs Kant's conception of a noumenal self as the nonnatural principle of ethical agency.[26] For Kant it solves the central problem that the agent, all of whose actions belong to the spatiotemporal-causal fabric of nature, must be autonomous and free at every juncture to do the right thing—a necessary condition for holding an agent responsible. (The noumenal self is also a theoretical interpretation of a commonsense summative conception of an agent's character: "*He* could not have done that, *that is not who he is*.") This eternal anchoring of responsibility provides a full alignment of the agent with the agent's own version of a prosocial, collaborative stance, but paradoxically seems to remove any ultimate *giving* or *taking* of responsibility—we simply are what we are, and our intentions and actions display what we are—or allows for it in an incomprehensible way that a narrative image could only misleadingly represent.

(Imagine two brilliant chess masters, well versed in each other's careers, who mentally play a whole game in a flash as their eyes meet. They immediately understood how *that* game would go. Did they *play* the game? Not in the normal sense; they shared a sort of architectural conception of it. Now, can we imagine that they flash-play on a second occasion with a different outcome? If this is possible, it is because their chess-player personae are multipotential—in the second game, perhaps player 1 is more defensive and player 2 is more audacious. It seems that Kantian eternal agents must be conceived as similarly multipotential, free within their noumenal dispositions, to allow for character improvement or conversion.[27] Eternity is not solid like a rock; as Plotinus suggested, it shimmers like a fire.)[28]

These different models of full responsibility respond to different human attitudes and cognitive styles. There would be one best model only if there were one best kind of human mind. The worldly ideal of a full portfolio of

---

26. On the problematic relationship in Kant between the noumenal grounding and phenomenal enactment of human intentions see Steven G. Smith, "Meaningful Moral Freedom: An Improved Kantian View," *International Philosophical Quarterly* 57 (June 2017): 155–72.

27. Kant, *Religion within the Boundaries of Mere Reason*, AA 6:47, 66–77.

28. Plotinus, *Enneads* V.4.2.

responsibilities and the metaphysico-religious ideal of eternal responsibility both have an affinity with the preference for limiting and balancing responsibilities; the other ideals appeal more to ambition, whether for self-realization or sympathy or rational control. I think that this is our best result, in this part of our inquiry: to see how the ideals are diversely attractive rather than to consolidate them or bolster the case for any at the expense of others. One might be compellingly inclined by a certain mode of responsibility to prefer one of these ideals. For example, the Kantian ideal speaks powerfully to and for ethical responsibility. But if we had sought to resonate with historical responsibility we might have embraced eternal responsibility as its perfected form, or perhaps a Gandhian ideal of being a great inheritor and adapter of cultural heritage, a "person of the age." In this way, too, the deep pluralism of responsibility is confirmed, even as its structure is recognized.

Spirits of Responsibility

The concern for responsibility is practical in a technical way, as a concern with getting needed things done, and practical also in a spiritual way in being a concern that we relate to each other with collaborative appreciation, staying invested in our interdependence. Thus there are two prime motivations of full responsibility ideals: hope for adequate solutions of all our problems, and ambition for the highest grade of socially engaged agency in dealing with our problems. These motivations are intersecting and mutually qualifying. If we are serious promoters of responsibility, we want neither a monarchic problem-solver sidelining the rest of us nor a cheery team of comrades who are useless.

An apt expression for our affirmative orientation to sharing is "spiritual," and accordingly an apt term for an enthusiastic or considerate way of doing things together is "spirit." There is a familiar conceptual alternative: one can posit that human subjects are cognizant of "values" of social relation and responsibility. But the "values" approach, though not without warrant, and despite its great intellectual convenience in many sorts of conversation, deceptively positions us as autonomous individual perceivers of possible directive touchstones rather than as members already of compelling relationships with other beings. In actuality we are moved, in something like the way the trees are moved together by the wind, to maintain mutually rewarding ways—when possible, *more* mutually rewarding ways—of sharing our existence in the world. Living this way, all forms of prosocial guidance have directive interest for us, and some have strict imperativeness. Customs can be perpetuated, laws can be adopted, virtues can be celebrated, and quasi-objective "values" can be posited, whenever this is helpful, as reminders of our insights about our sharing project. More basically important than any of these particular forms of best practice is our comprehensive sense of what we are properly about—what a sports team might call their "signature style of play" and what a society can nurture as its spirit or spirits.

There is an essential mystery in spiritual life for the obvious reason that it involves seeking, finding, and maintaining a genuine intentional concurrence with other agents who are free and incalculable. The purest example is in the dyad of lovers, irresistibly united by their spirit of love but at the same time excruciatingly aware that they have neither control of the relationship nor definitive knowledge of their motives. Something has them in its grip with a force as strong as life itself and a character as definite as their physical bodies; yet at certain moments the thing seems to have vanished, or to have changed surprisingly. On the large scale of a society, "law-abiding" is a mysterious style of concurrence for agents who long to go their own way and often do so; "freedom-loving" is mysterious for agents who often want predictability and security in their lives; and "peace-loving" is mysterious for agents whose peaceful moods alternate with harsh self-assertion. While appeals to these spirits may be platitudinous or in bad faith, the spirits themselves are powerful—they do in fact massively inspire conscientious choice and action—and in their absence the life of a society would be very different, if the society could function humanely at all (in what ways then *would* agents show consideration for each other, and what mutually affirming ways of acting *would* be available and sufficiently motivating?).

A spirit is, for the individual, a livable desirable life, desirable in being a felicitous plan for the sharing of life; an instituted ensemble of related spirits is a culture in which any number can dwell. (For example, spirits of dramaturgy, direction, performance, and set construction contribute to an inclusive spirit and indeed a culture of theater.) As a direction, a spirit is a rectitude, a standard to which relationships must conform (like respect for fellow citizens in the spirit of democracy); as a vitality, it is an optimism about reward in relationships. As we have observed about responsibility, spirit is a good-making condition for choice and action without guaranteeing the best.

In a society like ours that is animated partly by spirits of responsibility, it is possible to commend some choices, actions, styles of action, and agents as responsible and to criticize others as irresponsible. We can equally say—and this makes a good pairing, as a reminder that spirits must share spiritual space—that in a society like ours animated partly by spirits of enjoyment, it is possible to affirm some choices, actions, styles of action, and agents as joyous ("We must see the new Pixar movie!") and to criticize others as wet blankets.

Following the ideas we have of joy, we initiate each other into good times; following the ideas we have of serious collaborative engagement, we initiate each other into forms of responsibility. The premise of initiation is that the initiate is on the way to a *fuller* participation in a spirit, with the fuller discovery of subjectivity, agency, and relationship that the spirit supports. The progress toward fuller participation is endless: there is always some occasion of joy like the Iowa State Fair that I have yet to experience and some important function like being a ship's lookout that I have yet to take charge of. So an ideal of full responsibility cannot require that I have been fully initiated into a spirit of responsibility in the sense that I have no further discoveries to make or competencies to achieve; it requires only that I be well oriented and properly invested in realms of discovery that are proper to me.

What realms of discovery about action sharing *are* proper to me? There is a conventional wisdom about fulfilling standard worldly roles, but in religious perspective—somewhat surprisingly espoused by Aristotle—our spiritual aptitude connects us with divinity and eternity. "Nor ought we to obey those who enjoin that a man should have man's thoughts and a mortal the thoughts of mortality, but we ought so far as possible to achieve immortality and do all that man may to live in accordance with the highest thing in him."[29] It is true that for Aristotle the highest life is purely contemplative and not involved in action. But religious people generally tend to find a noble occupation for humans in fulfilling a role in the great divine work of world-making. In Christianity, although it is theologically contentious to speak of human collaboration with God, there is normally an appeal to play a certain proper part in the economy of God's work, such as in the apostle Paul's exhortation that everyone do their own kind of work as a member of the body of Christ (Romans 12:4–8) building on the one sound foundation that is Christ (1 Corinthians 3:7–15).[30] The divine and

---

29. Aristotle, *Nicomachean Ethics* X.7 1177b30. And this: "It is strange if someone thinks that politics or practical wisdom is the most excellent kind of knowledge, unless man is the best thing in the cosmos" (1141a20–22).

30. For a model Christian disagreement see John Paul II, *Of Human Work* [*Laborem Exercens*], Washington: United States Catholic Conference, 1981), and Stanley Hauerwas,

human contributions are asymmetrical, but there is still room for a divinely Directed human responsibility that is the highest of all responsibilities. This is part of "living in the Spirit."

The Protestant thinker Paul Tillich interprets Paul's metaphors of membership in a body and building on the foundation of Christ as the "theonomous" mode of life in which agents are unified with the ground of their being. Insofar as anything salvific is being done in our world, the ground of our being is present in the world as the acting Spirit that rectifies and animates all spirits. "The *nomos* (law) effective in it is the directedness of the self-creation of all life under the dimension of the Spirit toward the ultimate in being and meaning," where the various hampering estrangements of human existence are overcome.[31] In Tillich's conception we are not dominated by this greatest Spirit—that would be heteronomy, an estranging rule by an other—but we are enabled to participate in the Center of all centers thoughtfully and creatively. The responsibility part of that Spirit should be theonomous as well; that is the significance of the "members of one body" model of practical interdependence, and is reinforced by applying the standards of charity and faithful service to all worldly occupations.

A Great Spirit can be envisioned in various ways, not necessarily theistic. The *Zeitgeist* could be taken seriously again, in its directively serious depth—for example, in the Black Lives Matter and Me Too movements of the late 2010s. Democracy, socialism, and nationalism have been taken this way. Indeed, any directive vision at all, even that of a single book, or speech, or slogan, will function as a Great Spirit if it overridingly animates and steers a group's thought and practice. The overtly religious versions of Spirit will be distinguished by a footing in eternity and a transformation of the agentic situation—like the change from the rationalized interdependency model of responsible officeholders to the model of living in the body of the Savior, or the imperishable Self, or the Way. Ambitious political spirits might emulate the religious model, substituting history for eternity, or might instead take a procedural turn toward open access to collaboration, as in Habermasian discourse or Rawlsian public reason.

"Work as Co-Creation: A Critique of a Remarkably Bad Idea," in *Co-Creation and Capitalism: John Paul II's Laborem Exercens*, ed. John W. Houck and Oliver F. Williams (Lanham: University Press of America, 1983), 42–58.
31. Paul Tillich, *Systematic Theology*, Vol. 3 (Chicago: University of Chicago Press, 1963), 249; see also *Systematic Theology*, Vol. 1 (Chicago: University of Chicago Press, 1951), 84.

Your Vocation (in another sense)

> Loyalty to whatever in the established environment makes a life of excellence possible is the beginning of all progress.
>
> —John Dewey[32]

You have to develop an eye for them, and weigh them for their relative priority, but you live in a spiritual environment in which many well-defined forms of responsibility clearly make a more excellent life possible for you and everyone you care about. If you are generally loyal to the project of making the best of life then you will take on, or not try to evade, the responsibilities you think you can handle.

The question of your responsible life as a whole, your whole life as responsible, is on another plane, however. In theory, contemplating the responsibility dimension of life gives you a chance to shift from reacting to the responsibility opportunities and claims that present themselves to deciding proactively how responsible you want to be. To arrive at the most satisfactory decision, you would assess the whole range of opportunities for action sharing that are available to you as you endeavor to actualize your life on the basis of infinitely complex past realities and future possibilities; to guide this assessment, you would specify optimally all of your general practical commitments as reflective of your spiritual willingness to let yourself in for issues of relationship. But responsibility no more than spirituality is an issue that can be settled in a wholly self-initiated way; it has the nature of a response. A fully responsible life was not built as such; it got filled in.

You may be moved to respond, then, to the particular conflicts and uncertainties that emerge in your experience of responsibilities by contemplating the biggest picture; you may need some vision of a satisfactory whole of life to settle your responsible mind. If you do form such a response, you will almost certainly be responding favorably to a vision, or at least an appreciable attitude, that is already on offer in your environment—perhaps an ideal of passionate political activism (guided by a certain ideology), or of religious devotion (within a certain organization), or a popular image of a solid citizen or trend-setting celebrity. With an established option comes a presumption of time-tested human adequacy and the welcome prospect

---

32. John Dewey, *Human Nature and Conduct* (New York: Henry Holt, 1922), 21.

of sharing your life project with others. Nevertheless you are deciding for yourself. The life that you decide you can willingly live is, let us say, your *vocation*, that term now signifying not the solution of the coherence problem posed by our constant exposure to the calls of pragmatic responsibility but an answer to the question of the most appropriate whole qualification of your life by responsibility.

Your vocation for responsible life could be conceived as your "mission," using the model of a task ordered from a headquarters. A mission assumes a campaign to bring about some important state of affairs, so you will need to adopt some idea about the nature of the campaign, its objective, and the dimensions of your role in it. If you reflect fully on what this situation could be, you will find that you can think of the campaign as historic, possibly even eternal, and that the objective is to realize an optimal world (as a whole history and not merely as a last refinement) in part by drawing on your powers. But whether you can embrace such a view of the situation will depend on whether you can relate it supportively to what you most surely approve of (which should include responsible relationships with the others whom you know best or on whom you most depend—that is, relationships in which responsibility is least doubtful) and whether you can avoid the pitfalls of an abstractly or ideologically eternalizing distortion of responsible life-navigation.

Your vocation could be conceived as the creation of new values, using the Nietzschean model of overcoming humanity as we find it, or a lucid free endorsement of certain existing values, using the Sartrean model of avoiding bad faith. "Values" being not merely occasional and personal preferences but durable and sharable, you would be facing your fellow beings with a proposal for their concurrence, without any enforceable demand or guarantee.

Or your vocation could be conceived as life in a certain spirit. The basic premise of life in a spirit is not that quasi-objective commands or norms exist independently for our reference but that *we* exist; the first practical consideration is not simply that we have free self-determinations to make but that we experience our freedom in the midst of relating to each other in a range of ways. These ways are social habitudes, for an observer, but for us while we are living in such ways, sensitive to the occasion of relationship, they are spirits.

Living in a spirit is experienced as a fullness of life itself—what a good conversation has, what a good party has, and what a heroic team effort has such that each participant's life is additionally energized and complicated by the lives of others. Our interest in fullness in responsibility or joy is drawn by the general fullness of spiritual existence; rather than "grounding" us, it airily sweeps us up. There are proper limits to responsibilities, just as there are to good times, but the limits are auxiliary to the expansive adventure.

Epilogue

"What have I to do?" . . .
"You shall not withhold yourself."

—Martin Buber[1]

Am I doing enough? Are you? Are we? Which is more responsible: to keep pressing for new realizations, or to settle now on a reasonable "enough" so that we can deal with what is on our plate? There is no final answer. The principle of responsibility pushes us in both directions, toward unlimited responsiveness and all-out trying but also toward the calculable and feasible (fairly shared).

If you place yourself in a scene of infinite demand, like running for president or bringing humanitarian aid to a large suffering population, the question of doing enough may not arise because you will be constantly busy with what you know you need to do. Yet agents in these situations are sometimes haunted more strongly than anyone by the feeling that they could have done more. This is partly because they are engaged with huge demands, but it also reflects their seriousness about actual performance as opposed to mere orientation. They assess their fulfillment of responsibilities *to* their fellow agents by what they have been responsible *for* in the causal sense, the difference they have made in the world, subject to exacting standards of best practice. They may have produced results that the rest of us welcome and admire, but since they have assigned themselves *roles* that *were* demanding enough—at the top of the scale of practical ambition—they may never have been able to *do* enough to fulfill those roles. The lifesaver never

---

1. Martin Buber, "What Is to Be Done?" [1919], in *Pointing the Way*, ed. Maurice S. Friedman, 109–11 (New York: Harper & Row, 1963), 109.

saves all lives. Meanwhile those of us who are able to do enough in our accepted roles are prompted by the great examples to wonder what more we should ask of ourselves, what stronger realizations we can stand to have, and what disappointments we can bear.

"Political society exists for the sake of noble actions" (Aristotle).[2] We are still developing this idea. The arrangement of life that we could accept as optimal, that would be an unsurpassable political victory, would support all agents fulfilling in their own ways a humanly interesting full portfolio of serious responsibilities.

On the base of everyday collaboration we have made great experiments in enlarged responsibility including ethics, with its extension of responsible reckoning to all possible situations; democracy, with its determination to share active responsibility for worldly affairs among all members of a community; and religion, with its extension of responsibility from worldly affairs to the whole of time or eternity.

The initiation into responsibility is immeasurably important for our new members—no less important than their initiation into joy. Talking about the theme too much is numbing. But parents and teachers cannot plan too carefully for experiences of serious encounter with fellow agents. And everyone in our society, whatever their own stances, should be ready for friendly discussion when the young are ready to relate to our great experiments of ethics, democracy, and religion.

The great experiments are powered by a confidence we have gained in working together, but they are also driven by longing. So much is missing, so much is wrong. Who *will be* responsible for putting our world in better order? It is the question of every political election and implicitly the question in much moral deliberation and religious observance. The great question asked in *Night and Fog* as we contemplate Auschwitz, "Who is responsible?" is a pivot: one cannot help thinking of the causality and attributability of the huge crime, but then one is overtaken by the importance of trying in the future to persuade agents to accept responsibility for checking evil and enabling them to succeed.

---

2. *Politics* III.IX, trans. Benjamin Jowett, accessed October 20, 2021, http://classics.mit.edu/Aristotle/politics.html.

Appendix 1

Notes on Ethical Responsibility

The main purpose of this discussion is to mark some limitations of ethical reckoning that can be seen more clearly once we have conceived ethical responsibility as a form of responsibility distinct from other major forms.

Ethical Apriorism and Its Limitations

It seems that many of us are brought to ethical responsibility, to the extent that we are, in this way. As children, our understanding of action and the sharing of action expands in two stages. First, at animal learning level, we gather from the positive and negative reactions of others what kinds of actions are good ("*That's* a good girl") and bad. We can generalize to do *that* again or not to do *that*. Then we learn morality by being told, ideally-descriptively, "*We* don't do that," and prescriptively, "*You must not* do that." The force of this advice depends on understanding the reference of "we," which soberingly assembles everyone you ultimately have to deal with, and a broader reference of "that" applicable to any number of agents and occasions—"You must not do *that* ever again, not even if someone else is doing *that*; no one (in your agent category) should do *that*." At this stage we are still not being given responsibility, we are simply being constrained; if a reason is given, it is only to impress on us the constraint, implying that it has been thoroughly considered by the order giver or thoroughly discussed by the community. To assert or acknowledge a moral *duty* formalizes this kind of constraint. A duty positions us as accountable to the "we" in a completely asymmetric way. It remains nonnegotiable when we become one of its adult enforcers.

We can speak of specific responsibilities *for* the morally constrained life. A community leader may be assigned the role of enforcing moral standards. Parents may agree on different responsibilities in bringing up their children. With such responsibilities come occasions for individual moral problem solving. Yet they are instruments of the given moral program, strictly subordinated to it.

As *reflective* and *reasoning* adults, our position is different; we seek and may be provided general standards for our conduct that we ideally agree with and can independently adapt to new situations. On these terms it becomes *generally* appropriate to speak of responsibility, and because of its links with reflection and discussion it is more appropriate to qualify our responsibility—here, our responsibility to refrain from acts that we take to be generally unapprovable in our community—as "ethical" rather than as "moral." I will therefore interpret statements about "moral responsibility" as pertaining to ethical responsibility, except in cases where what is really meant is (1) moral duty as such, or (2) responsibility as such—for instance, in qualifying political responsibility as moral because it is responsibility. I beg the indulgence of anyone who, for other reasons, draws the "moral"/"ethical" distinction differently.[1]

Ethical responsibility will often take precedence over moral virtue or dutifulness because, as an issue decided by individuals in reasonable discussion, its commitments will tend to be more *humane*—more deeply and broadly considerate of the beings affected by moral constraints—than the commitments of received morality; for the same reason, the perspective of ethical responsibility can be *cosmopolitan*, supporting critical discussion across the boundaries of moral communities, whereas the priority for morality is the integrity of an existing community. But if the moral cohesion of an existing community seems threatened, moral responsibility will take precedence for everyone committed to defending that community. We see this struggle for precedence today between moral and ethical perspectives on sexuality.

The point of a conscious ethical stance is to prepare the self-governing individual agent for any eventuality and to make clear for all agents what they can require from each other and justify to each other. Its perspective

---

[1]. Notably, I am differing from the Hegelian association of the "moral" with the universal and the "ethical" with the concretely determined. But I am far from alone in distinguishing an intuitive and presumptive "morality" from a rationally reflected and argued "ethics."

is forward-looking, counterfactual, and universal: "What would be the right thing to do if one were in that kind of situation?" It is apriorist: knowing the universally valid ethical principles, the rational agent knows something crucial about how to make justifiable choices whatever the pragmatic data are. A Plan is always in place. (I do not say that the ethical agent always knows how to make justifiable choices, since the data may be somewhat intractable and the ethical conditions on justification may be necessary yet not sufficient for justification.) In the ideal ethical community that collectively sponsors the ethical project, agents are held responsible for following ethical norms; it is never acceptable to act without ethical permission. By implication, it is never acceptable to be unable to invoke a sound justifying principle, whether that be to universalize policies of action or to promote the greatest total happiness. The ethical community can insist on the agent's being conversant with abstract rules or values that demonstrably hold whether or not a given person or group thinks so.

It could be objected that many agents do not actually live in an ethical community, so defined, and that for some purposes no one does. Our society would not be viable if we did not live in a *moral* community in which authoritative constraints are widely accepted, that is clear; but the "ethical community" that would require acting on principle is merely a helpful fiction for the reflective minority, like "the Republic of Letters," and cannot be binding on all.

The objection contains a true perception of the limited *reach* of ethical *reasoning* in practice, but I think we cannot limit the *jurisdiction* of ethical *responsibility* on this ground inasmuch as the ideal of reflective participation in determining what is right and wrong is compelling for all rational agents for everyone they deal with, not only for themselves. Rational agents have a necessary interest in extending the circle of ethical discussion to as many other agents as possible in order to achieve the best alignment of their ideal with the actual community of interdependent action sharing. If agents do not share the relevant convictions, a crucial authenticity will often be lacking in normatively sensitive agreements among agents and in praise and blame.

But another sort of limitation does apply to the jurisdiction of ethical responsibility in principle, and that is its relative blindness to facts—not to facts in their specificity (for one can specify the referents of ethical judgments and their categories to any desired degree) or to facts as requisite for meaningful ethical evaluations (as for understanding how slavery in its many forms is an evil), but to facts in their status as being *actually* engaged by agents or *really* established as conditions for further meaningful action, as opposed to being *possibly* encountered. This is not to say that ethical evaluation does not touch actuality or reality at all. But strictly as an ethical subject, I know only that slavery is wrong and do not yet fully understand many of the conscientious choices people had to make in the midst of enslavement or how people living after enslavement would most responsibly build on that setup of their present.

I assume that ethical apriorism is fully appropriate for *ethics* in the stricter sense that distinguishes ethical from other major forms of responsibility. I have no new case to make for an ethical principle; my agenda is to support critiques of ethical apriorism that arise from other apprehensions of responsibility, not from alternative versions of ethics. For this purpose, it is useful to locate the telltale limits beyond which ethical reckoning loses its grip, unable to engage the actual and the real as such, in the formalist and consequentialist theories that most clearly assert the apriorism of ethics.

Kantian formalism requires commitment to the fair procedure of universalizing one's policies of action. Ethically eligible goals are whichever goals pass through the filter of strict fairness. Utilitarian consequentialism commits to the supreme goal of maximizing happiness (the total satisfaction of preferences) and endorses whichever policies of action pass the test of promoting this end better than alternative approaches.[2]

Kant believes that in practice we commonly determine right and wrong by applying the universalization test. Telling the truth and promise keeping are paradigmatic for universalizable policy. When one considers lying or breaking a promise, it is immediately evident that one would be unfairly exempting oneself from a necessarily universal rule. These are "perfect duties" to which there are no exceptions. Some choices, however, are ethically sensitive without being deducible from a properly universalized rule. For example, we have choices concerning how to be helpful to others in need. It is demonstrable that we ought to be willing to help, since it would be unfair to deny to others what we would inevitably want from them, but it cannot be determined in advance to whom, when, and how we ought to be helpful except in urgent life-saving cases. Thus benevolence is an "imperfect duty." We have reached the limit of reason's ability to prescribe the right action.

If we have a broader view of the issue of right action, we can see "imperfect duty" as a doorway from formalist ethics into other dimen-

---

[2]. I prefer the more subjective "happiness" or "satisfaction of preferences" formulation of utilitarianism to the "intrinsic value" formulation, which seems to me to disguise utilitarianism's weakness in explaining what is worthy of being preferred.

sions of responsibility.³ The apriorist ethical legislator uses the category of imperfect duty to allow latitude for approvable options. But in some actual situations, subject to historical conditions, responsible action does not have all that latitude; choice may be responsibly determined, yet not by general principle. If a fellow agent needs my help in an action we jointly have in hand, I do not have latitude to decide to be a helpful person differently. If I am a member of one historical community oppressed by another, I do not have latitude to relate to members of the two communities in exactly the same ways. Even if I can find a sound ethical rule to support my right course of action, that is not the kind of constraint I start with.

Meanwhile Mill's utilitarianism allows that we commonly do the right thing by following traditional moral rules, and that our attachment to these rules is a morally valuable sentiment for the most part. On the ethical plane these rules and feelings have their justification in promoting the general happiness. But no constraint, except for the supreme utilitarian rule, is necessarily justified always. Especially vulnerable to utilitarian override are the "special obligations" that agents have to their families or friends, or to their countries. Although particular relationships are subjectively important, and technically important as well in certain systems of practice (as in caregiving within families), they are not ethically sacrosanct. The long-term demand of utilitarianism is to revise our feelings and practices whenever that conduces to greater happiness.

"Special obligations" is a doorway from utilitarian ethics into other dimensions of responsibility.⁴ Utilitarianism requires that ethical decision makers always choose in favor of increasing the total happiness, which requires being free to override the demands of concrete relationships. Practical attachments to particular collaborators do not generate an all-things-considered ethical constraint. But in pragmatic and historical perspectives concrete collaborative relationships do generate ideal constraints. If a fellow agent or a historical community seems to need my loyal action now, I am not free to decide to promote the general happiness along a different line

---

3. For a clear ethicization of pragmatic responsibility as "imperfect duty" see Kant, *Groundwork*, AA 4:421–23, and *The Doctrine of Virtue*, and Patricia Greenspan, "Making Room for Options: Moral Reasons, Imperfect Duties, and Choice," *Social Philosophy and Policy* 27 (July 2010): 181–205.

4. On the problems special obligations raise for utilitarianism see Diane Jeske, "Special Obligations," *The Stanford Encyclopedia of Philosophy*, ed. Edward N. Zalta (Fall 2019), secs. 4 and 7, accessed October 20, 2021, https://plato.stanford.edu/archives/fall2019/entries/special-obligations/.

of action. I am not free not merely because I am fondly partial or dependent, or because I find value in a particular relationship,[5] but because I am responsible. Perhaps my multiple forms of responsibility are reconcilable, but ethics alone cannot guarantee that solution.

Both the formalist and consequentialist forms of ethical apriorism raise the specter of an insane infinity of responsibility: the conscientious agent would be required to figure out an optimal solution for every practical question in life, which would require infinite application to (1) analyzing action and consequences to identify all the variables that one needs to be thoughtful about, lest opportunities for better practice be missed; and (2) discovering all relevant facts in the world, including facts about the intentions and experiences of all other agents, in order to fashion a type-guided solution for every eventuality. (I am not even bringing up the worry that ethics demands infinite sacrifice of the agent's own material interest. An agent might allow reasonably for his or her own interest—but it would take infinite exertion to work out that answer!) A related specter is one of inhumanly cold impartiality, which could take the form either of legalism or opportunism.

We have a basic protection against the insanity of infinite responsibility in the structure of responsibility as such: to have responsibility is to be subject to a role prescription, and an agent's life never wholly coincides with a chosen or assigned role. If it did, we could not discuss with the agent how the role is being, or should be, fulfilled; the agent would not have a free perspective on it. We instantly sense an extraordinary and unsustainable condition when the difference between agent and role is suspended, even if the role, and sincerity in it, are of huge importance: it is alarming if an actor really becomes a character, it is dangerous if a leader says "I am the nation," it is sad when a tombstone says only "Loving wife."

We also have a protection against an overweening impartiality in ethical apriorism, with its commitment to perfectly general agent-neutral standards, in the particular loyalties of other forms of responsibility. In an ethical debate it may seem that a dash of legalism (unconditional commitment to following properly formed rules) is the needed antidote for reckless opportunism—and so one should be faithful to one's spouse, no matter how others are disadvantaged by that; or that a dash of opportunism (larger vision of the

---

5. I do not deny that finding value in a relationship gives a *reason* to be specially helpful to certain others, as Samuel Scheffler argues in "Relationships and Responsibilities," in *Boundaries and Allegiances* (Oxford: Oxford University Press, 2001), 97–110.

stakes, flexibility of approach) is the antidote for callous legalism—and so one should lie to a would-be murderer if that would probably save a life. The two ethical approaches do complement one another. But we also need help of another kind. To provide adequately for nonreckless and noncallous conduct we need to anchor some of our responsibilities in particular persons, situations, communities, and histories. It is indeed crucially supportive of responsible conduct that a Kantian must respect everyone's rational nature and that a utilitarian must care about everyone's happiness, and that their positions do not discriminate between agents at the level of the basic entitlement to consideration and the requirement to be considerate. We need ethics for this kind of scruple. But the other side of that impartial affirmation of everyone is an indifference that in some contexts is irresponsible.

Alternative Positionings of Ethics

Two other influential programs in ethics that are in instructive tension with ethical apriorism are virtue ethics and the ethics of care. Seen rightly, each conception illuminates the bounds of ethical responsibility.

Aristotle and Virtue Ethics

Along with identifying favored or disfavored types of action, a community will endorse qualities like "brave" and "honest" and stigmatize qualities like "cowardly" and "hypocritical," encouraging its members to be or not be those kinds of person. The greatest classical ethicist, Aristotle, drawing on the Greek moral discourse of virtues and vices, locates the reliable guide to right choices in the wisdom that finds the right settings for those socially sensitive personal qualities.

It is possible to take up Aristotelian "virtue ethics" as an ethical alternative to modern deontology and consequentialism, the idea being that we can generally determine the right thing to do by considering what the virtuous person would do. But there are reasons to think that this approach misunderstands the program of the *Nicomachean Ethics*.[6]

There is an ambiguity right off the bat in contemplating an "ethics of virtue" if, as modern ethicists tend to assume, the purpose of ethics is to

---

6. Aristotle, *Nicomachean Ethics*, trans. Harris Rackham (Cambridge, MA: Harvard University Press, 1934).

determine which actions are justifiable. For actions motivated by virtue do not seem to be coextensive with actions with ethical justification, nor is there a necessary demand that they be, inasmuch as the main point of admiring or despising people is to determine membership and rank, not to prescribe actions, and the main point of ethical justification is to prescribe actions that ought to be performed no matter who performs them. Nevertheless the ethical importance of virtue is clearly immense. Our character qualities and the qualities of our fellow agents determine more than any other factor the likelihood of approvable actions being performed. (This is true even if the classical Chinese Legalists are right and the most important character quality is docility in submitting to state regulation.)[7] More intimately, the character qualities of agents determine the better or worse tenor of our partnership in life as we experience it at any moment—whether it is trustful or distrustful, harmonious or discordant, encouraging or depressing, instructive or distracting. Further, it can be argued that the best hope for acceptable *interpretations* and *implementations* of ethical principle, in the many cases where ethical principles can be turned different ways or solutions must be somewhat innovative and intuitive, lies in agents of virtuous character, whose good dispositions protect against many ethical misfortunes and are always good in themselves. I hope to have shown in chapter 1 that our assumptions and aspirations regarding authentically responsible conduct sink a root in good character, which aligns responsibility-oriented approaches to life guidance with virtue ethics. The lack of a tight correspondence between approvable character qualities and approvable actions may be taken as an indication that virtues transcend modes of responsibility; virtue theory is perhaps better seen as a part of general responsibility theory than as a version of ethical theory.

Confusingly for readers of his "ethics," Aristotle makes it clear that virtue does not run only in an ethical channel. He portrays at least three different virtuous lives: that of an ordinary citizen, that of the political leader, and that of the philosopher. The political leader's virtue could perhaps be encompassed by ethics if we take Aristotle's moralistic view of politics; but

---

7. "When the sage rules the state, he does not depend on people to do good for him, but utilizes their inability to do wrong. If he depends on people to do good for him, we cannot even count ten within the state, but if he utilizes the people's inability to do wrong, the whole country may be regulated. . . . People are originally submissive to power and it is truly easy to subdue people with power." *The Han Feizi*, in *A Source Book in Chinese Philosophy*, ed. Wing-Tsit Chan (Princeton: Princeton University Press, 1963), 252–61, 253, 258.

the philosopher is another story. The life of philosophical study (*theoria*) is praised as the life that most fully realizes "the virtue of the best part of us" (1177a14) and as superior to other good lives on grounds that do not seem prosocial at all: it is more pleasant, more self-sufficient, more leisurely, and links the agent to that which is greater than human beings, popularly pictured as the "blessed" life of the gods (1178b).

To be virtuous is to be admirable, not necessarily to be responsible.[8] We might wish to say that humans fall short of excellence if they fail in responsibility, but Aristotle's ethics is not designed to make that point. His survey of the virtues is guided much more by concerns for self-control and self-satisfaction. Tellingly, the virtue related to the assignment of honor, *megalopsuchia*, has to do with one's sense of the honor one deserves rather than with honoring others (1107b).[9] It is true that several important Aristotelian virtues clearly overlap with our general ideal of responsible relations among agents, including truthfulness and justice; and Aristotle's politician is conspicuously responsible in being dedicated to promoting the good life for the whole community. But the paramount virtue of theoretical wisdom and the supremely self-sufficient, leisured life of the thinker devoted to *theoria* seem remote from responsibility as we think of it. Aristotle implicitly dismisses the idea that the supremely excellent gods would bear responsibility: "all forms of [morally] virtuous conduct seem trifling and unworthy of" them (1178b).

One can imagine—at a stretch—two Aristotelian appeals for *theoria* involving responsibility. One is that we would be letting ourselves and the human race down if we did not fulfill our best potential (1178a). Another is that neglecting *theoria* would be failing to give due regard to God or the gods, since "the man who pursues intellectual activity . . . is also the man most beloved of the gods" (1179a). I will not push those thoughts further. Aristotle's model of a plurality of forms of virtue, of which moral virtue is but one, is not a theory of plural forms of responsibility. It is at most a premonition of one.

---

8. Note the emphasis on display: "The liberal man will need wealth in order to do liberal actions, and so indeed will the just man in order to discharge his obligations (since mere intentions are invisible, and even the unjust pretend to wish to act justly); and the brave man will need strength if he is to perform any action displaying his virtue; and the temperate man opportunity for indulgence: otherwise how can he, or the possessor of any other virtue, show that he is virtuous?" Aristotle 1178a.

9. On honoring others, see Aristotle 1165a.

Ethics of Care

The so-called ethics of care became an ethical theory option in the wake of Carol Gilligan's 1982 study of women's moral perspectives on abortion, *In a Different Voice*.[10] Gilligan found that a concern for the well-being of particular persons and relationships was consistently in the foreground of women's moral reasoning, in contrast to an emphasis on rights and formal justice in men's. She argued that the pattern observed in women is not merely a weakness or a female bias, as it tends to be seen in male-dominated ethics, but an equally valid approach to moral life complementary with a justice-oriented approach. Other feminists, including Nel Noddings and Virginia Held, embraced care as a properly dominant approach to the moral life.[11]

Like Aristotle's virtue theory, the orientation to care is agent-relative and allows variation in individual agents' solutions, but it involves a very different agent ideal, a relationship-centered counterpoint to Aristotle's program of self-perfection. Caring begins in receptive attention to the needs of another and is confirmed in attachment to the other's well-being and being occupied with meeting the other's needs. For Noddings, caring is a "natural" sensibility and passion,[12] not only an immediate sympathy with others when they are present but also a longing for relatedness. An ethical "best self" ideal of principled agency may be added to our sympathetic feeling to motivate a properly ethical program of caring, but ethical caring remains dependent on natural caring and serves it. If acting as a principled carer requires an agent to harm someone, as in the extreme example of a woman who kills her abusive husband in defense of herself and her children, the agent feels ethically diminished rather than justified.[13]

Significant work has now been done on developing the care perspective into full-fledged ethical and political programs. Although care ethics is needs-oriented rather than rights-oriented, it arguably produces action

---

10. Carol Gilligan, *In a Different Voice* (Cambridge, MA: Harvard University Press, 1982).

11. Nel Noddings, *Caring: A Feminine Approach to Ethics and Moral Education* (Berkeley: University of California Press, 1984); Virginia Held, *The Ethics of Care: Personal, Political, and Global* (Oxford: Oxford University Press, 2006).

12. Noddings, *Caring* 79. She links this idea to Hume's argument for a necessary basis of moral life in natural feeling. David Hume, *An Inquiry Concerning the Principles of Morals* [1751] (Indianapolis: Library of Liberal Arts, 1957), 6.

13. Noddings, *Caring* 102.

prescriptions very similar to those of deontological ethics.[14] But Noddings continues to call attention to the difference between the interest in persons and relationships and the interest in justification and principle. There are telltale divergences between what caring would prompt her to do, prioritizing the needs of the living beings with whom she is presently dealing, and what Kantianism or utilitarianism would require. For example, she says she would tell a lie to protect her cat and will not accept global do-goodism as an ethical priority.[15]

The formula for being the most responsible sort of agent includes both competence and a disposition to be helpful. Aristotelian virtue is above all a cultivation of admirable competence, while ideal caring is above all a cultivation of sincere sympathy: that is a way of placing the two perspectives together in a harness of responsibility. But caring is essentially close to the spirit of responsibility in a way that Aristotelian virtue is not. The project of mastering and effectively using the best means of serving others, including an ego ideal of rational agency, grows naturally out of sincere sympathy, whereas the service of others is a contingent element in the Aristotelian plan for rationally optimized life and is missing altogether from the life considered most blessed.

Like other key terms in our directive discourse, *caring* has a broader and a narrower sense. The narrower sense is powerfully represented by the mother who finds herself in the prototypical role of carer for her newborn; this is an intense case of pragmatic responsibility and can serve as a constant reminder of the peremptory relevance of present practical needs.[16] The ethics of care can be seen as a project of deriving ethical responsibility from pragmatic responsibility. Meanwhile caring in a broader sense can plausibly

---

14. Michael Slote, *The Ethics of Care and Empathy* (New York: Routledge, 2007).

15. Noddings, *The Maternal Factor* (Berkeley: University of California Press, 2010), 236, 239.

16. Consider Hans Jonas's appeal to the newborn as a base for responsibility in *The Imperative of Responsibility*, trans. Hans Jonas and David Herr (Chicago: University of Chicago Press, 1984), 130–34. "The always-acute, unequivocal, and choiceless responsibility which the newborn claims for himself stands out as utterly beyond comparison. The newborn unites in himself the self-accrediting force of being already there and the demanding impotence of being-not-yet; the unconditional end-in-itself of everything alive and the still-have-to-come of the faculties for securing this end. This need-to-become is an in-between, a suspension of helpless being over not-being, which must be bridged by another causality" (134). Noddings's emphasis, in contrast, is on the infant's "sweet" availability for relationship, compelling for one-caring who longs for relationship (*Caring* 52, 89).

be regarded as coextensive with prosociality or spirituality, the general presupposition of all forms of responsibility. The general directive in many of our early promptings by others must have been "You should care" more than "This is the correct type of action." It is caring in this sense that can plausibly be claimed to be a necessary foundation for morality and all humane cooperation.[17] In neither of these senses is the import of caring strictly moral or ethical. Yet proponents of an "ethics of care" have accepted the challenge of formulating a general validation of a disposition that elevates particular relationships over ethical universality and impartiality.[18]

---

17. Held writes: "Care seems to me the most basic of moral values. Without care as an empirically describable practice, we cannot have life at all since human beings cannot survive without it. Without some level of caring concern for other human beings, we cannot have any morality" (79).

18. Held: "As Brian Barry expresses this view, there can be universal rules permitting people to favor their friends in certain contexts . . . but the latter partiality is morally acceptable only because universal rules have already so judged it. The ethics of care, in contrast, is skeptical of such abstraction and reliance on universal rules and questions the priority given to them. To most advocates of the ethics of care, the compelling moral claim of the particular other may be valid even when it conflicts with the requirement usually made by moral theories that moral judgments be universalizable, and this is of fundamental moral importance" (11).

Appendix 2

Notes on Historical Responsibility

The Historical Dimension of Responsibility

I am a college professor. My opportunity to act in this great role—possibly also my doom, if the educational culture changes—I owe largely to the previous envisionings and efforts of many agents in the past. Because I work in the humanities it is natural for me, and a disciplinary scruple as well, to be mindful of the historical context of my work. When I think of defending academic freedom, for example, I think of joining John Dewey in defending academic freedom, which requires further thought about how the situation has developed between his time and mine. Does this mean that I am responsible *to* John Dewey (and certain other past agents) for keeping up the defense of academic freedom?

In one obvious sense I cannot be responsible *to* anyone who no longer exists; I cannot be responsible *for* them either, as they are beyond my power of helping or hurting. In another sense, though, Dewey is still present (he is "relevant"), his legacy is still up for grabs, and I can indeed help or hurt the cause of which he and I are both sponsors. He and I share the intention that our society reap the benefits of academic freedom. If I, as an academic and AAUP member (which means that I have signed on for the program that Dewey supported), do not defend academic freedom when occasion arises to do so, then I am letting my cosponsor down; I am worsening the chances that what we were both working for will be a long-term success.

Suppose I *am* complicit in the decline of the Deweyan academy. It might be that I had a different vision for the academy that was arguably just as good, or a nonacademic vision for my own career that arguably had just as much value. It might be, however, that I just selfishly kept my head down during episodes of censorship. Among the sad aspects of my conduct would be a form of irresponsibility that is distinctively historical, based on my involvement in a long-term compound collaboration.

Suppose instead that I defend the Deweyan academy. I might have pragmatic reasons for doing so based on imminent dangers to some present efforts at my school; I might have ethical reasons based on respect for persons, or contracts, or the truth. But I also might amplify my defense by testifying to the long-term campaign of the AAUP as an essential part of the historic contribution of my profession. Among the strengths of my appeal and my character, then, would be a form of responsibility that is distinctively historical.

When I take the historical perspective, my opportunity to teach is not merely to make an honorable living; it is like the opportunity an athlete has when joining a team in the middle of a memorable season. I depend on predecessors not only for what they have created that I can take over, but for what they have done that I can join with.

The Roots of Historical Responsibility

Historical responsibility in its fully reflected form is highly discretionary and for many people remote. Even academics are in practice quite free not to feel responsible for the history of their profession. But historical responsibility has roots in social life that are not remote at all.

AGENTIC IDENTITY

That I share the world, my theater of action, with other agents gives me compelling reason to keep track of what the others have done; otherwise there is much I would fail to understand practically about my present situation and future prospects. In theory, I would be best equipped if I knew *all* the performed actions (in their contexts) and the implied capacities and intentions of *all* those agents; in practice, I hope to approach this ideal with relatively full knowledge of the agents who most directly impinge on me.

The other agents are not merely phenomena to be studied or things to deal with. In sharing the world practically, we share webs of action that enable and elaborate almost everything interesting that we do; our social mode of life guarantees that our instigations of change in the world and the intentions we form for those actions are extensively interrelated. I need to know the intentions of other agents because I understand that the others are cosponsors of shared actions on which the feasibility and significance of my own actions depend. We are cosponsors in that we have some agreement on doing what we are doing; what we agree about is solidarity (sharing in burdens and benefits) and liberty (sharing out what can be individually appropriated from our efforts). To know that my neighbor does not intend to move the broken-down cars out of his front yard is to know that he and I have different visions for the appearance of our neighborhood and that my home beautification efforts may be somewhat in vain.

I want to talk to my neighbor about the cars; I want to see if we can have a meeting of the minds. *Who* is this fellow? How do I consider him most accurately—not his feelings, but his agency? I know how to acquire some of the knowledge I need: I can learn his name and occupation and place him with a family and a certain array of lifestyles. I can ask other neighbors about their dealings with him and learn about his manner of speaking, his demeanor, his possible plans. I establish *who* he is, as a cosponsor of neighborhood life, on a platform of establishing his *history* as embedded in the larger careers of relevant groups and institutions.

The idea of "who" a person is, this thick and practically charged version of personal identity, implies a necessary connection between being appreciably *someone* and being historically responsible, at least in a causal sense of responsibility. For if I were not supposing that shared conditions for action had been affected over time by the intentions and actions of my neighbor, I would not be able to infer his stance and potential as a cosponsor now. I might get a useful sense of him on first meeting, or from a reported single conversation in which he seemed to display an attitude toward the cars issue, or from finding out that he is the deputy mayor of our town. From several such data points, together with my general knowledge of human nature and culture, I could construct an image of him on which I could predicate a plan of approach. But that would be a far cry from *knowing him*, in the sense that involves being able to speak to who he is and having an overall estimate of him; and it would be better to know him.

(It would be better to know myself, too. But I can press toward this particular encounter without giving much thought to myself, beyond trying to be honest and fair.)

If my neighbor says to me in a challenging way, "You don't know who you're dealing with," then *he* supposes—unless he is bluffing—that his agentic considerability has been built up and manifested historically. But neither in my assessment of him nor in his self-advertisement is there any interest yet in assigning him responsibility for a historical state of affairs. History comes in only as evidence for his practical personality as it now obtains.

Nevertheless, the question of historical significance arises with any showing of a historical performance, and the question of proper continuation: Will he keep on in his irascible independence? Or will he turn over a new leaf and be neighborly? This is an ethical question about better or worse conduct, but it is also a historical question about a better or worse career, and not just one person's career. It sets us both up as potentially responsible for long-term developments: what long-term program has each of us, consciously or not, coherently or not, been carrying out? Intentionality and activity on that scale could fill out the strongest sense of "who" we are.

Involvement

Suppose that my neighbor is indeed the deputy mayor, and that this fact makes it impossible to ignore another historical question, namely, whether he shares responsibility for the recently discovered illegal awarding of contracts by the city administration. Am I dealing with a crook—a crook still enjoying the fruits of a crime? He is on record claiming that he had nothing to do with the impropriety, but further inquiry leads me to think that he must have been *involved*. To think of him as "involved" in "what was going on" is not only to think of a causal historical responsibility that goes toward determining who he is and what he might be blamed for, it is also to be moved to assign responsibility to him to act properly with regard to the continuation of that significant accumulation of action.

The strongest assertion of involvement asserts cosponsorship, of which there are degrees. Some members of the city administration might have been involved in the corrupt scheme merely as blindly operating parts of the mechanism, such as mailing out checks. It would be odd to characterize them as presiding over or owning the action. Some might have been wittingly yet unwillingly involved. They were just following orders—yet they were part of the team that was intentionally overseeing the action. And some others must have been all in, full sponsors for maximum profit. Their culpability varies, yet all of these agents *are* the ones who *did* the actions that together constituted the bad action. Some who need not repent of it will quite rightly regret it and feel that the most appropriate continuation of their involvement would be reparative in some way—not necessarily "righting the wrong" according to a justice calculation (which might not be feasible anyway) but changing the city atmosphere for the better.

It is the nature of our social life that we participate in many constructions of shared action, in our families first of all and then in a variety of other enterprises. We do not intentionally assign or accept responsibility for many of these participations because we do not think that things could have gone differently or that anyone would have wanted things to go differently. It would seem overly dramatic to say that we were "involved" in them; or it may suggest an element of discretion that seems out of place ("I was very involved in raising my children"). But some of our participations seem elective and worth building on or explicitly renouncing. For example, a young girl goes to a preschool in her neighborhood that her parents chose for its convenience; as a young woman, she goes to a college that she has chosen for its philosophy of higher education. Afterward she makes donations to the college, not to the preschool. The preschool program seems generic and she takes it for granted; the college program seems distinctive and to deserve being extended for the benefit of others. She is an "involved" alumna and glad to be recognized in those terms.

A political leader might try to convince us that we are all involved in a national history and an active national project, like the American Manifest Destiny. A religious leader might describe a great whole of shared action that so enfolds and commands our present lives that we feel unable to separate ourselves from it, like (for biblical Yahwists) Yahweh's project of establishing the Israelites in Canaan. The latter case shows how historical responsibility can become the idiom of all responsibility, so that the essence of right is to participate faithfully in the people's long-term project.

Causes and Results

Any definite shared action that can be presented to others as something to subscribe to is a *cause*. A cause has immediate practical significance as a promising platform for collaboration; it is also appreciable in historical perspective as part of a story worth telling about how the world came to be as it is in some significant respect.

"Help me thread this needle" proposes a cause that may be compelling at a particular moment. Perhaps you *can* help! You also might be able to do something enterprising for the good of the cause like finding a better needle. Any cause has pragmatic significance as a summons and a doable thing that we can attend to. And the spirit of attending to causes can grow—for a historically sensitive agent into great long-term collaborative accomplishments, for an idealist as far as the True Cause.

> Loyalty begins . . . in elemental forms. A cause fascinates us—we at first know not clearly why. We give ourselves willingly to that cause. Herewith our true life begins. The cause may indeed be a bad one. But at worst it is our way of interpreting the true cause. (Royce)[1]

A broadly and strenuously compelling sort of cause is to right a wrong, which will most often be viewed as a matter of ethical responsibility. Ethical causes are optimally short-term by their very nature, since justice delayed is justice denied. The campaign to end legal chattel slavery is a good example of an ethical cause, though it extended over many years. Any cause, even an objectionable one like preserving a slave society, has an ethical aspect in that it can be presented as being worthy of someone's participation. If agents are allocating their time and energy to a cause—if they envision the activity as a unit of their collaborative experience—then they are also on the plane of reckoning what is worth doing, and their possible investment can be critically discussed.

Another sort of cause is to make an improvement in society and is probably longer-term—for example, to commit more resources to remembering legal slavery and attending constructively to its legacy, including making reparations to descendants of slaves. This can be called a historical cause. While the reparations movement clearly shares an ethical concern about injustice with the abolition movement and may even use the language of "righting a wrong," it does not have the clear path to righting a wrong that abolitionism had with its demand to free the slaves. For there is vast social discretion in deciding the magnitude and formation of the reparative effort and who in particular should be burdened and benefited by it. Efforts to construe the legacy of slavery as a solvable problem of just deserts are predictably unsuccessful.[2] To abandon the cause, however, would seem to its subscribers *historically* irresponsible as it would leave their society's largest web of collaborative relationships in an unacceptable condition.

---

1. Josiah Royce, *The Philosophy of Loyalty* (Nashville: Vanderbilt University Press, [1908] 1995), 178.
2. See Steven G. Smith, "Historical Rightness," *Soundings* 98 (Spring 2015), 127–45.

We live in the sphere of historical responsibility to the extent that we lend ourselves to causes, both at the front end, in trying for and succeeding with collaborative accomplishments that will become elements of long-term accomplishments, and at the back end in retrospective assessment, sifting the stories that explain who we are and who we should try to be.

Just as I've been able to use a historically pregnant conception of "cause" in this discussion rather than the cause of cause-and-effect, so I can use the correlated historical conception of "result" in the sense of meaningful outcome or upshot for the collaborative community. Historically minded subscribers to a cause see the success of their effort as a notable result in large perspective; they want to be responsible for that result, not merely as a good deed in their ethical portfolios but as a "great" change or preservation in the world that they were involved in achieving. The same public-spirited mentality can be found even at the level of helping a friend thread a needle. "We figured it out—it was great!" and "We couldn't figure it out—it was pitiful!" are historically responsible assessments of results.

Here "great" and "pitiful" are evaluations at opposite ends of the greatness scale, which is a scale of historical evaluation. The distinctive interest of historical evaluation is in the fullest possible realization of agency, as this is revealed in complex collaboration; the "greatest" events and times are those with strong, interesting actions by the most impressive ensemble of agents, while the "darkest" parts of history are those marked by silence, stagnation, diminution, and meaningless loss of agents and restriction of things that can be done. While the earliest history writing was prompted by the ambitions of kings for extraordinary large-scale accomplishments, we now write history to recognize what the diversely sourced large-scale results of our communities' endeavors have been. This consciousness of larger-scale significance has filtered down to everyday practice where almost anything we set ourselves to do can turn out in some small way "great," and being "a great friend" or "a great colleague" is an important goal within reach.

Cognizance

Our historical attention is dominated by compounds of action that capture the imagination and can be variously evaluated and built upon. The atoms in these molecules, one might say, are the facts of what was done and what happened, part of the larger realm of already-constituted things that *are so*. We often think of it as a matter of intellectual responsibility to be aware of what is so and faithful to it in our representations, and our ideal of intellectual responsibility is often tied to the general ethical requirement to be truthful and adequately informed relative to the demands of a situation. But this branch of ethical responsibility rests on a foundation of historical responsibility in several connections: (1) that we are scrupulously aware of the already-achieved givens in our world that we are building with, on, or over, as is required in our being responsible *for* the accumulation of shared action (a requirement violated by "fact-free" fantastical politics); (2) that we are serious students of the facts of history that are the achievements of our earlier fellow agents, *with* whom we share historical responsibility; and (3) that we are seriously in conversation with *their* efforts to understand the facts and responsible *to* them as interpreters of the world. Thus to teach the history of slavery without acknowledging that there was opposition to slavery in classical Greece (an example from Simone Weil)[3] is objectionable ethically as a false communication but also historically as disrespecting earlier participants in a great conversation. Ethical responsibility without historical responsibility is unreliable.

The Farmer's Historical Responsibility

The great human communities act on a time scale longer than anyone's life. Our built environment makes this point palpable for us at any given moment, but even before we lived in houses and towns, we followed hunting and gathering itineraries and used practices that our forebears had worked out and that we handed along to our children. The multigenerational coherence of a way of life is an essential practical concern for a community purely for assurance of survival; it is also spiritually essential that the living maintain an affirming relationship with the dead, honoring their share in the larger action. Without this relationship with our forebears, our own brief, skewed, and flawed lives are not part of something more established and valuable.

Yet there is no full guarantee of survival or value for anything living. Any unit of historical enterprise, including a whole people, is a site of trial and possible failure. A common site of trial and failure in agricultural soci-

---

3. Simone Weil, *The Need for Roots*, trans. Arthur Wills (New York: Harper & Row, 1952), 38. She argues that Jacques Maritain could properly be taken before a public tribunal for presenting Aristotle's belief in the naturalness of slavery as representative of his civilization, despite Aristotle's own admission that "some people assert that slavery is absolutely contrary to nature and reason" (*Politics* I.3).

eties is the family farm. Appeals to historical responsibility are important in preserving such an enterprise, as I imagine in the following case.

An aging farmer now lives alone on his inherited family farm. He hires the help he needs. His wife of thirty years left him; she wanted a different life. His children, now grown, have all decided to live elsewhere.

He has appealed to his wife to honor their previous work on the farm and their marriage by continuing to nurture these large investments. Needs for improvement can be addressed, he promises. But she replies that the past is no prologue for her, her interests are completely different, the time has come to develop her life along new lines. He feels that she is slighting him, and the farm too, outrageously; how can he and the farm now count for so little?

He has appealed to his children to carry on with the farm so that their ancestors' investment in it won't be thrown away. He makes a historic settlement appeal: "There have been Smiths in this valley since before the Civil War." They are indifferent to that fact because they have no interest in living anywhere near there. He makes historic business appeals: "We have been supplying the community with food for generations"; "We have given summer work to the youth." They reply that someone else can better fulfill that community role, given their lack of interest. He asks why they would not want to be part of historic excellence: "We're known for operating a model farm." That type of excellence, though impressive in itself, does not align with their own affinities for excellence, they say. Finally, he argues that if he dies without succession, the farm (*where they grew up*, and with all its other admitted values) will probably die with him, as the land, conveniently not very far from town, will probably be taken over for a shopping center or a subdivision. That would be a shame, they say, but still we don't feel we have to bind ourselves to the farm. Furthermore—this is an ethical counterappeal—the farmer should be more considerate of their wishes and respect their autonomy.

The children do admit that the end of the farm would be a *shame*; we can tell from this that they are not historically insensitive. From the farmer's perspective, though, they are historically irresponsible. Underneath the specific historical and economic points he makes is the premise of family continuity—how can we stay effectively related to the ancestors and the values they introduced into our shared life? How can we be confident that our children will thrive if they "stray," striking out along new paths? How can we be impressed and reassured by the values realized in our children's lives if they are disconnected from the values realized in earlier family lives?

I imagine that a historical responsibility counselor would advise the farmer and his straying relatives to develop a more flexible and variegated image of the family career. It has been possible for many parents to make this adjustment, so that they can narrate the new initiatives of their children as though they were great new conquests by the family. The counselor would probably also point out that no family lives where it always lived; emigration and innovation have been required of all. (The farmer thinks: Yes, but why break off this great episode of family collaboration unnecessarily?) Whether the farmer can be reconciled to a more flexible view of family flourishing, given the strength of his appreciation for the values of the family farm, is uncertain. But whichever view he finally takes could be prompted most of all by a tug of historical responsibility, either of a farm-centered kind or of a family-centered kind.

The children, meanwhile, though lacking in historical responsibility as prescribed by their father, are not lacking in familial piety, a historically responsible glue for most families. They will continue to call, write, visit for Christmas, and look through the family photo album, not only in fondness but thinking of that as the right pattern of conduct.

One can imagine the wife experiencing this situation very differently. She might say that her husband's historical claim is false, because he made purely selfish, economically motivated decisions to maintain a regime on the farm that had nothing to do with respect for historical continuity, and abusive, because he interfered with his wife and children's development of interests and capabilities that deviated from his own selfish plan. These negatives could be the truth of her experience even as historical responsibility is the truth of the farmer's own experience. When we listen to the participants in a shared action we often learn that there is no single truth of motivation and no single dominant value in the complex web of collaboration. But even in the murkiest situations responsible agents cannot ignore any right- and wrong-making factors of which they are aware; and so they may disagree with each other very seriously, perhaps hopelessly.

The National Leader's Historical Responsibility

Nations are dangerous grounds for historical responsibility claims. If a national leader says that such-and-such must be done to fulfill the national mission, or to keep faith with the national heritage, or to restore the national honor, we ought to be wary, because we ought to know how readily that type of politics leads to oppression and violence. On the other hand, a nation without honor is a dispiriting home for its people—in one important way, not a home at all; a nation without a heritage has no identity to contemplate; and a nation with no mission at all is an impossibility.

States and other institutions are founded and terminated according to their rationales; we only need to maintain an institution so long as someone thinks it is a good idea. Families, however, go back forever in human time (though in changing forms) and have an unquestionable mission of continuing. Nations do not go back forever, but in the respect that they seem to have emerged in associations among families, they partake of this unquestionableness—they will certainly claim a share of the earth's resources and a share of human action, just because they exist. Yet the *performance* of a nation can always be questioned. Since it takes care of its essential business—maintaining cooperation among families, settling them, mobilizing them, representing them—in certain ways and not in other possible ways, with a certain accumulation of results rather than other conceivable accumulations, it is subject to evaluation as a historical project (*will* Abraham's descendants be as numerous as the stars?) and its specific practical objectives and methods can always be adjusted (*will* the Mosaic covenant be observed?). Anyone who accepts the status of national leader accepts one of the largest shares of individual responsibility for envisioning and executing the national project.

It is part of Abraham Lincoln's exceptional significance as an American leader that he seemed to sincerely and thoughtfully assume historical responsibility. That was part of the force of his assertion in 1861 that he had "never had a feeling politically that did not spring from the sentiments embodied in the Declaration of Independence."[4] In his 1858 Senate contest he said:

> My countrymen, if you have been taught doctrines conflicting with the great landmarks of the Declaration of Independence; if you have listened to suggestions which would take away from its grandeur, and mutilate the fair symmetry of its proportions; if you have been inclined to believe that all men are not created equal in those inalienable rights enumerated by our chart of liberty, let me entreat you to come back. Return to the fountain whose waters spring close by the blood of the Revolution.[5]

---

4. Abraham Lincoln, speech of February 22, 1861 at Independence Hall, accessed October 20, 2021, http://www.abrahamlincolnonline.org/lincoln/speeches/philadel.htm.

5. Lincoln, speech of August 17, 1858, accessed October 20, 2021, https://www.nps.gov/liho/learn/historyculture/declaration.htm.

Lincoln's appeal to the principles of the Declaration is powerfully *ethical* because the ethical rightness of recognizing certain inalienable rights is what makes the Declaration an "immortal emblem of humanity" and not merely the charter of a single group. Further, calling the emblem "immortal" and its principles "sacred" lifts the appeal into dimensions of eternal and religious responsibility, for whoever is willing to go there.[6] But Lincoln also gave the ethically and religiously emphatic notion of the Declaration's "immortality" a historically specific birth in the American Revolution and a historically optimistic extension to everyone living in the future.

> I have often inquired of myself, what great principle or idea it was that kept this Confederacy so long together. It was not the mere matter of the separation of the Colonies from the motherland; but that sentiment in the Declaration of Independence which gave liberty, not alone to the people of this country, but, I hope, to the world, for all future time.[7]

There we see the exceptionally ambitious and in certain ways exceptionally threatening American mission, its vehicle a people's growing complex of action facilitated by the American state: to secure the rights enunciated in the Declaration of Independence for all humans. A great issue that no responsible American leader can properly dodge is how the American nation should comport itself in relation to founding principles conceived "with a decent respect for the opinions of mankind" as globally relevant and historic, building on what Americans have done to this point. It is a spectacular example of the irreducibly historical responsibility that any nation imposes on its leaders.

Historical Injustice and Historical Jeopardy

The essential historically responsible question is, "Given what has happened and given our prospects, how can we best contribute to the most ideally satisfactory whole of shared action?" This question looks deceptively like an ethical question, but its referent "the whole of shared action" makes it reach far beyond ethical practicality.

---

6. Ibid.

7. Lincoln 1861.

The whole of shared action takes in the whole relevant past, in which countless agents and their actions can no longer be perceived or directly reacted to, across which there are profound differences in applicable values, and about which there will be endlessly conflicting interpretations. We are in the somewhat frustrating position of simply wondering about or marveling at cultures and life-experiences that are alien to us; we are in the more uncomfortable position of contemplating past crimes and disappointments in our own largely understandable past that we cannot now rectify, even though we are still practically connected with them. American slavery, for example, has left a legacy of unacceptable social relations in American life and so is not only a historical dark age of oppression and personal tragedies to be regarded sadly but a "historical injustice" to be regarded intolerantly. Awkwardly, we cannot make anywhere near a complete determination of the harms done by slavery or the profits wrongly taken from it, nor can we make an uncontroversial determination of causal and ethico-legal connections between the slavery actions that are clearly unacceptable and present actions that seem unacceptable in a related way. Our very commitment to personal autonomy and giving citizens equal chances prevents us from imposing "the sins of the fathers" on anyone now living.

Because slavery is part of American history, a historically responsible American leader will take the legacy of slavery seriously and propose a collective action that places the whole of the American action in a more acceptable state in this connection. Which action is most feasible and appropriate is a political question, of course, but a historically motivated one. On a smaller scale, collectives with a historic involvement in slavery can take constructive action that is emblematic of the right kind of national action, leading the leaders. For example, Brown University prepared a "Slavery and Justice Report" documenting Brown's early reliance on slaves and slave-trading wealth, part of a larger Africana studies initiative. At Georgetown University, students and the administration have proposed programs of monetary reparations for descendants of slaves once owned and sold by the school.[8] These actions do not purport to "right the wrong" of enslavement,

---

8. On the Brown initiative see Joanne Melish, "Recovering (from) Slavery: Four Struggles to Tell the Truth," in James Oliver Horton and Lois E. Horton, eds., *Slavery and Public History* (New York: The New Press, 2006), 119–25; Paul Davis, "Slowly, Brown Starts Fulfilling Its Vow of Atonement," *Providence Journal*, April 26, 2010; and on the difficulties in institutional follow-through, Sydney Ember, "The Forgotten Report: Slavery and Justice at Brown," *Brown Daily Herald*, May 24, 2012. The work of the Brown committee studying the legacy of slavery is posted at http://brown.edu/Research/

but they are self-substantiatingly "right things to do" in that a piece of history is now more cognizantly "confronted" and taken up for further development along more acceptable lines, bent toward justice even if not fulfilling justice, by agents taking the responsibility implied by belonging to that historical complex.

"The whole of shared action" also takes in the whole future with which we have any possible connection. It is very hard to make definite plans for a future more than a generation away; "the world we give our grandchildren" is a way of referring to the future that takes us to the limit of meaningful anticipation. It is very hard to say what we owe future people who not only are not yet in our scene, making the basic claim to consideration that living beings make—who do not even have the substance to be a "who" in our reckoning—but, supposing such beings will exist, might have very different needs and preferences from ours.[9] Nevertheless it seems impossible to dispute that it would be wrong of us to burden future generations with a time bomb of toxic waste, or to set in motion a humanly disastrous climate change. No responsible person would be complacent about being involved in a mass extinction, even if the extinction takes place over centuries. As with historical injustice, and for much the same reasons, the devices of ethical responsibility are unequal to the challenge: we cannot determine what agents owe. But here too we nevertheless see problems that need to be addressed if we have historical awareness of the larger formation of our shared action—problems that are awkwardly diffuse for ethical assessment but amply clear to anyone who sees the general superiority of times of thriving, expanding agency to times of shrunken agency.

Historical responsibility is not an arbitrary conceit. We sometimes must take our bearings by considering how actions we might perform now or in the future belong to a large accumulation of actions, and how some of the feasible extensions of that accumulation would be more ideally satisfying than others. We do sometimes appeal to our fellow agents to be mindful of a larger shared action in a *responsible* way, concerned to rectify their relation-

---

Slavery_Justice/, accessed October 20, 2021. For the Georgetown discussion see Susan Svrluga and Nick Anderson, "Georgetown Has a Plan to Help Descendants of Enslaved People," *Washington Post*, October 31, 2019.

9. On these issues see Steven G. Smith, "What We Have Time For: Historical Responsibility on the Largest Scale," *Journal of the Philosophy of History* 13 (June 2019): 163–82.

ships with other agents with whose efforts their own efforts are practically linked. We do overcome skepticism and deep disagreement about historical truth with ascertainments of undeniable historical involvement. And our appeals are sometimes successful: we preserve historic structures, we create historical exhibits and observances, we make formal apologies, we institute programs of reconciliation, we guard against future harm.

In a modern society there is no obvious way for an ordinary agent to get in trouble for lack of historical responsibility; there is no scheme in which such responsibility is assigned and monitored. For lack of a scheme of assignment, and because it is impossible to say exactly what constitutes fulfillment of historical responsibility (though we recognize historically respectful intent when it is manifested), it might be argued that while historical *piety* is a real and valid motivation, historical *responsibility* is an unusable idea. Historical piety could attach to anything in the past at all; all the individual and occasional variation in its expression does not contradict its nature. In a sphere of responsibility we ought to be able to compare definite specifications for action with actual performance and find the performance acceptable or not.

It seems that we do indeed have specifications for historically responsible action at the level of civic leaders and leaders of major institutions. There is a strong expectation that a national leader will make historically cognizant gestures and statements on certain occasions—national holidays, international visits, when treaties are signed, when war threatens. A religious leader is expected to interpret current issues in relation to a historic tradition's goals, standards, and accomplishments. There are analogies to this in any field of endeavor, even at the level of the family reunion. To the extent that we conscientiously follow such leadings, we do accept roles in a scheme of historical responsibility. We understand that the state of long-term endeavors in which our own endeavors are embedded cannot simply be taken for granted: historic societies and factions are competitive threats to each other; historic guidances are precarious as circumstances change. We also have reason to follow the best available leadings for the sake of rectifying our own unavoidable involvements in the development of shared action.

Improvised historical responsibility can easily become problematic, as with the farmer I imagined who invokes historical responsibility against his wife and children. We are very aware that he is possibly abusing his personal discretion to mount such a claim to constrain them. He is acting like the leader of a people in a way that is not automatically appropriate in our culture. But he *is* the senior family member onsite at that family's longest-established home. To that extent his claim is at least intelligible. His claim is even exemplary in bringing up a kind of concern that should not be ignored. It would be shortsighted and unfair on our part to think that his self-responsible sense of who he is amounting to as an agent could be separated from his exercise of historical responsibility for his family.

Who are we? What are we involved in? What are we about, and what have we wrought? An agent who completely declines historical responsibility can largely disregard these questions. From the point of view of someone wholly occupied with immediate tasks, such as catching dinner or making payroll, such questions may seem idle. And yet a hunter might have a practical need to understand why the game are getting harder to find, and an employer might need to understand why a business has lately become more prosperous or less—perhaps due to external circumstances and perhaps due to changes in oneself. Because of our social and temporally extended mode of living, questions of historical action tend constantly to arise for us; and agents who are disposed to act responsibly will tend to take such questions seriously as bearing on their responsibility.

In sum: We normally must *assume* that *someone* in our community—a leader—is historically responsible, as we cannot be indifferent to the status of long-term shared actions in which we realize our own lives are embedded and in which we have involvements that are approvable or not.

We naturally *hope* that we ourselves can be on the right side of history, in every form of history that is relevant to us, and that we ourselves can make an appreciable positive difference to historic action.

Appendix 3

Notes on Religious Responsibility

Exemplars of Religious Responsibility

> Responsibility affirms: "God is acting in all actions upon you. So respond to all actions upon you as to respond to his action."
>
> —H. Richard Niebuhr[1]

Several of the lines of aspiration for full responsibility arouse interests that are possibly best handled by adopting religious conceptions that purport to bring our understanding to its true ultimate reference points. The most estimable model of responsible agency, an agent who approvably attends to the preponderance of what is done in the universe, whom one would wholeheartedly imitate as best one could and who would be able to hold one ultimately responsible ("the hearing, the sight, and the heart, all will be questioned," Quran 17:36), would be a god—a responsible kind of god. The most trustworthy headquarters, providing ideally benign and coherent direction to all responsible endeavor, would be a divine mind or Heaven. The most legitimate scheme of standards and retribution would be a cosmic law of karma or a divine providence. The community to whom the most responsible service is rendered would be an eternal communion of the living and the dead. The personal mobilization by which an agent would most responsibly serve others, in the most authentic individual relation with

---

1. H. Richard Niebuhr, *The Responsible Self* (New York: Harper & Row, 1963), 126.

the Ultimate, would be that of a saint. And the most responsive human agent would be the one who senses need and opportunity in all directions always—that "God is acting in all actions upon you," as Niebuhr put it. As all responsible subjects are aware of playing a role in something working out—historically, in the accumulated reality of shared action; politically, in a comprehensive actualization of shared actions; ethically, in the generally right formation of action, with principal relevance for the future—religiously, one plays one's responsible part in the working out of everything. Religion is adhesion to the eternal plan. Religious reasoning has this anchor and guide rope.

There is a kind of religious vocation, that of the monk or martyr, for which the main theme of responsibility is preferring eternity to the existing world. This is a bold embrace of a superior responsibility, but not a fullest responsibility.

Some religious styles of responsibility are limited by special religious considerations, such as the controlling power of God or the distorting power of sin in human life; here, too, the ideal of fullest responsibility seems out of place.

To see how a life geared to full responsibility might take a religious shape—distinctively motivating as a strong type of personal fulfillment, and yet shadowed by the distinctive danger that it is perhaps the worst of all overreachings, or the worst of all exposures to a crushing excessive demand in responsibility, or the grossest evasion of worldly problems—let us consider first how the agentic God may be thought to exercise a supreme responsibility and then how some traditional human heroes of religious responsibility bear an amplified kind of responsibility while not absconding from their more ordinary responsibilities.[2]

1. *God.* Because God is thought to be a uniquely necessary eternal being on which all other beings depend, God's action does not enter the arena of responsibility in the same way that the actions of human producers or controllers do. Even if God is one of the characters in the story, God is the maker of the story.

There is a potent parable of divine responsibility in Quran 18:65–82. A mysterious unnamed "servant of God" who has been granted godlike judgment lets Moses observe some of his interventions in the affairs of

---

2. This section draws on my article "Responsibility in Religiosity," *Religious Studies* 57 (June 2021): 249–65.

others to show that while divine determinations are not wholly outside human comprehension they are not within it either. The servant of God inflicts destruction and death on seemingly innocent victims and spares the guilty, always with an arguably benign (not *patently* benign) longer-term rationale. The point may be that God cannot be second-guessed. That part of holding-responsible is impossible between ourselves and God. The world is surpassingly good when most fully considered, for which we thank and respect God; but the reason that we accept God's rule without criticism is not that God passes our own value-maximizing test but that humans cannot authoritatively discern either the facts of the case or the values at stake as the eternal World Sponsor can. Among ourselves, responsible collaboration generally requires that the collaborators can always reexamine and renegotiate their goals and methods, but that feature of responsibility is here suspended: we can only try to attune ourselves better to God's eternal determinations.[3]

If one's conception of divine eternity is that all beings are simultaneously present for God, then the divine service of others would seem to be best described as *pragmatically* responsible. The Mahayana idea of the Buddha's flexible employment of "skillful means" in aiding sentient beings toward enlightenment seems to suppose a fundamental pragmatism. But the resemblance to human pragmatic responsibility is deceptive here, because human pragmatic reckoning in its strong bias toward what is near at hand is a function of our ignorance (especially of competing goods), just as any other human mode of responsible reckoning copes with our ignorance of fact and of the future. Perhaps the closest resemblance would be with *political* responsibility, which factors the claims of factual and possible action sharings together with the immediate consequences of present action sharing. But a decisive difference remains, barring a deliberate contraction of divine power and knowledge to make room for true contingency and uncertainty: the divine agent always already has, and is, the solution of every problem. We have not (except in imagining) deployed God, as we deploy other agents, to a role in the hope that God will do well for us in that role. One cannot bring a problem to God for responsible handling in the same way that one approaches another agent.

---

3. It is not an uncontroversial point, but there is a long tradition in Abrahamic theology of interpreting scriptural stories of negotiation between humans and God (as in Abraham's intercession for Sodom in Genesis 18) as indications of the progress of human realization of what God eternally determines.

2. *Abraham.* In the Abrahamic traditions the ideal of a responsible collaborative relationship with the world's Creator/Ruler/Redeemer is paradigmatic, despite the asymmetry between the human and divine positions. The responsibility comes to a person as an amazing opportunity of service, a divine election. In Genesis 12–25, the first written Abraham story, the prophet's conduct is conspicuously responsible in that he harkens to an authoritative voice ("Here am I" is his signature utterance), accepts his election despite its difficulty, and works hard in his own way to fulfill its mandate. His responsibility is also appreciably religious in quality in the extraordinary behavior it supports, seen above all in his willingness to intercede for the Sodomites and to sacrifice his son Isaac.

Abraham's task is to migrate at the age of seventy-five to another country where he can become the father of a great nation and a blessing to the world. He is up for it.[4] He is not a free adventurer, however. He is responsible for an extended family and is repeatedly challenged to find resources for them and to protect them. As he prospers, he becomes responsible for the management of wealth (13:2); as his power grows, he becomes responsible for resolving intergroup conflicts in Canaan (14). In the episode of being asked to father a child with the servant Hagar (16) he is portrayed as responsible to his wife Sarah.

Abraham's partnership with God is formalized in a covenant, for which the declared basis is God's reckoning of Abraham's righteous faithfulness in the relationship (15). The covenant imposes on Abraham's descendants a magnification of the burden of the worldly responsibility Abraham has already shouldered successfully, being in charge of a large land full of peoples. To violate or forget the covenant will have ethical and spiritual meanings in this tradition, but in the first place, it means defecting from the economic and political project of holding this land. A barrier to defection is set up in the mandated sign of the covenant, male circumcision (17); Abraham's people will wear a sort of livery of their Commander in their very skin, making their commitment to the relationship irrevocable.

In the Sodom story (18–19), we see that Abraham's special relationship with God does not make him either self-centered, in playing his great role, or abject in his complete surrender. Because his divine partner is "the judge of all the earth [who must] do what is just" (18:25), he is bound to plead strenuously for the lives of the Sodomites whom God intends to punish, for the

---

4. According to a later tradition, he is disgusted by the idolatry in his home setting. See Genesis Rabbah 38; see also Quran 6:74 and 21:51–57.

sake of the righteous among them. Thus the "suspension of the ethical" that Kierkegaard thought was implied by Abraham's willingness to sacrifice Isaac as commanded by God (22) is not definitive of Abraham.[5] His willingness to sacrifice his son puts him in a religiously responsible position of emblematic self-mortification that will be seen again in Hosea, Jeremiah, Ezekiel, and Jesus. And it dramatizes the extreme insecurity of living on the basis of divine promises. But he is a comprehensively responsible person, even as he acts with extraordinary venturesomeness and resignation in his partnership with God.

3. *Aeneas.* Virgil and presumably the *Aeneid*'s first audience imagine Aeneas as a responsibly disposed human being—his epithet is *pius*, "dutiful"—tested by the heaviest possible loading of responsibilities. He is an answer to the question "How much responsibility can one person bear?" as he has hard-to-fulfill responsibilities in every major dimension of human existence: as a son, father, and husband charged with the safety of his family during the destruction of Troy; as a military captain and expedition leader driven by storms around the dangerous Mediterranean; as a lover of the formidable, forbidden Dido; as a representative of Troy and father of a new nation in a hostile land; and as a servant of conflicted transcendent powers. All of these responsibilities are visited on him unsought; he takes them on as the perfect good sport. Yet he is a real human with the imperfections especially of a warrior, as shown in his later battle scenes where bloody *furor* gets the better of his *pietas*.

Aeneas is a man who has religious duties and fulfills them, performing appropriate sacrifices and faithfully executing his god-given mission. But he has no choice about these matters. Where he impressively shows that he is responsible in a religious way is not so much by praying or sacrificing on suitable occasions as by addressing the ghosts of his father and the jilted Dido in Book VI. He faces up to them, and the issues associated with them, in their placement among the dead in Hades and in their ghostly sempiternity. Another Trojan might believe in ghosts due to an overactive imagination or a literal understanding of ghost tales, but ghosts for Aeneas *are* persons, persons now dead, whom he *ought (always) to face*. Even if you do not believe in ghosts you can appreciate how this part of Aeneas's experience is essential to his full extension of responsibility.

---

5. Accordingly, Levinas adopts the Sodom story as the definition of Abraham's responsibility. "Kierkegaard: Existence and Ethics," in *Proper Names*, trans. Michael B. Smith (Stanford: Stanford University Press, 1996), 66–74, 74.

Aeneas will pay any personal price to fulfill his responsibility. Virgil's Jupiter is so impressed by this that he tells Juno that in the end the Romans will surpass the gods in godliness (*pietate*).[6]

4. *Kongzi*. Unlike Abraham or Aeneas, Kongzi as we find him in the *Lunyu* is an intellectual. Unable to practice his profession as a government adviser, he is not responsible for any practical affairs, which is precisely his trial: he must prove his concern for the community, his fidelity to sound principles, and his competence in articulating them by maintaining himself with no social support beyond a small circle of similarly marginal scholars. What keeps him going, and what qualifies him as a paragon of religious responsibility, is his intimacy with a greater being: "Heaven produced the virtue that is in me. Huan-Tui—what can he do to me?" (7.22)[7]

The Heavenly virtues taught by Kongzi are intensely responsible: considerateness (*ren*), appropriateness (*yi*), reciprocity (*shu*), filial piety (*xiao*).

> [Kongzi's disciple] Zeng said, "I daily examine myself [to determine] whether, in transacting business for others, I may have been not faithful [and] whether I may have not mastered and practiced the instructions of my teacher." (1.4)

So important is the principle of responding satisfactorily to one's fellow beings that emphasis is laid on correct facial expressions (16.10; or demeanor, 2.8) and consistency in mourning long after one's parents have died (1.11).

Over and above his teachings of personal responsibility, Kongzi embodies maximal devotion to a classic tradition. "Extreme is my decay. For a long time, I have not dreamed, as I was wont to do, that I saw the duke of Zhou" (7.5). This is something like a Jew saying, "I have not thought of Sinai."

In accepting the oversight of Heaven and the restraint of a canonical tradition of Heavenly wisdom, Kongzi in a certain way immobilizes himself like King Shun who merely sat on his throne facing south in order to rectify all of China. That is the strategy and value of the *sage*, to be a luminous fixed point of reference: "He who exercises government by means of his virtue may be compared to the north polar star, which keeps its place and all the stars

---

6. Aeneid 12.839.

7. Huan Tui seems to have been a government official who threatened him. Kongzi quotations are taken from *The Analects of Confucius*, trans. James Legge, accessed October 20, 2021, http://oaks.nvg.org/analects-legge.html.

turn towards it" (2.1). At the same time, Kongzi exhibits reassuring human-level responsibility as an active learner (5.27) and passionate friend (11.8).

5. *Dharmakara.* The king-turned-monk who became Amitabha, the Buddha of the Pure Land, is a hero of religious responsibility in that the felt necessity of saving all suffering beings carried him into Buddhahood. Like the Buddha (once a prince), he steps out of worldly responsibility to take up spiritual responsibility. In his religious position he is a pure type of one who cares infinitely and practically (like a perfect king) about his fellow beings. He focuses all the energy of his good disposition on the goal of liberation for all, as expressed in his vow.

> [On] the strength of the determination I will assume . . . I will have a magnificent field, the best and highest. And in this most noble beautified high seat of awakening will be found the incomparable bliss of the state of nirvana. And I will purify this field so that in it all living beings will reach nirvana. Living beings will gather from the ten directions, and once they are here will quickly prosper in bliss. (Larger Pure Land Sutra §19 [7–9])[8]

By vowing to assure the liberation of others, Dharmakara intends to assume responsibility even for their responsibility.

> [Vow #23] May I not awaken to unsurpassable, perfect, full awakening if, after I attain awakening, the roots of merit of the bodhisattvas in my Buddha-field will not appear in whatever form they wish them to grow, even as their wish arises . . .

> [Vow #43] May I not awaken to unsurpassable, perfect, full awakening if, after I attain awakening, living beings in another Buddha-field will hear my name and yet the root of merit that comes with hearing my name will not be enough to give them possession, until they have attained the highest limits of the essence of awakening, of the root of merit which is joy and delight in the conduct of the bodhisattva.[9]

---

8. Larger Pure Land Sutra, trans. by Luis O. Gómez, in *Land of Bliss* (Honolulu: University of Hawai'i Press, 1996), 67.
9. Larger Pure Land Sutra, trans. by Gómez, *Land of Bliss*, 72, 75.

Dharmakara is an ambiguous *human* exemplar because he can become the divine Amitabha only by realizing a perfect intention to exercise a more-than-human power of salvation. On his human side, he wholeheartedly wants this. Fortunately there is a bridge between the human yearning of Dharmakara and the divine power of Amitabha in the Buddhist dharma, the supremely helpful conception of the situation as a gateway through which one can aim one's passion for enlarged responsibility toward a reality of love greater than belief or statement. In keeping with his name, "treasury of dharma," Dharmakara makes himself a meritorious repository of the supreme wisdom, rising to the challenge of spiritually powering the fulfillment of his outsized vow by practicing the virtues of bodhisattvas for aeons.[10] In an illuminating Buddhist way he agreeably does what we all (ideally) would say must be done.

6. *Miaoshan.* By the twelfth century CE the legendary Chinese princess Miaoshan was identified with Guanyin, the Buddha of the Thousand Eyes and Arms (originally Avalokiteshvara) who hears all cries of suffering and can help everyone.[11] As a Buddha, Guanyin is a cosmic principle of compassion; as a human incarnation of that compassion, Miaoshan makes classic human choices and so serves as a human hero. She refuses to be married, on the grounds that marrying would fail to address her fellow beings' three great misfortunes of aging, sickening, and dying. She maintains this stance despite severe persecution by her father, who eventually becomes so exasperated that he orders her execution. At this crisis point her "merit" (or we could say her exemplary responsibility) takes her to hell, where she vows to save everyone whose plight she sees; her goodness turns hell into a heaven. Back on earth, when her father comes to his own crisis of sickness, she sacrifices her eyes and arms for his benefit, thus demonstrating that Buddhist compassion grounds true filial piety (rebutting a standard Confucian objection to Buddhism).[12] Once she is miraculously restored and reconciled with her parents, her relentless instruction enables her father to choose the

---

10. Larger Pure Land Sutra, trans. by Gómez, *Land of Bliss*, 174–75.

11. See Glenn Dudbridge, *The Legend of Miaoshan*, rev. ed. (Oxford: Oxford University Press, 2004), and Will Idema, *Personal Salvation and Filial Piety: Two Precious Scroll Narratives of Guanyin and Her Acolytes* (Honolulu: University of Hawai'i Press, 2008).

12. For the objection see Han Yu, "Essentials of the Moral Way," trans. Charles Hartman, in William Theodore de Bary and Irene Bloom, eds., *Sources of Chinese Tradition*, 2nd ed. (New York: Columbia University Press, 1999), 569–73 (early 9th century).

path of perfection after all. She has fulfilled an ideal filial responsibility for her parents' responsibility.[13]

Miaoshan/Guanyin's explicit vows of compassionate responsibility propose a logic in the popular conception of sharable merit that is not merely wishful or sensuous: the fundamental salvific possibility to be embraced is not someone else's beneficence by which one would be helped, but rather one's own assumption of benevolent responsibility.

Miaoshan is like Dharmakara in being conceived at an extreme of human responsibility reaching into divinity. (In fact Avalokiteshvara and Amitabha are regularly associated in the Pure Land divine trinity.) But the monk Dharmakara embodies responsibility in a furiously masculine way, wishing to be the greatest of all Buddhas, acquiring exceptional merit through aeons of dharma study and piling up impressive vows that he will benefit everyone. He is the bodhisattva ideal of thrilling aspiration, whereas Miaoshan/Guanyin is the bodhisattva ideal of *having heard*, being wholly cognizant of need and responsible to meet it as it presents itself.[14] And whereas Dharmakara fits into a scheme of roles and tasks only by the special arrangement of Buddhist monasticism, Miaoshan is plainly legible to us as a responsible daughter.

In summary comparison: Dharmakara and Miaoshan are specialists in compassion. They are an opposite type from Aeneas and Abraham, who are

---

13. Dudbridge, 108. In one version of the story, Miaoshan gives her blessing to the executioner sent by her father and assumes the enormous demerit of what he meant to do—see Stephen Levine, *Becoming Kuan Yin* (San Francisco: Weiser, 2013), 33–34. Here too she takes responsibility for someone else's responsibility.

14. She is represented in one account as a modest sort of perfection-seeker: "I desire nothing more than a peaceful retreat on a lone mountain, there to attempt the attainment of perfection. If some day I can reach a high degree of goodness, then, borne on the clouds of Heaven, I will travel throughout the universe, passing in the twinkling of an eye from east to west. I will rescue my father and mother, and bring them to Heaven; I will save the miserable and afflicted on earth; I will convert the spirits which do evil, and cause them to do good. That is my only ambition"—"The Goddess of Mercy," trans. E. T. C. Werner, in *Myths and Legends of China* [1922], chap. 10, accessed October 20, 2021, www.sacred-texts.com/cfu/mlc/mlc12.htm. According to Sherin Wing, however, the definitive Buddhist account of Miaoshan in the twelfth century portrays her as a hero of *male*-gendered religiosity, making much the same moves in her situation that Shakyamuni Buddha would; the point is to show the superiority of Buddhism to family-prioritizing Confucianism. "Gendering Buddhism: the Miaoshan Legend Reconsidered," *Journal of Feminist Studies* 27 (2011): 5–31: 25.

pragmatically righteous while fulfilling great plans for nations. Kongzi has a desirable serenity that one would not attribute to the swelling Dharmakara, the self-mutilating Miaoshan, or the crisis-plagued Aeneas or Abraham. He stands as proof of concept for a calm, diligently conversational style of responsibility. But all of these religious heroes display an extraordinary profundity of responsibility, changing the parameters of responsible life to fit with religiously expanded conceptions of life and the world while remaining in continuity with a variety of human susceptibilities and ultimate values. They all realize an extraordinary agent power in being a crucial divine instrument (the progenitor of a nation, the enlightener of a society) or the wielder of divinely granted power (a Savior).

That the exemplars of religious responsibility are like each other in seeming to hit a maximum of responsibility does not prevent there being a great difference between Aeneas's reverent relationship with his father and Miaoshan's patronizing relationship with hers, or between Kongzi's affiliation with impersonal Heaven and Abraham's personal loyalty to Yahweh. We cannot assume that a certain emphasis in religious responsibility will always underwrite the same ideology or promote the same conduct. On the other hand, we can recognize a general constraint in religious responsibility if it is predictable that religious motivations will be at least partly convergent in the dimension of respect for others and conscientiousness; and this does seem to be predictable. While Aeneas and Miaoshan might disagree strongly about how to relate to one's father, I expect that they would agree strongly on the importance of the issue and recognize each other's religious seriousness in that vein.

The Threat of Religious Responsibility

A positive view of expansive responsibility must be qualified by awareness of the real possibility of becoming trapped in an unwholesome version of it. The Aztecs' avowed responsibility to perform massive human sacrifice is one example;[15] the Catholic responsibility for dead relatives exploited by

---

15. We are told that the Aztec high priest would instruct a new ruler in this responsibility (or, he would more likely say, *duty*): "You must see to it that the sun and earth continue on their courses . . . consider, Lord, that you must toil in order that the sun god not lack his [human] sacrifice of blood and food that he needs in order to continue on his course and shed his light on us; you must do the same for the earth goddess, that she may give us provisions." *Memoriales de Fray Toribio de Motolinía*, quoted and

Johann Tetzel's racket in indulgences is another; the responsibility felt by an evangelist to convert persons all over the world, believing they will otherwise be rejected by God eternally, is another. Even in currently thriving versions of world religions, a doctrine of sin or karma conceived as a fully amplified acceptance of responsibility can in practice be an immobilizing burden.

These perils lend force to the argument that the very idea of full responsibility, whether for blame or ambition, is false and monstrous—false because no finite cause by itself determines any result at all, let alone an eternal result, and monstrous because no one could retain either a reasonable humility or a reasonable degree of autonomy believing that personal successes and failures have infinite good and bad consequences.

But full responsibility does not seem a necessarily faulty ideal if appropriate allowances are made for finitude, including realism about one's own capacities, a vocational orientation to prioritizing the more urgent needs of fellow beings nearest to hand (under normal circumstances), and an open-mindedness about how the eventual results of our actions will be good enough. In forming responsible life plans, many of us will find the congenial role models of "heroes" more helpful than exceptional "saints."[16] But the exceptional exemplars serve well for instruction and discussion purposes, partly because they are widely honored and partly because they challenge us from positions right at the apparent limit of feasibility. We might wish to imitate them to some extent without expecting to equal them.[17] How then *could* we take a measure of direction from the examples of Abraham, Aeneas, Kongzi, Dharmakara, or Miaoshan without being intoxicated by fantastic power or crushed by excessive demand?

The Aeneas model is daunting. Staggering out of Troy with his father on his back and his little boy in tow, horrifically losing touch with his wife, his story starts out almost as a sick joke about an overburdened man. His signature accomplishment, founding a state, is attributable to him only with the huge qualification that it requires divine intervention. But this is not a problem with the spiritual relevance of the *Aeneid*, this is its point: Virgil conceives Aeneas, proxy for Augustus, at a unique extreme of responsibil-

---

translated in Benjamin Keen, *The Aztec Image in Western Thought* (New Brunswick: Rutgers University Press, 1990), 112.

16. A. I. Melden, "Saints and Supererogation," in Ilham Dilman, ed., *Philosophy and Life: Essays on John Wisdom* (Dordrecht: Springer, 1984), 61–81.

17. Linda Zagzebski, *Exemplarist Moral Theory* (Oxford: Oxford University Press, 2017), 23–27.

ity. No one other than a Roman emperor will ever be responsible for the happiness of the world. In ordinary life one can try to be a good son, or father, or captain, but one gets onto Aeneas's plane only by extraordinarily taking responsibility for everything. A Stoic consenting to Fate makes this move in a way.

Dharmakara is another borderline case because he steps over into divine perfection at the point of realizing full responsibility and can fulfill his intention only by doing this. If we take his human limitations seriously while he is on the human side of that border, we can say he has a feasible version of full responsibility insofar as he is allowed to express his intention hopefully, that is, uncertainly, and with a benevolence and plan that are still vaguely general, not yet specified for the needs of actual beings. We too can take a hopeful and broadly benevolent stance toward a world full of sentient beings.

Of the five human exemplars under review, it seems to me that Kongzi has the most to say about a feasible and wholesome version of responsibility, thanks to his reverence for the traditional forms of appropriate conduct (compare the Roman *decorum*). Even more than for Aeneas, for Kongzi the format of the responsible life is already established with human-scaled specificity. Indeed, Confucianism is so well scaled to the ethos of a human society that it need not be viewed as a religion at all. It does sometimes present as religious, and there are religious notes of exceptional sensitivity and yearning in the *Lunyu*.

> With a great sigh Yan Hui lamented, "The more I look up at it the higher it seems; the more I delve into it, the harder it becomes. . . . The Master is skilled at leading me on, step by step." (*Lunyu* 9.11)

But even the most devoutly responsible Confucian does not plunge into the hurricane of universal need *in the manner of* a bodhisattva; instead, the mission is to tend relations with one's parents, children, spouses, siblings, rulers, and subjects according to the evolved norms of good Chinese society. (The Confucian point seems to have been taken to heart in Miaoshan's story, where it was possible to combine filial piety with bodhisattva excellence.)

If my general conceptual proposal is correct, placing responsibility in a definite collaborative scheme secures the normal basis for any assigning or holding of responsibility, including religious responsibility. Those who espouse a more abstract, ideally stronger principle of responsibility like Buddhist compassion or Christian charity may be well positioned to criticize the Confucian endorsement of existing social forms. But we may then ask them to provide their own solution to the problem of the human scaling of responsibility. For Christians, Jesus's parable of the Good Samaritan (Luke 10:25–37) might offer one of the most characteristic answers, combining a standard issue of responsible orientation ("Who is my neighbor?") with practical realism ("A man fell into the hands of robbers, who stripped him, beat him, and went away, leaving him half dead") and the elements of the unexpected and the transcending: the respectable citizens do not help the stricken man but the despised outsider does, investing time and money in the rescue.[18]

---

18. Compare Anguttara Nikaya 5:162: [Shariputra:] "How should you get rid of resentment for a person whose behavior by way of body and speech is impure, and who doesn't get an openness and clarity of heart from time to time? Suppose a person was traveling along a road, and they were sick, suffering, gravely ill. And it was a long way to a village, whether ahead or behind. And they didn't have any suitable food or medicine, or a competent carer, or someone to bring them to the neighborhood of a village. Then another person traveling along the road sees them, and thinks of them with nothing but compassion, kindness, and sympathy: 'Oh, may this person get suitable food or medicine, or a competent carer, or someone to bring them to the neighborhood of a village. Why is that? So that they don't come to ruin right here.' In the same way, at that time you should ignore that person's impure behavior by way of speech and body, and the fact that they don't get an openness and clarity of heart from time to time, and think of them with nothing but compassion, kindness, and sympathy." Trans. Bhikkhu Sujato, at SuttaCentral, https://suttacentral.net/an5.162/.

Bibliography

Aiken, William. "Human Rights in an Ecological Era." *Environmental Values* 1 (Autumn 1992): 191–203.
Alfano, Mark. "Towards a Genealogy of Forward-Looking Responsibility." *The Monist* 104 (2021): 489–509.
Arendt, Hannah. *The Human Condition.* Chicago, IL: University Press of Chicago, 1958.
Aristotle. *Nicomachean Ethics.* Trans. Harris Rackham. Cambridge, MA: Harvard University Press, 1934.
———. *Politics.* Trans. Benjamin Jowett. Accessed October 20, 2021. http://classics.mit.edu/Aristotle/politics.html.
Auhagen, Elisabeth, and Hans-Werner Bierhoff, eds. *Responsibility: The Many Faces of a Social Phenomenon.* London: Routledge, 2001.
Barry, Andrew, and Lucy Kimbell. "Pindices [Personal Political Indices]." In Latour and Weibel, 872–73.
Bauer, Joanne R., and Daniel Bell. *The East Asian Challenge for Human Rights.* Cambridge, UK: Cambridge University Press, 1999.
Beckwith, Frances J. "Does Judith Jarvis Thomson Really Grant the Pro-Life View of Fetal Personhood in her Defense of Abortion? A Rawlsian Assessment." *International Philosophical Quarterly* 54 (2014): 443–51.
Benhabib, Seyla. *The Rights of Others.* Cambridge, UK: Cambridge University Press, 2004.
Biggs, M. Antonia, et al. "Women Seek Abortions for a Variety of Complex Reasons." In *Abortion*, ed. Tamara Thompson, 34–53. Greenhaven, MI: Farmington Hills, 2015.
Bird, Otto A. *The Idea of Justice.* New York: Frederick Praeger, 1967.
Birnbacher, Dieter. "Philosophical Foundations of Responsibility." In Auhagen and Bierhoff, 9–22.
Bourne, Randolph. "Twilight of Idols." *The Seven Arts* 11 (October 1917): 688–702. Accessed on October 20, 2021. http://www.expo98.msu.edu/people/bourne.htm.

Brandom, Robert B. *Making It Explicit*. Cambridge, MA: Harvard University Press, 1994.

———. *A Spirit of Trust*. Cambridge, MA: Harvard University Press, 2019.

Bratman, Michael. *Shared Agency*. Oxford, UK: Oxford University Press, 2014.

Brown University Steering Committee on Slavery and Justice. Accessed October 20, 2021. http://brown.edu/Research/Slavery_Justice/.

Buber, Martin. "What Is to Be Done?" [1919] In *Pointing the Way*, ed. Maurice S. Friedman, 109–11. New York: Harper & Row, 1963.

Bujalski, Andrew, writer and dir. *Support the Girls*. New York: Magnolia Pictures, 2018.

Burrell, David. *Knowing the Unknowable God: Ibn Sina, Maimonides, Aquinas*. Notre Dame, IN: University Press of Notre Dame, 1986.

Carens, Joseph. *The Ethics of Immigration*. Oxford, UK: Oxford University Press, 2013.

Collingwood, R. G. *The New Leviathan*. Oxford, UK: Oxford University Press, 1992.

Critchley, Simon. *Infinitely Demanding: Ethics of Commitment, Politics of Resistance*. London: Verso, 2007.

"Critical Reaction to *24*." Wikipedia. Accessed October 20, 2021. https://en.wikipedia.org/wiki/Critical_reaction_to_24#Torture.

Croce, Benedetto. *Politics and Morals*. Trans. Salvatore J. Castiglione. New York: Philosophical Library, 1945.

Daly, Mary. *Gyn/Ecology. The Metaethics of Radical Feminism*, rev. ed. Boston, MA: Beacon, 1990.

Dansby, Colin. "Lupita's Dress: Care in Time." *Hypatia* 19 (Fall 2004): 23–48.

Darwin, Charles. *The Descent of Man*. London: Penguin, 2004.

Davis, Paul. "Slowly, Brown Starts Fulfilling Its Vow of Atonement." *Providence Journal*, April 26, 2010.

Delcker, Janosch. "The Phrase that Haunts Angela Merkel." politico.eu, August 19, 2016. Accessed October 20, 2021. https://www.politico.eu/article/the-phrase-that-haunts-angela-merkel/.

Denbow, Jennifer M. "Abortion as Genocide: Race, Agency, and Nation in Prenatal Nondiscrimination Bans." *Signs* 41 (Spring 2016): 603–26.

Derrida, Jacques. "Faith and Knowledge: The Two Sources of 'Religion' at the Limits of Reason Alone." Trans. Samuel Weber. In Jacques Derrida and Gianni Vattimo, *Religion*, 1–78. Stanford, CA: Stanford University Press, 1998.

DeWeese, Garrett J. *God and the Nature of Time*. Aldershot, UK: Ashgate, 2004.

Dewey, John. *Human Nature and Conduct*. New York: Henry Holt, 1922.

———. "Outlines of a Critical Theory of Ethics." In John Dewey, *The Early Works, 1882–1898*, Vol. 3, ed. Jo Ann Boydston, 349–86. Carbondale, IL: Southern Illinois University Press, 2008.

Dewey, John, and J. H. Tufts. *Ethics* [1908]. N.p.: Okitoks, 2017.

Dudbridge, Glenn, trans. *The Legend of Miaoshan*, rev. ed. Oxford, UK: Oxford University Press, 2004.

Dworkin, Ronald. *Law's Empire*. Cambridge, MA: Harvard University Press, 1986.

Elis, Niv. "Fewer than Half of Workers in 'Good' Jobs." *The Hill*, October 23, 2019. Accessed October 20, 2021. https://thehill.com/policy/finance/467126-fewer-than-half-of-workers-in-good-jobs-survey.

Ember, Sydney. "The Forgotten Report: Slavery and Justice at Brown." *Brown Daily Herald*, May 24, 2012.

Fain, Haskell. *Normative Politics and the Community of Nations*. Philadelphia, PA: Temple University Press, 1987.

Firestone, Shulamith. *The Dialectic of Sex*. New York: William Morrow, 1970.

Fischer, John Martin, and Mark Ravizza. *Responsibility and Control*. Cambridge, UK: Cambridge University Press, 1998.

French, Peter A., and Howard K. Wettstein, eds. *Forward-Looking Collective Responsibility. Midwest Studies in Philosophy*, Vol. 38. Boston, MA: Wiley, 2014.

Friedrich, Carl J., ed. *Responsibility*. New York: Liberal Arts, 1960.

Fritsch, Matthias. "Sources of Morality in Habermas's Recent Work on Religion and Freedom." In *Habermas and Religion*, ed. Craig Calhoun, Eduardo Mendieta, and Jonathan VanAntwerpen, 277–300. Cambridge, UK: Polity, 2013.

Gandhi, Mohandas. *An Autobiography: The Story of My Experiments with Truth*. Boston, MA: Beacon, 1957.

Gilbert, Margaret. *On Social Facts*. Princeton, NJ: Princeton University Press, 1989.

———. *A Theory of Political Obligation*. Oxford, UK: Oxford University Press, 2006.

Gilligan, Carol. *In a Different Voice*. Cambridge, MA: Harvard University Press, 1982.

Glendon, Mary Ann. *A World Made New: Eleanor Roosevelt and the Universal Declaration of Human Rights*. New York: Random House, 2001.

"The Goddess of Mercy." In *Myths and Legends of China* [1922], trans. E. T. C. Werner, chap. 10. Accessed October 20, 2021. www.sacred-texts.com/cfu/mlc/mlc12.htm.

Gómez, Luis O., trans. *Land of Bliss*. Honolulu, HI: University of Hawai'i Press, 1996.

Good Jobs Institute. "What Is a Good Job?" Accessed October 20, 2021. https://goodjobsinstitute.org/what-is-a-good-job/.

Goodin, Robert E. *Protecting the Vulnerable*. Chicago, IL: University of Chicago Press, 1985.

Greenspan, Patricia. "Making Room for Options: Moral Reasons, Imperfect Duties, and Choice." *Social Philosophy and Policy* 27 (July 2010): 181–205.

Habermas, Jürgen. "A Genealogical Analysis of the Cognitive Content of Morality." In *The Inclusion of the Other*, ed. Ciaran Cronin and Pablo De Greiff, 3–46. Cambridge, MA: MIT Press, 1998.

Han Feizi. *The Han Feizi*. In *A Source Book in Chinese Philosophy*, ed. Wing-Tsit Chan, 252–61. Princeton, NJ: Princeton University Press, 1963.

Han Yu. "Essentials of the Moral Way." Trans. Charles Hartman. In William Theodore de Bary and Irene Bloom, eds., *Sources of Chinese Tradition*, 2nd ed., 569–73. New York: Columbia University Press, 1999.

Hart, H. L. A. *Punishment and Responsibility*. New York: Oxford University Press, 1968.
Hauerwas, Stanley. "Work as Co-Creation: A Critique of a Remarkably Bad Idea." In *Co-Creation and Capitalism: John Paul II's Laborem Exercens*, ed. John W. Houck and Oliver F. Williams, 42–58. Lanham, MD: University Press of America, 1983.
Hegel, G. W. F. *Elements of the Philosophy of Right*. Trans. H. B. Nisbet. Cambridge, UK: Cambridge University Press, 1991.
Held, Virginia. *The Ethics of Care: Personal, Political, and Global*. Oxford, UK: Oxford University Press, 2006.
Hershenov, David. B. "Abortions and Distortions: An Analysis of Morally Irrelevant Factors in Thomson's Violinist Thought Experiment." *Social Theory and Practice* 27 (January 2001): 129–48.
Hildebrand, Dietrich von. *Ethics*. Chicago, IL: Franciscan Herald, 1953.
Hobbes, Thomas. *Leviathan*. New York: E. P. Dutton, 1950.
Hoekstra, Kinch. "Athenian Democracy and Popular Tyranny." In *Popular Sovereignty in Historical Perspective*, ed. Richard Bourke and Quentin Skinner, 15–51. Cambridge, UK: Cambridge University Press, 2016.
Horton, John. *Political Obligation*. 2nd ed. New York: Palgrave Macmillan, 2010.
Hrdy, Sarah. *Mothers and Others: The Evolutionary Origins of Mutual Understanding*. Cambridge, MA: Harvard University Press, 2009.
Hume, David. *An Inquiry Concerning the Principles of Morals*. Indianapolis, IN: Library of Liberal Arts, 1957.
Husak, Douglas. "Why There Are No Human Rights," *Social Theory and Practice* 10 (1984): 125–41.
Idema, Will, trans. *Personal Salvation and Filial Piety: Two Precious Scroll Narratives of Guanyin and Her Acolytes*. Honolulu, HI: University of Hawai'i Press, 2008.
Israel, Ron. *Global Citizenship*. N.p.: CreateSpace, 2012.
———. "The Rights and Responsibilities of Global Citizenship." Accessed October 20, 2021. https://www.theglobalcitizensinitiative.org/index.php/the-rights-and-responsibilities-of-global-citizenship/.
Jeske, Diane. "Special Obligations," *The Stanford Encyclopedia of Philosophy*, ed. Edward N. Zalta (Fall 2019). Accessed October 20, 2021. https://plato.stanford.edu/archives/fall2019/entries/special-obligations/.
John Paul II. *Of Human Work* [*Laborem Exercens*]. Washington, DC: United States Catholic Conference, 1981.
Jonas, Hans. *The Imperative of Responsibility*. Trans. Hans Jonas and David Herr. Chicago, IL: University of Chicago Press, 1984.
Jovanović, Miodrag A. "Recognizing Minority Identities through Collective Rights." *Human Rights Quarterly* 27 (May 2005): 625–51.
Kant, Immanuel. *The Doctrine of Virtue*. Trans. Mary J. Gregor. New York: Harper, 1964.

———. *Groundwork of the Metaphysic of Morals*. Trans. H. J. Paton. New York: Harper, 1964.

———. *The Metaphysical Elements of Justice*. Trans. John Ladd. Indianapolis, IN: Bobbs-Merrill, 1965.

———. "To Perpetual Peace." In *Perpetual Peace and Other Essays*, trans. Ted Humphrey, 107–43. Indianapolis, IN: Hackett, 1983.

———. *Religion within the Boundaries of Mere Reason*. Trans. Allen Wood and George di Giovanni. Cambridge, UK: Cambridge University Press, 1998.

Keen, Benjamin. *The Aztec Image in Western Thought*. New Brunswick, NJ: Rutgers University Press, 1990.

Kennett, Jeanette. *Agency and Responsibility*. Oxford, UK: Oxford University Press, 2001.

Kierkegaard, Søren. *Practice in Christianity*. Trans. Howard V. Hong and Edna H. Hong. Princeton, NJ: Princeton University Press, 1991.

Kirkman, Maggie, et al. "Reasons Women Give for Abortion: A Review of the Literature." *Archives of Women's Mental Health* 12 (December 2009): 365–78.

Kongzi. *The Analects of Confucius*. Trans. James Legge. Accessed October 20, 2021. http://oaks.nvg.org/analects-legge.html.

———. *The Analects of Confucius*. Trans. Arthur Waley. New York: Vintage, 1938.

Korsgaard, Christine. *Self-Constitution: Agency, Identity, and Integrity*. Oxford, UK: Oxford University Press, 2009.

LaFleur, William R. *Liquid Life: Abortion and Buddhism in Japan*. Princeton, NJ: Princeton University Press, 1992.

Latour, Bruno. *Reassembling the Social*. Oxford, UK: Oxford University Press, 2005.

Latour, Bruno, and Peter Weibel, eds. *Making Things Public: Atmospheres of Democracy*. Cambridge, MA: MIT Press, 2005.

Lenk, Hans, and Matthias Maring. "Responsibility and Technology." In Auhagen and Bierhoff, 93–107.

Levinas, Emmanuel. "The Ego and the Totality" [1954]. In *Collected Papers*, trans. Alfonso Lingis, 25–45. The Hague, the Netherlands: Martinus Nijhoff, 1987.

———. "Kierkegaard: Existence and Ethics." In *Proper Names*, trans. Michael B. Smith, 66–74. Stanford, CA: Stanford University Press, 1996.

———. *Otherwise than Being or Beyond Essence*. Trans. Alfonso Lingis. The Hague, the Netherlands: Martinus Nijhoff, 1981.

———. *Totality and Infinity*. Trans. Alfonso Lingis. Pittsburgh, PA: Duquesne University Press, 1969.

———. "The Trace of the Other." Trans. Alfonso Lingis. In *Deconstruction in Context*, ed. Mark C. Taylor, 345–59. Chicago, IL: University of Chicago Press, 1986.

———. "Transcendence and Height." In *Emmanuel Levinas: Basic Philosophical Writings*, ed. Adriaan T. Peperzak, Simon Critchley, and Robert Bernasconi, 11–32. Bloomington, IN: Indiana University Press, 1996.

Levine, Stephen. *Becoming Kuan Yin*. San Francisco, CA: Weiser, 2013.

Lévy-Bruhl, Lucien. *L'idée de responsabilité*. Paris: Hachette, 1884.
Leys, Wayne A. R. "Platonic, Pragmatic, and Political Responsibility." In Friedrich, 71–83.
Lincoln, Abraham. Speech of February 22, 1861 at Independence Hall. Accessed October 20, 2021. http://www.abrahamlincolnonline.org/lincoln/speeches/philadel.htm.
———. Speech of August 17, 1858 at Lewistown, Illinois. Accessed October 20, 2021. https://www.nps.gov/liho/learn/historyculture/declaration.htm.
List, Christian, and Philip Pettit. *Group Agency: The Possibility, Design, and Status of Corporate Agents*. Oxford, UK: Oxford University Press, 2011.
Locke, John. Second Treatise of Civil Government. In *Two Treatises of Government*. Cambridge, UK: Cambridge University Press, 1960.
MacBride, Fraser, ed., "Forward-Looking Accounts of Responsibility." *The Monist* 104, no. 4 (2021).
Machiavelli, Niccolò. *The Prince*. In *The Portable Machiavelli*, trans. Peter Bondanella and Mark Musa. London: Penguin, 1979.
MacIntyre, Alasdair. "*Sophrosune*: How a Virtue Can Become Socially Disruptive." In *Midwest Studies in Philosophy*, Vol. 13, ed. Peter A. French, Theodore E. Uhling Jr., and Howard K. Wettstein, 1–11. Notre Dame, IN: University of Notre Dame Press, 1988.
Marcel, Gabriel. "On the Ontological Mystery." In *The Philosophy of Existentialism*, trans. Manya Harari. New York: Citadel, 1956.
May, Larry. *Sharing Responsibility*. Chicago, IL: University of Chicago Press, 1992.
McKenna, Michael. *Conversation and Responsibility*. Oxford, UK: Oxford University Press, 2012.
McKeon, Richard. "The Development and the Significance of the Concept of Responsibility." *Revue Internationale de Philosophie* 11 (1957): 3–32.
McPherson, Thomas. *Political Obligation*. London: Routledge & Kegan Paul, 1967.
Melden, A. I. "Saints and Supererogation." In *Philosophy and Life. Essays on John Wisdom*, ed. Ilham Dilman, 61–81. Dordrecht, the Netherlands: Springer, 1984.
Melish, Joanne. "Recovering (from) Slavery: Four Struggles to Tell the Truth." In *Slavery and Public History*, ed. James Oliver Horton and Lois E. Horton, 103–33. New York: The New Press, 2006.
Mendus, Susan. "The Magic in the Pronoun 'My.'" *Critical Review of International Social and Political Philosophy* 5 (2002): 33–52.
Miller, Richard W. *Globalizing Justice*. Oxford, UK: Oxford University Press, 2010.
Morgenthau, Hans J. *Politics among Nations: The Struggle for Power and Peace*. New York: McGraw-Hill, 1993.
Neuhäuser, Christian. "Structural Injustice and the Distribution of Forward-Looking Responsibility." In French and Wettstein, 232–51.
Niebuhr, H. Richard. *The Responsible Self*. New York: Harper & Row, 1963.

Nietzsche, Friedrich. *On the Genealogy of Morals.* Trans. Walter Kaufmann and R. J. Hollingdale. New York: Random House, 1967.
Noddings, Nel. *Caring: A Feminine Approach to Ethics and Moral Education.* Berkeley, CA: University of California Press, 1984.
———. *The Maternal Factor.* Berkeley, CA: University of California Press, 2010.
Nussbaum, Martha. *Frontiers of Justice.* Cambridge, MA: Harvard University Press, 2006.
"Obama: That's Not Who We Are." apnews.com, December 9, 2014. Accessed October 20, 2021. https://apnews.com/article/637247cb92a7471293b076ddc5aa54eb.
Okin, Susan Moller. *Justice, Gender, and the Family.* New York: Basic Books, 1989.
O'Malley, Pat. "Responsibilization." In *The Sage Dictionary of Policing*, ed. Alison Wakefield and Jenny Fleming, 276–78. London: Sage, 2009.
Padgett, Alan G. *God, Eternity, and the Nature of Time.* New York: St. Martin's, 1992.
Pennock, J. Roland. "The Problem of Responsibility." In Friedrich, 3–27.
Peterson, Dale. *The Moral Lives of Animals.* London: Bloomsbury, 2011.
Pettit, Philip. *A Theory of Freedom.* Cambridge, UK: Polity, 2001.
Pevnick, Ryan. *Immigration and the Constraints of Justice.* Cambridge, UK: Cambridge University Press, 2011.
Plato. *Crito.* In *Euthyphro, Apology, Crito, Phaedo, Phaedrus.* Trans. H. N. Fowler. Cambridge, MA: Harvard University Press, 1977.
———. *Republic.* Trans. Chris Emlyn-Jones and William Preddy. 2 vols. Cambridge, MA: Harvard University Press, 2013.
Plotinus. *Enneads.* Trans. A. H. Armstrong. 7 vols. Cambridge, MA: Harvard University Press, 1966–1988.
Posner, Eric A. *The Twilight of Human Rights Law.* Oxford, UK: Oxford University Press, 2014.
Prinz, Jesse J. "Is Empathy Necessary for Morality?" In *Empathy: Philosophical and Psychological Perspectives*, ed. Amy Coplan and Peter Goldie, 211–29. Oxford, UK: Oxford University Press, 2011.
Raffoul, François. *The Origins of Responsibility.* Bloomington, IN: Indiana University Press, 2010.
Rawls, John. "The Idea of Public Reason Revisited." In *Collected Papers*, ed. Samuel Freeman, 573–615. Cambridge, MA: Harvard University Press, 2001.
———. *Justice as Fairness: A Restatement.* Ed. Erin Kelly. Cambridge, MA: Harvard University Press, 2001.
———. *The Law of Peoples.* Cambridge, MA: Harvard University Press, 1999.
———. *Political Liberalism*, expanded ed. New York: Columbia University Press, 2005.
———. *A Theory of Justice.* Cambridge, MA: Harvard University Press, 1971.
———. *A Theory of Justice*, rev. ed. Cambridge, MA: Harvard University Press, 1999.
Renzo, Massimo. "Associative Responsibilities and Political Obligation." *The Philosophical Quarterly* 62 (January 2012): 106–27.

Ricoeur, Paul. *Interpretation Theory.* Fort Worth, TX: TCU Press, 1976.

———. "What Is a Text?" In *Hermeneutics and the Human Sciences*, ed. John B. Thompson, 145–64. Cambridge, UK: Cambridge University Press, 1981.

Robichaud, Philip, and Jan Willem Wieland, eds. *Responsibility: The Epistemic Condition.* Oxford, UK: Oxford University Press, 2017.

Rosenau, James N. "Governance, Order, and Change in World Politics." In *Governance without Government*, ed. James N. Rosenau and Ernst-Otto Czempiel, 1–29. Cambridge, UK: Cambridge University Press, 1992.

Rossi, Enzo, and Matt Sleat. "Realism in Normative Political Theory." *Philosophy Compass* 9/10 (2014): 689–701.

Roth, Hans Ingvar. *P. C. Chang and the Universal Declaration of Human Rights.* Philadelphia, PA: University of Pennsylvania Press, 2016.

Rousseau, Jean-Jacques. *On the Social Contract.* Trans. John T. Scott. In *The Major Political Writings of Jean-Jacques Rousseau*, 153–272. Chicago, IL: University of Chicago Press, 2014.

Royce, Josiah. *The Philosophy of Loyalty.* Nashville, TN: Vanderbilt University Press, 1995.

Saad, Lydia. "Americans Still Oppose Overturning *Roe v. Wade.*" Gallup News. Accessed October 20, 2021. https://news.gallup.com/poll/350804/americans-opposed-overturning-roe-wade.aspx.

Saward, Dudley. *Bomber Harris.* New York: Doubleday, 1985.

Scanlon, Thomas. *What We Owe to Each Other.* Cambridge, MA: Harvard University Press, 1998.

Scheffler, Samuel. "Relationships and Responsibilities." In Scheffler, *Boundaries and Allegiances*, 97–110. Oxford, UK: Oxford University Press, 2001.

Schweickart, David. *After Capitalism.* 2nd ed. Lanham, MD: Rowman & Littlefield, 2011.

Sen, Amartya. *The Idea of Justice.* Cambridge, MA: Harvard University Press, 2009.

Sessions, George. "Shallow and Deep Ecology: Review of the Philosophical Literature." In *Ecological Consciousness*, ed. Robert C. Shultz, 391–462. Washington, DC: University Press of America, 1981.

Simmons, A. John. "Associative Political Obligations." *Ethics* 106 (January 1996): 247–73.

———. *Moral Principles and Political Obligations.* Princeton, NJ: Princeton University Press, 1979.

Singer, Peter. *Expanding the Circle: Ethics and Sociobiology.* New York: Farrar, Straus & Giroux, 1981.

———. "Famine, Affluence, and Morality." *Philosophy and Public Affairs* 1 (Spring 1972): 229–43.

Singh, Satwant. "The Court Statement of Satwant Singh." Accessed October 20, 2021. http://panthic.org/articles/2275.

Sleat, Matt, ed. *Politics Recovered: Realist Thought in Theory and Practice*. New York: Columbia University Press, 2018.
Slote, Michael. *The Ethics of Care and Empathy*. New York: Routledge, 2007.
Smiley, Marion. "Future-Looking Collective Responsibility: A Preliminary Analysis." In French and Wettstein, 1–12.
Smith, Adam. *The Wealth of Nations*. New York: Random House, 1994.
Smith, Steven G. *The Concept of the Spiritual*. Philadelphia, PA: Temple University Press, 1988.
———. "Historical Rightness." *Soundings* 98 (Spring 2015): 127–45.
———. "Meaningful Moral Freedom: An Improved Kantian View." *International Philosophical Quarterly* 57 (June 2017): 155–72.
———. "Responsibility in Religiosity." *Religious Studies* 57 (June 2021): 249–65.
———. *Scriptures and the Guidance of Language*. Cambridge, UK: Cambridge University Press, 2018.
———. "The Structure of Unlimited Action Sharing." *Philosophical Frontiers* 4 (July–December 2009): 57–71.
———. "What We Have Time For: Historical Responsibility on the Largest Scale." *Journal of the Philosophy of History* 13 (June 2019): 163–82.
Sneddon, Andrew. "Moral Responsibility: The Difference of Strawson, and the Difference It Should Make." *Ethical Theory and Moral Practice* 8 (2005): 239–65.
Spinoza, Benedict de. *Ethics*. Ed. Matthew J. Kisner. Cambridge, UK: Cambridge University Press, 2018.
Stilz, Anna. "Why Do States Have Territorial Rights?" *International Theory* 1 (2009): 185–213.
Strawson, P. F. "Freedom and Resentment," *Proceedings of the British Academy* 48 (1962): 1–25.
SuttaCentral. Accessed October 20, 2021. https://suttacentral.net/.
Svrluga, Susan, and Nick Anderson. "Georgetown Has a Plan to Help Descendants of Enslaved People." *Washington Post*, October 31, 2019.
Talbert, Matthew. "Moral Responsibility." *The Stanford Encyclopedia of Philosophy*, ed. Edward N. Zalta (Winter 2019). Accessed October 20, 2021. https://plato.stanford.edu/archives/win2019/entries/moral-responsibility/.
Thomson, Judith Jarvis. "A Defense of Abortion." *Philosophy and Public Affairs* 1 (1971): 47–66.
Thoreau, Henry David. "Civil Disobedience." In *Civil Disobedience and Other Essays*. Mineola, NY: Dover, 1993.
Tillich, Paul. *Systematic Theology*, Vol. 1. Chicago, IL: University of Chicago Press, 1951.
———. *Systematic Theology*, Vol. 3. Chicago, IL: University of Chicago Press, 1963.
Twain, Mark. *Life on the Mississippi*. New York: Collier, 1917.
van Ackeren, Marcel, and Martin Sticker. "Kant and Moral Demandingness." *Ethical Theory and Moral Practice* 18 (2015): 75–89.

van Every, Dale, Irwin Shaw, and Sidney Buchman. *The Talk of the Town* screenplay. Culver City, CA: Columbia Pictures, 1942.
Vázquez-Arroyo, Antonio. *Political Responsibility.* New York: Columbia University Press, 2016.
Vernon, Richard. "Obligation by Association? A Reply to John Horton," *Political Studies* 55 (2007): 865–79.
Vincent, Nicole A. "A Structured Taxonomy of Responsibility Concepts." In *Moral Responsibility: Beyond Free Will and Determinism*, ed. Nicole A. Vincent, Ibo van de Poel, and Jeroen van den Hoven, 15–35. Dordrecht, the Netherlands: Springer, 2011.
Viola, Herman J. *Little Bighorn Remembered.* New York: Crown, 1999.
Vogelmann, Frieder, *The Spell of Responsibility: Labor, Criminality, Philosophy.* Trans. Daniel Steuer. London: Rowman & Littlefield, 2017.
Waller, Bruce. *Against Moral Responsibility.* Cambridge, MA: MIT Press, 2011.
Walzer, Michael. *Just and Unjust Wars.* New York: Basic Books, 1977.
———. *Spheres of Justice.* New York: Basic Books, 1983.
Watson, Gary. "Two Faces of Responsibility." *Philosophical Topics* 24 (1996): 227–48.
Weber, Max. "Politics as a Vocation." In *From Max Weber: Essays in Sociology*, ed. H. H. Gerth and C. Wright Mills, 77–128. New York: Oxford University Press, 1948.
Weil, Simone. *The Need for Roots.* Trans. Arthur Wills. New York: Harper & Row, 1952.
Wellman, Christopher Heath, and Phillip Cole. *Debating the Ethics of Immigration: Is There a Right to Exclude?* Oxford, UK: Oxford University Press, 2011.
Williams, Bernard. "Realism and Moralism in Political Theory." In *In the Beginning was the Deed*, ed. Geoffrey Hawthorn, 1–17. Princeton, NJ: Princeton University Press, 2005.
Williams, Garrath. " 'Infrastructures of Responsibility': The Moral Tasks of Institutions." *Journal of Applied Philosophy* 23 (2006): 207–21.
———. "Responsibility as a Virtue." *Ethical Theory and Moral Practice* 11 (2008): 455–70.
Wing, Sherin. "Gendering Buddhism: the Miaoshan Legend Reconsidered." *Journal of Feminist Studies* 27 (2011): 5–31.
Yanagisako, Sylvia. "Family and Households: The Analysis of Domestic Groups." *Annual Review of Anthropology* 8 (1979): 161–205.
Yeoman, Ruth. "Conceptualising Meaningful Work as a Fundamental Human Need." *Journal of Business Ethics* 125 (2014): 235–51.
———. *Meaningful Work and Workplace Democracy.* Houndsmill, UK: Palgrave, 2014.
Young, Iris Marion. *Justice and the Politics of Difference.* Princeton, NJ: Princeton University Press, 1990.
———. *Responsibility for Justice.* New York: Oxford University Press, 2011.
Zagzebski, Linda. *Exemplarist Moral Theory.* Oxford, UK: Oxford University Press, 2017.

Index

abortion, 48 n.5, 62–67, 106, 110–114, 135
Abraham, 150, 185, 193 n.3, 194–195, 199–200
action sharing, 7, 12, 17, 46–47; ethical, 28, 47, 77, 165; in families, 109–110; Gilbert on, 81; historical, 47, 90, 175–190; military, 92; political, 72, 74, 83 n.27, 88, 90, 95, 103, 110, 120; pragmatic, 47–48, 66, 90; scales of, 5–6, 47–48, 54–55; schemes for, 6, 11, 22–23, 27, 77, 103, 109, 121, 38. *See also* collaboration
actuality (ontological), 45–46
Aeneas, 150, 195–196, 199–202
Agathocles of Syracuse, 70 n.3
Aiken, William, 130 n.41
Amitabha, 197–199
Anderson, Marc, 25 n.26
Arendt, Hannah, 72
Aristotle, 70, 140–142, 148, 156, 162, 169–173, 182 n.3
Arjuna, 106
al-Assad, Bashar, 126
Augustus, 201
autonomy, 20, 29, 67, 118 n.18, 149, 153–154, 183, 187, 201
Avalokiteshvara, 146, 198–199
Aztec sacrifice, 200

Barry, Andrew, 69 n.1
Barry, Brian, 174 n.18
Bauer, Jack, 86
Bauer, Joanne R., 129 n.39
Bayezid II, 127 n.32
Beckwith, Frances J., 63 n.19
Bell, Daniel, 129 n.39
Benhabib, Seyla, 105 n.1, 124
Biggs, M. Antonia, 112 n.14
Bird, Otto A., 75 n.7
Birnbacher, Dieter, 21 n.17
Bismarck, Otto von, 87 n.33
Bourne, Randolph, 52 n.7
Brandom, Robert B., 16 n.3, 25 n.25
Bratman, Michael, 81 n.22
Brown University initiative, 187
Buber, Martin, 161
Buddha, 193, 197, 199 n.14
Bujalski, Andrew, 118 n.19
Burrell, David, 151 n.24

capitalism, 96–97
Carens, Joseph, 129 n.38
causes (ethical and historical), 179–181
character (personal), 66, 86, 153, 170, 176
citizenship, 78–79, 83–85, 95, 96 n.38, 98 n.41, 120–124, 135; global, 125–126, 131–132, 135
civil disobedience, 84–86

Cole, Phillip, 129 n.38
collaboration, 10, 21–28, 32, 34–37, 44, 47–49, 121, 139; and cooperation, 10–12; established formats for, 56; and ethical evaluation, 80; in families, 104, 111–112, 184; with God, 156, 193–194; and historical responsibility, 180–181; and immigrants, 123; and jobs, 116–117; and obligation, 62; in organizations, 104, 119; political, 76, 83 n.27, 88, 98; and religious responsibility, 202; and trust, 58. *See also* action sharing
Collingwood, R. G., 27 n.27, 120 n.22
community, 104, 129; eternal, 191; ethical, 37, 165; as *Gemeinschaft* and *Gesellschaft*, 40–41; global, 104, 125, 128, 131–133; of helpfulness, 24; historical, 167, 182; ideally inclusive, 2; of love, 108; and morality, 164–165; political, 77, 80, 89, 91, 120–124; and responsibility, 7; solidarity of, 20
competition, 45, 49, 72, 105–108, 123, 133–134, 189; and cooperation, 50–51, 105
Confucius, *see* Kongzi
consequentialism, 166–169
contracts, 22, 25, 33, 43, 115
Creon, 74, 96
Croce, Benedetto, 93
Curtis, Edward, 92 n.35

Daly, Mary, 74 n.6
Dansby, Colin, 47 n.4
Darwin, Charles, 49, 57 n.12
Delcker, Janosch, 127 n.33
democracy, 41, 73, 79, 84, 120–121, 135, 162; economic, 119 n.21
Denbow, Jennifer M., 65 n.22

Derrida, Jacques, 4, 5 n.8, 144 n.7
DeWeese, Garrett J., 152 n.25
Dewey, John, 15 n.2, 25 n.25, 52 n.7, 158, 175
Dharmakara, 197–202
Dickens, Charles, 96
divorce, 109
Dostoevsky, Fyodor, 96
duties, 15–17, 19, 65–66, 86, 129, 140–141; civic, 84; ecological, 130; to family, 106–107, 121; moral, 163–164; and obligation, 78–79, 81; perfect and imperfect, 55, 166–167; religious, 195, 200 n.15
Dworkin, Ronald, 80

empathy, 57–59
eternity, 150–153, 156–157, 192–193
ethics, 1–4, 7, 28, 43, 45, 112–113, 129–130, 162–174; applied, 61; of care, 45, 112, 172–174, 186; in Confucianism, 144; ecological, 130; and ethos, 56; and historical responsibility, 180–182, 186–188; in Kant, 144–145, 149, 153; in Levinas, 144, 151; in Machiavelli, 93 n.36; in Mill, 167; and political responsibility, 73–88, 127; and pragmatic responsibility, 48, 60–67, 173; and religious responsibility, 194–195; and values, 42; of virtue, 169–171; in Weber, 2–3, 93, 94 n.37, 141
expediency, 5, 45, 70, 73

Fain, Haskell, 125 n.29
fairness, 48, 74–77, 79, 82, 108, 125, 161; and abortion, 113; in Kant, 32, 166; and policy on migrants, 130, 132; in Rawls, 75–77, 127 n.35; and work, 119; in Young, 146. *See also* reciprocity

family, 26, 44, 55, 62, 72, 104–114, 120–121, 124, 135; in Aristotle, 140; in Buddhism and Confucianism, 198–199; and historical responsibility, 183–184, 189–190; and nations, 185
feeling, 57–59; in ethics of care, 172; in utilitarianism, 167
Firestone, Shulamith, 108 n.7
Fischer, John Martin, 23 n.23
Foster, Diana Greene, 112 n.14
freedom, 15–17, 21 n.19, 29, 159; and abortion, 63; academic, 175; and determinism, 12; in human rights, 127
friendship, 44, 54, 61, 85, 104, 108, 174 n.18; civic, 98 n.41; in Confucianism, 143
Fritsch, Matthias, 17 n.8

Gandhi, Indira, 87
Gandhi, Mohandas, 147–148
Georgetown University initiative, 187
Gilbert, Margaret, 12, 78 n.17, 80–82
Gilligan, Carol, 112, 172
Glendon, Mary Ann, 99 n.42, 128 n.37
God, 105, 150–152, 156, 191–195, 201
Goodin, Robert E., 21 n.18
Gorbachev, Mikhail, 134
Gould, Heather, 112 n.14
Greenspan, Patricia, 167 n.3
Guanyin, 146, 198–199

Habermas, Jürgen, 17 n.8, 29, 157
Han Feizi, *see* Legalism (Chinese)
Han Yu, 198 n.12
Harris, Sir Arthur ("Bomber"), 3, 87
Hart, H. L. A., 15 n.2, 19 n.14, 23 n.21
Hauerwas, Stanley, 156 n.30

Hegel, G. W. F., 16 n.3, 25 n.25, 52–53, 106, 164 n.1
Held, Virginia, 172, 174 n.17–n.18
heritage, 92, 124, 154, 184–185
heroes, 92, 94; of religious responsibility, 194–201
Hershenov, David B., 64 n.20
Hildebrand, Dietrich von, 57 n.11
historical injustice, 187–188
Hobbes, Thomas, 21 n.19, 31–35, 71, 74, 77, 79–80, 122 n.24, 131
Horton, John, 80 n.18, n.20, 81 n.23
Hrdy, Sarah, 66 n.24
Hume, David, 172 n.12
Husak, Douglas, 127 n.34
Huxley, Aldous, 108

identity, collective, 90–92, 97, 106
immigration, 60–61, 120–124, 129–130, 135
Israel, Ron, 125 n.31, 132 n.42

Jefferson, Thomas, 91
Jellyby, Mrs., 96
Jeske, Diane, 167 n.4
jobs, 22–23, 115–119, 135, 139
John Paul II, 156 n.30
Jonas, Hans, 21 n.18, 173 n.16
Jovanović, Miodrag A., 107 n.4
justice, 29, 71–72, 75, 146–147, 172; ecological, 130; ethical, 88; global, 127–130, 146; liberal, 11; as "moral" (in Rawls), 75–76; political, 73, 75; pragmatic, 89; in social contract theory, 79

Kannon, *see* Guanyin
Kant, Immanuel, 31–35, 93 n.36, 105, 122 n.24, 144–145, 148–149, 153, 166–169, 173
Kennett, Jeanette, 23 n.23
al-Khidr, *see* servant of God

Kierkegaard, Søren, 150–151, 195
Kimbell, Lucy, 69 n.1
King, Martin Luther Jr., 94–96
Kirkman, Maggie, 112 n.14
Kongzi, 142–143, 145 n.10, 147–148, 150, 152, 196–197, 200, 202
Korsgaard, Christine, 18 n.12

LaFleur, William R., 48 n.5, 110 n.10
Latour, Bruno, 13 n.14, 146 n.15
Lee, Robert E., 94, 96
Legalism (Chinese), 170
Leibniz, G. W., 153
Levinas, Emmanuel, 4, 5 n.8, 17 n.8, 144, 151, 195 n.5
Levine, Stephen, 199 n.13
Lévy-Bruhl, Lucien, 18 n.10
Leys, Wayne A. R., 85 n.29
liberalism, 11, 75, 98–99, 107–109, 118, 128
Lincoln, Abraham, 185–186
List, Christian, 37 n.34
Locke, John, 77, 122 n.24, 131
loyalty, 2, 60, 69, 82, 121, 124, 158, 180

Machiavelli, Niccolò, 70, 71 n.4, 74, 85 n.29, 93 n.36
MacIntyre, Alasdair, 16 n.4
Malthus, Thomas, 49
Marcel, Gabriel, 22
Maritain, Jacques, 182 n.3
May, Larry, 36 n.33
McKenna, Michael, 20 n.16
McPherson, Thomas, 78 n.16
Melden, A. I., 201 n.16
Mendus, Susan, 44 n.1
Merkel, Angela, 126–127, 134
Miaoshan, 198–200, 202
Mill, John Stuart, 167
Miller, Richard W., 124 n.27
monarchy, 72–73, 79

moral (versus ethical), 163–165; in Rawls, 75–76
moralism (political), 4, 8, 75–77, 93 n.36; in Aristotle, 170
Morgenthau, Hans, 76 n.13
Moses, 192

nationalism, 131, 157, 184; in Hegel, 52–53
nations (rationale), 125 n.29, 134, 179, 184–185
nativism, 133
Neuhäuser, Christian, 36 n.33
Niebuhr, H. Richard, 191
Nietzsche, Friedrich, 17 n.7, 159
Noddings, Nel, 172–173
Nussbaum, Martha, 108

Obama, Barack, 86 n.31, 134
obligation, 16, 61–62, 78–79, 82–83; associative, 80–81, 84; in Gilbert, 81; political, 78–84, 86, 88; special, 44–45, 167
Okin, Susan Moller, 108 n.6, 110 n.9
Orbán, Viktor, 126
organizations, 22, 27, 89, 104, 114–119, 135

Padgett, Alan G., 152 n.25
Paul (the apostle), 156–157
Pennock, J. Roland, 15
Peterson, Dale, 66 n.24
Pettit, Philip, 17 n.6, 21 n.19, 37 n.34
Pevnick, Ryan, 124 n.27
Plato, 30, 71, 73, 84, 88, 108
Plotinus, 153
politics, 2, 5, 13, 69–70, 85, 87, 120, 135; classical view, 138; modern, 75, 79
Posner, Eric A., 99 n.43
possibility (ontological), 45–46
pragmata, 46

pragmatism, 51–52, 89, 193
public sphere, 69, 104
Pulaski, Mr., 137

Ravizza, Mark, 23 n.23
Rawls, John, 11, 75–77, 78 n.17, 98 n.40–n.41, 127, 131, 157
realism: political, 4–5, 8, 71–73, 76–77, 88, 93; pragmatic, 51
reality (ontological), 45–46
realization: collective, 33–35, 96–99; historical, 36, 90–91; political, 94, 96–98, 128; practical, 30
reciprocity, 9, 76, 79, 82, 98 n.41, 127, 131; in Kongzi, 143–144, 196
refugees, 123–124, 126–134
religion, 42, 59, 146–147, 150, 156, 162, 191–203; and historical responsibility, 189; and politics, 99, 115, 138; in Lincoln, 186; and spirit, 157
Renfro, Jack, 142
Renzo, Massimo, 83 n.26
responsibility, 1–8, 15–28; affective, 57–59; agency, 37–41; civic, 84–88; collective, 35–41; distributed, 149; domains, 4; family, 26; humanly scaled, 202–203; in language, 8–10; monism of, 1, 4, 7, 45; shared, 33–38, 56, 146–147
responsibilization, 17
results (historical), 181
revolution, 85–86; in Dostoevsky, 96
Ricoeur, Paul, 150 n.21
rights, 6, 66, 97; constitutional, 94; and decency, 65–66; and ethics of care, 172; human, 77, 99, 104, 122, 126–132; in a job, 23; and liberalism, 98, 107; to life, 63–64; in Lincoln, 185–186
roles, 7, 18 n.12, 19–22, 26–29, 35–36, 137–138, 149, 161, 168; and associative obligation, 80; in language, 8–10; as natural, 17; in religion, 156, 199
Roosevelt, Theodore, 92 n.35
Rosenau, James M., 125 n.30
Rossi, Enzo, 76 n.12
Roth, Hans Ingvar, 128 n.37
Rousseau, Jean-Jacques, 21 n.19, 149
Royce, Josiah, 180

saints, 192, 201
Sartre, Jean-Paul, 159
Scanlon, Thomas, 82 n.25
Scheffler, Samuel, 45 n.2, 168 n.5
Schweickart, David, 119 n.21
scripturalism, 147, 150
Sen, Amartya, 19
servant of God, 192–193
Sessions, George, 130 n.41
Shun, 143, 196
Simmons, A. John, 78 n.15–n.17, 80 n.19–n.20
Singer, Peter, 128, 146 n.15
Singh, Satwant, 87 n.34
slavery, 165–166, 180, 182, 187
Sleat, Matt, 76 n.12
Slote, Michael, 173 n.14
Smiley, Marion, 36 n.33
Smith, Adam, 96
Smith, Steven G., 2 n.2, 13 n.14, 146 n.15–n.16, 150 n.21, 153 n.26, 180 n.2, 188 n.9
Sneddon, Andrew, 24 n.24
social contract theory, 36–37, 79–80
Social Darwinism, 49, 52
socialism, 96–97, 157
Socrates, 71, 84, 88
Spinoza, Benedict de, 74
spirit and spirits, 154–157, 159–160
Stapledon, Olaf, 146–147
Staples, Sam, 20
Sticker, Martin, 145 n.12

Stilz, Anna, 122 n.24
Stoicism, 202
Strawson, P. F., 13 n.13, 20 n.16, 21 n.19
sympathy, 57–59, 172–173

Tetzel, Johann, 201
theonomy, 157
Thomson, Judith Jarvis, 63–66
Thoreau, Henry David, 20, 84
Thrasymachus, 71–72, 74, 88
Tillich, Paul, 157
trust, 9–10, 16, 32, 35, 41, 58, 191
Tufts, J. H., 15 n.2
Twain, Mark, 56

Unger, Peter, 64 n.20
Universal Declaration of Human Rights, 99, 118, 128–129
utilitarianism, 37, 145, 147, 166–169, 173

values, 7, 41–42, 59, 84, 118 n.18, 154–155, 159
van Ackeren, Marcel, 145 n.12
Vázquez-Arroyo, Antonio, 75 n.8
Verkhovensky, Pyotr, 96
Vernon, Richard, 81 n.23
Vincent, Nicole, 18 n.9

Virgil, 195–196, 201
virtue, 16, 19, 21; in Aristotle, 169–171, 173; of citizenship, 96 n.38; of the collective, 90; in Kongzi, 142, 196; moral, 164; political, 96; pragmatic, 55
vocation, 52–57, 158–159
Vogelmann, Frieder, 17 n.7

Waller, Bruce, 12 n.12, 28
Walzer, Michael, 3 n.4, 121 n.23, 123 n.26
Watson, Gary, 18 n.11
Weber, Max, 2–3, 51, 93–94, 141
Weil, Simone, 182
Welty, Eudora, 142
Williams, Bernard, 5 n.9
Williams, Garrath, 4 n.7, 20 n.15, 115 n.15
Wing, Sherin, 199 n.14

Yanagisako, Sylvia, 106 n.2, 111 n.11
Yeoman, Ruth, 118 n.18
York, Alvin, 27
Young, Iris Marion, 38 n.36, 96 n.38, 146, 147 n.17

Zagzebski, Linda, 201 n.17

www.ingramcontent.com/pod-product-compliance
Lightning Source LLC
Chambersburg PA
CBHW020652230426
43665CB00008B/404